Policing the Police

A Nation's Cry

James Vadackumchery

2003

Kaveri Books

New Delhi - 110 002

First Published in 2003
ISBN 81-7479-060-8

Published by : Rakesh Goel
Kaveri Books
4697/5-21 A, Ansari Road,
New Delhi - 110 002 (India).
Tel.: 328 8140, 324 5799 Fax: 011 719 9029
e-mail: kaveribooks@vsnl.com

Printed at : Chawla Offset Printers, Delhi - 110 052

PRINTED IN INDIA

To

Mary

Neethu and Neethie

Contents

Preface

Police, *Pujarees* and Politicians— all of them enjoy a lot of power and authority to establish peace, harmony, welfare and human co-existence. Do they? All of them are to establish human rights, social justice, cultural development etc. But, do they? Police crimes have been a reality since the inception of the police. Communal riots and religious bigotry could be seen from time immemorial. Political atrocities have been very atrocious and, so to say, the crimes committed by the 3 *Ps* in the world might be more than perhaps the same committed by the *non-Ps* in human history. Is it true? There is lack of policing in the police, religion and politics. If the 3 *Ps* would have taken a different approach, certainly the history of the world would have been different today.

The rule of law must be geared to the rule of justice and that is what is meant by policing. The police is the agency, the law is the means and justice is the end in policing. The British Indian police had a limited objective and they owned loyalty only to imperial values. In such a system, the British Indian police did not think much about policing the police; rather were concerned with policing the society for achieving the colonial interests. Ideologically, the police in India was the police in London, but operationally it was different in the subcontinent and in Great Britain. Policing the police has been the aim of the British in London whereas it was not so in India. Police the police and thereby police the society - this idea worked well in England and they have the London bobby today. The police in the bullock-cart India did many things which the police in the GSLV - India cannot and should not follow. We cannot put a bullock-cart in a space shuttle and call it a satellite. Likewise, the police in free India have bullock-cart laws - the Police Act-1861 to guide them during the third millennium.

The history of the police from its beginning is a history of dissatisfaction among the lower level functionaries. They were paid low salaries and were forced to work in very dissatisfactory working environments. The British understood it and every now and then they increased their salary - with a meagre increase - and they always saw to it that they remained desperate in life. Corruption became a part of their lives and certainly the British could not police the police. There are many instances to show that the colonial police - including the colonial constabulary - usurped the role of the judge, jailor and executioner. David Arnold writes: "police power could not be precisely controlled by law-makers and magistrates. Much of the impact of the police lay in their unlicensed petty tyranny, their corruption and brutality ... the British, by the very nature of the police institution they created, sanctioned their continuance" (cf. Police Power and Colonial Rule: Madras: 1859-1947, Oxford University Press, 1986). The questions which are asked by researchers are: "Can the law-makers and the judiciary control police power and their doings?; what about the unlicensed petty tyranny, corruption and brutality?" In practice, allegations are heard against the police today and they point to the fact that there exists a lack of policing in police. One of the allegations is that the democracy's police today do not exclusively work for the cause of justice. Most of them have self and vested interests which are political, financial, personal, etc. Some policemen/officers have their political contacts with the affluent and the influential, a nexus with undesirable elements in society including underworld criminals, crime-syndicates and so on, and they probably perform their job with the patronage they receive from such unprincipled men. The police extends support to them and they ensure protection to the police. In a way, they are in a vicious circle and they work for their mutual benefits and advantage.

The police in a democracy stands between the people and the people's Government in power. For the common man, each member of the police service symbolizes the power of the Government. Politicians become very powerful in a democracy and therefore the police as the symbol of the State's power becomes the "yes men" of the politicians. They may overlook even the control of the judiciary and of the press when they get political support. It is not surprising that anti-police slogans are frequently shouted by the people and politicians in the opposition.

The British introduced the subordinate police and the superior police. The former consisted of the constables and headconstables then and they made up the bulk of the police force in British India. The Torture Commission - 1855 noted the abuses of the police which were indicative of the lawlessness in the law enforcement department. The British created a structure of supervision and control over the subordinate police, and the Police Commission: 1902-03 wanted to make the supervision and control more absolute. History shows that the superior police misused the subordinate police in many ways and the subordinate police worked in an atmosphere of terror, fear and deterrence from above. When India became independent, politicians too became very powerful and the members of the subordinate police became their men and thus the members of the subordinate police and politicians at various levels started to work together for their mutual advantage. The members of the superior police too started establishing nexus with politicians of various levels. Ultimately, the members of the subordinate police, superior police and various political parties came under the same umbrella. Together, they started enforcing law and their "collaboration" resulted sometimes in lawless law enforcement. Whenever a political party comes to power, it sees to it that some of the partymen are recruited to police service at the subordinate level and the intention is to see that they have their adherents in the police even when they go out of power. Police the police or politicize the police - the politicians want the latter, for a politicized police may serve their interests better than a policed police. True or false, there is a growing feeling today that every political party in power wants to enlist as many party men as possible in the police service so that their political interests are served with police power and authority. Can the police do justice to people in such situations? How effectively can the Constitution of India and the laws made under the Constitution of India control the police?

The British recruited uneducated and illiterate policemen. For, they wanted such people to protect their interests. Evidently, they created a brutal police force. After India became independent, the political masters came in place of the British masters during the pre-independent India and they wanted to create a police force which might serve their interests. Political interests and police functions cannot go hand in hand so much so that one had to be sacrificed if the other had to be achieved. Political interests cannot be sacrificed for maintaining police functions and precisely therefore the police have to tune their functions to serve the interests of the political party in power. This is what is seen today so much so that policing the police becomes a difficult, if not an impossible, task.

The British wanted an army-like police force in India. They appointed many army officers to the superior police. They wanted military criteria for recruitment and training. Even today, the physical standards prescribed for lower level functionaries in the police are almost the same as those intended for armymen. The training too closely follows the same as that for the army. The civil police in a democracy is not and must not be the army of the Country. The objective of a civil police service in a democracy is certainly different from the same of the army in a Country. Somehow or other, this idea was not accepted and consequently, democratic India created an army-like police service even after her independence in 1947. As a result the police resorted to army tactics and strategies to police the people. People and politicians objected to such people-unfriendly attitudes/approaches by the police. The people and the politicians accused the police of lack of policing within the police organization. The accusations were not altogether baseless. The Central Committee on Police training (Gore Committee) appointed by the Government of India in 1971 recommended to reorient the attitude of the police and they suggested many inservice courses for the purpose. An army-like behaviour is unwarranted in the civil police and it can help the police to become people-unfriendly in a democracy. The functions of the army and the civil police are different and are not even distantly related. In order to police the society, why do the police have recourse to military tactics and strategies? But the police did not study the strategies and tactics which are different from those of the army. The people in a democracy found the police resorting to army tactics and strategies and therefore they demanded the police to police the police first before they started policing the society. The police did not get the public acceptance for the work they did honestly for the people. In the army, there exist no political masters whereas in the police, there are. The civil police is not the army and the army is not the civil police. The armymen are trained to fight against the enemies; the policemen are trained to serve the people. The motives and attitudes of the armymen are different from those of the policemen. The policemen are interested in the welfare and human coexistence of the people with whom the politicians too are concerned. Hence, policing the police to police the people becomes essential and inevitable. The policeman is very careful or ought to be extraordinarily careful about his self-image whereas the armyman is not. For, the policeman works among his own people and amidst his own population. The policeman is not a warrior in a democracy, rather is the servant of the people. The more he serves the people, the more self-image and social prestige he derives. He can achieve them only if he polices himself and his organization. Self-esteem and social prestige for the policeman are bound up with his social awareness and service-mindedness in the present day. It was not so in the colonial past. The illiterate or marginally educated constables whose pay was notoriously low had fantasized self-esteem and social prestige whenever they behaved rudely with the people. They were British Government servants then, whereas they are public servants in the democracy today. The British terrorized the constabulary, and by doing so they made attempts to police the police. To quote David Arnold again: "Although low pay was an acknowledged cause of laxity and corruption in the force, senior police officers tried to impose discipline on the force through a harsh system of departmental punishments. It was typical of the Colonial regime as a whole to believe that Indians could only be made to behave as the British wanted them to through fear and coercion: the punitive character of colonial law enforcement and maintenance of 'order' thus had its counterpart in the punitive discipline exercised within the police department".

Policing the police by punitive methods was the British style of administration. When India became independent, the administration followed the same pattern and wanted to see that the police was policed. Even today, allegations are raised sometimes that the police is overpunitive to police the police. The police administration both in pre-independent and post-independent India could not understand that punitive methods to police the police were counterproductive. For example, in Madras Police Administration Report - 1867-68, one takes note of the fact that nearly half of the policemen were fined for minor offences. Demotions and dismissals were frequently resorted to. Some policemen resigned or deserted. The impact of applying excessively punitive strategies was counterproductive.

Again, in Madras Police Administration Report: 1901, it is seen that there was a change in the punitive mentality of the police administration. As a result, dismissals and desertions came down. Nevertheless, the constabulary was dissatisfied with the methods of policing the police. They took sick leave and some absented themselves without leave. In the *Crime in India - 1998,* it may be observed that a lot of policemen are departmentally punished. In the democracy, the policemen often approach political leaders to escape from punishment and studies show that the punitive approaches of police administration pave the way for establishing a nexus with the politicians. The police-politician nexus and dependability become matters of critical importance and serious consequences in these days and the days to come. Police Associations formed make the nexus stronger. The constables/officers express their grievances through their associations. The chain of institutional command and control from the director general of police to the constables are now said to be shaken. There is a growing feeling now that the subordinates are not amenable to strict supervision, control and guidance from the higher-ups in police service. Policing the police thus becomes an item of priority in the police service now.

New definitions are given to "policing the police". Policing the police means a service with adequate control over lawlessness in the service. Policing the police has three dimensions which are: (1) policing the self, (2) policing the police department and (3) policing the society in a people-friendly way. Policing the self means a lot and includes principally self-control. Policing the police department means controlling the members in the service for harmony and human coexistence. Policing the society means rendering police service in a human rights friendly and just way to the people.

The Europeans ruled over the Indians during the colonial regime. The whites were officers (superior police) and the Indians were constables (subordinate police). The Indian Police Commission: 1902-03 made a tripartite division in the police. Accordingly, those Indians who were better educated and having social positions higher than the constables were recruited as intermediaries between white superintendents and Indian constables. The white superintendents realized that there was lack of policing in the constabulary and one of the prime reasons was the dearth of communication between the two levels. Hence, in order to effect adequate control and supervision and thereby to police the constabulary, Indians were enlisted at the intermediary levels. Of course, there were white officers too at the intermediary levels. The European intermediaries were given preferential treatment and were given better salary than the Indian intermediaries. Certainly the double standard in the approach could cause only dissatisfaction among the Indians. Drunkenness among the European intermediaries was notorious. Drunkenness, indiscipline, chronic indebtedness and corruption were vogue among them. They were rude and spoke filthy and abusive language to the Indians. Even today, the police - especially those who are in the middle and lower levels - are blamed for their frequent use of foul language and epithets. People are found to keep away from the police as they cannot tolerate the police language which has a notorious meaning in the dictionary and the meaning is "indecent language". A policed police service cannot use such expressions to the people they serve. Of course, the Indian Penal Code-1860 had enacted a provision to punish the people who uttered indecent language or expressions. But, the law was ineffective as far as the policemen/officers were concerned. Almost the same situation continues even today when India has accepted human rights laws and individual dignity.

The post of sub-inspectors was sanctioned by the Government in 1905. As a result, candidates holding at least an S.S.L.C (a pass) came to occupy the newly created posts of the sub-inspectors. One of the intentions for creating the post was to enlist officers directly as sub-inspectors in the police. It was presumed that such newly recruited officers would be men of good moral character. However, it was later noted that the sub-inspectors who were directly recruited were not up to the mark. They possessed higher qualifications (S.S.L.C.) and therefore they looked down upon their subordinates. They were disinclined even to talk to their constables. They had such an EGO in them that they did not even respect the constables. They were relatively better educated and came from middle class families and from higher castes. The constables had the peasant or labour class background. The constables were excessively docile, submissive and obedient to their European masters while the newly enlisted sub-inspectors were not. As a consequence, suspicion and hostility between the middle and higher levels in the police came into being. The superior police ranks knew well that some of their middle level functionaries were better educated and smarter than many of them. They did not like it and, therefore, they purposely saw to it that the middle level officers were humiliated. They initiated disciplinary actions against the middle level police functionaries just to show and convince them that they were administratively higher than the smarter or smartest sub-inspectors in the police.

Even today, there exists a situation wherein one takes note of interpersonal rivalry between the ranks in the police service. In 1912, a lot of allegations were raised against the newly enlisted sub-inspectors. The allegations were that they were corrupt and cruel to the people. They employed torture on the people. The *Indian Patriot* in 1913 wrote: "honest men cannot serve in the police". There are any number of research studies and public opinion surveys to show how the lower, middle and top level police functionaries behave these days. They show that something is lacking in the police and probably, it is nothing but lack of policing. How many policemen/officers are detected and punished for committing crimes which may include corruption, torture, manipulation of records, false registration of cases and involvement in nexus crimes ? What Colonel Hearn, the Inspector General of Police in 1876, said about the police in India then is found to be true even during 2002. In 1876, he used the words "corruption, oppression, inefficiency, etc.," about the police and he said that the corruption, oppression and inefficiency made "a blot upon the face of the country and a curse to the people". How far is his observation true with respect to the police today? The answer to the question will show the extent of policing within the police service.

The police force was considered as a coercive weapon of the colonial Government. They created the armed reserves and armed battalions (paramilitary sections) within the police organization. The police force was given an army like-training. They considered the police as a quasi-military force. The British used the police as a coercive arm of the State in the suppression of demonstrations, disturbances and law and order situations. In order to suppress the demonstrations/disturbances, the British wanted able bodied men at lower posts than the troops. If needed, the British wanted to utilize the police for military operations. Hence, they were given quasi-military arms, training and discipline and were called the police. They were not taught or told about the finer points in human behaviour. They did not know how to investigate crimes scientifically. They were not the civil police. Policing the armed police was different from policing the civil police. As the paramilitary police force was intended to be a coercive organ of the British, they resorted to coercive tactics whenever they dealt with the civilians. It was not policing, rather it was a police raj under deterrence.

When India became independent, the same pattern of policing continued. The democracy's police in India had a broader perspective than suppression and oppression. They were to protect the people and ensure their social welfare. The role and functions of the police changed a lot, but the police did not realize their duties in a democracy. A new Constitution came into force and the people of India enjoyed equality, freedom, dignity, etc., as guaranteed by the Constitution. The police were entrusted with the safeguarding of the fundamental rights of the people. The police were thus policed first as Art. 38 of the Constitution states: *"the State to secure a social order for the promotion of welfare of the people"*.

"The State shall strive to promote the welfare of the people by securing and protecting as effectively as it may a social order in which justice social, economic and political, shall inform all the institutions of the national life".

The police were thus to promote the welfare of the people by establishing a social order in which justice was everything. The power vested with the police ought to be used in favour of those who are the ultimate donors of the power to the police. It is the people of India who empower the police to exercise powers and precisely therefore the police become answerable/accountable to their masters/patrons who are the people themselves. In such a state of affairs, there is no scope for a suppressive or oppressive policing. Torture and use of third degree methods become meaningless and the need for a policed police service becomes essential. Justice to the people is the first Constitutional promise and the police is to offer justice to people. Any type of police cannot do so. The policed police will accept that justice is the foremost human right. Police crimes have no scope in such a situation. The police will invite contempt unless they become justice friendly. The police during the British raj was accountable to the British Government, whereas the police in democratic India is accountable to the people of the country.

All police power is a people's trust in a democracy and precisely therefore the police power has a fiduciary component. The people believe that their police will exercise their powers as per the law and procedure established by law. In such a system, lack of policing in police service has no scope or relevance.

Do the police maintain their dignity and decorum? Last week when I engaged a session for the vertical interaction course for the officers of the Indian Police Service at the Institute of Management in Government, Thiruvananthapuram, I said that the press often brought out lack of policing in the police department. I had any number of paper cuttings with me to establish my point of view. The paper cuttings relate to misbehaviour towards women and children to nexus criminality and police sponsored terrorism/fake encounters. Immediately, an inspector general of police said: "The press exaggerates any news against the police". Another inspector general of police sharply reacted and said: "behind the exaggerated version of the press, there is a lot of truth". Ultimately, they reached a consensus and it was that the police needed policing them first before they policed the society. For, almost everyday the people read the news about the drunken behaviour of the policemen, illegal arrests, unauthorized detentions and use of torture by policemen. Apart from the individual misconduct of the policemen/officers, there is a dimension of institutional accountability to the people. The people invest huge amounts of money on the police and they expect polished and policed behaviour from the institution of the police. The police are the subjects of people's audit and any policeman/officer who misuses his power/abuses his authority is an offender under the law and therefore he must be amenable to punishment. He must keep himself away from lawless, immoral, undesirable and unbecoming conduct.

A few days ago, I found a street corner meeting in front of a police station. I found a politician of the opposition party speaking against police atrocities and he blamed many policemen/officers by names. He said that they were animals in police uniform. I learnt later that the police officers whose names were publically announced as people-unfriendly and crime-prone were not disturbed at the platform utterances. For, they were supported by the politicians of the ruling front. Politicians encourage and condemn police crimes and so long as the drama continues, it may be difficult to police the police. In a private conversation with a senior police officer, the question of policing the police came up. I could understand that the senior police officer did not like the topic and therefore he said: "first let the legislators police themselves in the Houses". Yes, there is a point in what he said. The law makers violate the laws, call others by rude epithets, throw microphones, damage furniture, cause injuries to fellow legislators and they become instant heroes and leaders in a democracy. Likewise, a law-abiding policeman/officer becomes a misfit in the police service! People have a mental picture of a policeman/officer and there they do not see a policed policeman/officer. Anandswarup Gupta writes: "The Indian police have no doubt served India well and truly in many important and vital respects since independence, particularly in the control of agitations and disturbances of a wide variety, in the preservation of India's integrity and unity and in the protection of her borders, but in the routine tasks of policing, they are still the object of public distrust and condemnation, if not hated; and the unfortunate fact remains that they are still in search of a new identity, a new image, a new aim and a new technique".

More than 50 years are now over since India became independent and the police is in the third millennium. Yet, the police experiences an identity crisis. What exactly is the role of the Indian police? - suppression? - oppression? - employment of brute force? Or public service and people friendly approaches? An identity crisis comes into being when there is no clarity in the objectives of the police service. If the objectives are not clear, then there will not be any policing within the police organization. This is what did happen to the Indian police. The Police Act-1861 had an oppressive and repressive police force in mind. The objective was clear then. But in Indian democracy, the police are not oppressive and repressive. We have today the armed police. They are a force. Their objectives are different from those of the local police who are concerned with the detection, prevention and investigation of crime and criminals. They must be human rights friendly. The Rapid Action Police, Commando Police and so on have different objectives which are different from those of the local police or Thana police. The Traffic police are different from the Tourist police with different objectives. The intelligence police are different from the juvenile police. How can all of them be put under a Police Act? Necessarily, they will face an identity crisis. The word "Police" is a generic term which cannot be equally applied to all categories of police in a democracy. As it is today, there exists a total confusion. The traffic police think that they are the law-and-order police and the law-and-order police think that they are the riot police. Because of the identity crisis and confusion in their objectives, they resort to many means and methods which are not people friendly in a democracy. I have noticed the traffic policemen shouting at the road users with epithets - the tourist police speaking foul language - the law-and-order police interacting with people in a filthy and vulgar way. As they are confused about their role and functions, they resort to the same means and methods to police the society. While doing so with the show of their muscle power, they forget the objectives and experience an identity crisis. After India became independent, some guidelines are given from time to time for proper behaviour. The guidelines may be perfect in all respects, but their implementation is dismal. Why? This is due to the identity crisis. The human content in police transactions is more important than the muscle and brute contents. On certain occasions, as Shakespeare said - 'the police can be mad, but there should be a method in madness!' The police may be active, but not effective. And if that happens, then what is the ultimate advantage? In all situations, there is only one correct way for doing a thing and that must be done in a people friendly manner. The policemen/officers who suffer from an identity crisis may be doing the correct thing, but in a wrong way? They create a bad image for the police. A bad police image means lack of policing the police in a democracy. They must learn the Preamble to the Constitution of India and then create a police image. The Preamble reads: "We, The people of India, having solemnly resolved to constitute India into a Sovereign Socialist Secular Democratic Republic and to secure to all its citizens:

> *Justice, social, economic and political;*
> *Liberty of thought, expression, belief, faith and worship;*
> *Equality of status and of opportunity;*
> *and to promote among all*
> *Fraternity assuring the dignity of the individual and unity and integrity of the Nation...*

and the policemen in democratic India have no objectives other that what are stated in the Preamble to the Constitution of India. The British police and the Indian Police Act - 1861 did not have such sublime objectives. The Constitution of India speaks about Justice, Liberty, Equality, Fraternity, Dignity, Unity and Integrity of the Nation. If the policemen respect them, they will not experience any identity crisis and will be able to project an enviable police image. Studies conducted to learn about the lack of policing in the police show that the police in free India :

(1) register false cases, do not register true cases, conduct perfunctory investigations, do not conduct just and fair investigations, concoct evidence, manipulate records, torture suspects and commit human rights violations. If the findings are true, then how do the police ensure justice to the people as envisaged by the Constitution?

(2) do not take adequate interest in the prevention of crimes, patrolling and beat, collection of criminal intelligence; rather they take interest in involving themselves in the commission of nexus crimes, corruption, Mafia crimes, crime-syndicate, etc. If so, how do the police protect the liberty of the people as envisaged by the Constitution.

(3) do treat differently and unjustly the people, especially the poor and the downtrodden. They become susceptible to political influence and the influence of the affluent. The differential treatment is a threat to equality as envisaged by the Constitution.

How can the police guarantee the dignity of the people if they do not show due respect to them, if they insult them, if they humiliate them?

The Preamble of the Constitution contains everything the police must perform, and certainly it removes the identity crisis in any policeman/officer in democratic India. The British pattern of policing was not the pattern of policing in democratic India. Nevertheless, the administration did not realize it as early as 1947 when India became independent or as early as 1950 when the Constitution of India came into force. Although the objectives of policing changed a lot, there was no attempt made to enact new legislations to translate the newly accepted police objectives to real work situations. The tragic effect was that the police in India continued to behave in the same way as they used to be in pre-independent India. As a result, the oppressive and repressive police force of British India could not become people friendly in democratic India. The police had a bad image, but the police blamed the mirror for the true reflection. They said that the people were bad and therefore they deserved a bad police force. "As the people, so the police" - attitude did not ensure justice, liberty, equality and dignity as guaranteed by the new Constitution of India. The policemen were worried about their image in democratic India; nevertheless, they were not found worrying about the reality behind the reflected image. The reality was, perhaps, more horrible than the reflection. Custodial deaths, custody-rapes, blinding episodes, torture in custody, etc., were realities, but some of them were not properly reflected. The victims of police abuse of power/misuse of authority will, in all probability, malign the police at every conceivable opportunity. P.S. Bawa, a senior police officer of the Indian Police Service writes: "After I had finished training in the State Police College, my friend said: 'Meharban, you must have learnt the choicest abuses and the most effective methods of torture'. I was stunned by the remarks. He was thoroughly mistaken. 'These are perhaps the only two things they do not teach you at the college. Believe me, we are not trained to be sadists'. I told him. 'But then these must be taught to the constables' schools', he insisted. 'No, not there even'. I told him. But you can't say these things don't happen. There are tortures in police custody; people are insulted in public; there are brutal beatings and all that. Yes, he was correct". If Bawa is correct, then a question is raised and that is: "what type of policing is there in the police?". He enumerates a number of atrocities committed by the police which include: 'shaving of the head of the people taken into police custody, beating a person who fell into an open drain while escaping from a lathy charge, towing of cars in such a way that the lamps of the vehicle get smashed in transit, handcuffing a person just for humiliating him, keeping a person under incommunicado detention, etc'. No policed police may do such acts in any civilized country or if at all they do so, they may have to face severe consequences.

I have heard some policemen/officers talking wildly against human rights friendly approaches in the police service. For them, "old is gold" and they advocate a brute and muscle approach to various categories of offenders and people. They are people who want to regress into the old strategies which are proved to be ineffective and people unfriendly. They argue that the new methods do not solve the problem - as if the old strategies could solve the problems ! Resistance to change is seen, but change becomes inevitable to progress and development. The Protection of Human Rights Act - 1993 has come into force and the Act is intended, among other things, to police the police. The courts are making new laws and are giving new directives to police the police. The legislatures bring new laws to police the police. The police departments issue many circulars and rules to police the police. The press and the media bring many news items to police the police. Researchers and scholars conduct many studies for the same. Human rights activists, non-governmental organizations and the United Nations insist on the police to be human rights friendly. The United Nations have brought out many declarations and conventions in this aspect. The national and international communities are making serious and genuine attempts in this respect. All of them want the police to become sensitive to issues, individuals and events. To quote P.S. Bawa once again: "There are certain activities which are objectionable. You cannot accept them. Sometimes policemen break the queue, they get into the bus from the wrong end, try to jump in or out of a bus while it is moving, turn a blind eye to a problem which ought to engage their attention, stand in a corner doing nothing when the traffic is heavy and undirected, and so on". To what he has observed to show lack of policing in police, we may add many more. People who closely observe the policemen/officers make complaints that :

(1) Some conduct patrolling without any purpose. They move from one place to another in a ritualistic way.

(2) Some policemen keep their patrol vehicle in places where they remain ideally and in a ritualistic fashion.

(3) Some policemen come in patrol vehicle to wayside shops to smoke cigarettes, to drink soft drinks, to enjoy refreshments, etc., without making payments.

(4) Some police officers enjoy traffic concessions by misusing police vehicles, policemen and lights on police vehicles.

(5) Some policemen/officers take a 'don't care attitude' to complainants and service seekers to police aid posts. They sleep there and show no concern to people's needs.

(6) Some policemen chew *paan* and throw the spit on the road, park the vehicle at a "No Parking" zone, behave in a drunken way, make vulgar comments on women/girls to which the people develop a scorn.

Little things the policemen do - namely, entering a theatre without purchasing tickets, travelling in an omnibus without paying, renting out a car without paying the full rent, purchasing provisions without payment, etc., have adverse effects on the police image and exhibit the non-policing of the police. The hardening of human behaviour and the projecting out of the image of a tough man is not policing. Creating anxiety and apprehension among the people that something bad may happen if they don't entertain a policeman properly is not policing. Journalists take photographs of police action during a law and order situation. Getting angry at it, some policemen/officers snatch the camera and expose the films to light. No policeman is above law and whenever a civilian questions the authority of a police officer to behave the way he does, he may get angry and beat him in public. People are taken to police stations and locked up in half-nakedness. Pressuring them to starve there and to remain there in humiliating conditions without the minimum human comforts, refusing to grand bail in bailable offences, showing a blind eye to the women in police custody to attend to their special needs during menstural periods, forcing people to stay in police stations on the pretext of verifying the address/status of sureties even when that is not required, shouting at way-side vendors, foot-path sellers, fellow drivers and road-users, etc., are not policing or polished ways of policing. They are manifestations of aggressiveness and abuse of power. The arrogance of the police ego must not go to the extent of showing animal instincts and misuse of powers, "I will show him who I am" - "I will teach him a hard lesson" - "I will show the power of my uniform" - attitude is dangerous. The law is not what the police do-rather it is what the law is.

The Police Act-1861 makes the police an efficient instrument for the detection and prevention of crimes. But how? One sees the words like "obey, execute", etc., and the Act contains aggressive and authoritative expressions. The Act does not show respect to human dignity and human rights. The Act has been in existence for one and a half centuries and so far could not carve out a policed police service. An Act which could not bring out a policed police service for a hundred and fifty years cannot think about a people friendly police service ever in the future. The Act could create, as the researchers find, a crude, rude, rough, offensive and authoritarian police force with a culture which is not people friendly - a culture which accepts maltreatment of offenders, which promotes corruption and corrupt practices, which is devoid of courtesy and good manners, which does not value police duties as a service to the people. Still, the Act treats the police as a force - a coercive force to suppress and oppress the people. Indian democracy's police did not make any conscious and serious attempts to get out of the shell of the Police Act-1861. The inherited evils continue to rule the police subculture. The service aspect of the police has not given precedence over the "brute force aspects" of police work.

This book "Policing the Police: A Nation's Cry!" is a millennium wish and exposes the state of affairs in policing the largest democracy by a police force which came into existence by virtue of the Police Act-1861. A police force which is not policed well cannot render police service in a people friendly way. For nearly a century and half, the people of this country suffered the police, of course with a lot of complaints, allegations and accusations against them. Now the society pressures the police to render services and the police services are compared with the those that are offered by the police in developed countries, especially in democratic nations. The services rendered by the police outside India and those offered by the police in India are the same. Nevertheless, the manner in which the services are given, delayed, or refused is different. Why? Policing the police or lack of policing the police becomes a topic of discussion. The services are in many areas - viz., in law and order, in administration of penal justice, juvenile justice, gender justice, human rights justice, victim justice, social justice, etc. The objectives are different and in India the same police offer all kinds of justice and they are far away from being satisfactory - that is what the people complain of. For example, the social commitments of the police have increased manifold after India became independent. The police have new responsibilities. A number of social legislations come into being and certainly each legislation causes disturbance in the society. The police in India work under the Police Act-1861 and they know coercive techniques and strategies. They are of a questionable nature to ensure the desired results in social change. Studies reveal that the undemocratic methods sometimes resorted to by the police pave the way for widespread corruption and malpractices in the police service. The National Police Commission: 1977-81 think that police enthusiasm to bring quick social changes in a quick way lowers the department's image in the eyes of the common man. The Commission feels that misplaced authority affects police public relations adversely and damages the department's credibility. Only a well policed police service can administer social justice. What about juvenile justice? Police Act-1861 never thought anything about the concept of juvenile justice. An Act which was brought to oppress and suppress the Indians by the British did not think about correctional justice. The punitive police was not meant for it. As early as in 1920, the Madras Children Act which was enacted on a provincial basis brought the concept of juvenile justice; nevertheless the punitive police were not meant for it. As early as in 1960, the Central Children Act was enacted to administer juvenile justice. Many States had their Children Acts. Correspondingly, no change was seen in the traditional police in the Country. Many nations instituted special juvenile police specially qualified in dealing with neglected and delinquent children for the same. They wanted first to police the police for policing children who needed special care. In India, the 1861 police who were to police the society in the British way continued to police children who needed special care. The international community (The General Assembly of the United Nations) on 29, November, 1985 adopted Standard Minimum Rules for the Administration of juvenile justice and subsequently India enacted the Juvenile Justice Act-1986 to administer juvenile justice. The U.N.'s Rules insisted: "In order to best fulfil their functions, police officers who frequently or exclusively deal with juveniles or who are primarily engaged in the prevention of juvenile crime shall be specially instructed and trained. In large cities, special police units should be established for that purpose". Though 15 years are now over after the Juvenile Justice Act - 1986 came into force, no State Governments, I think, have policed their police to police the neglected and delinquent children with a correctional perspective. As the police are the first points of contact with the juvenile justice system, it is most important that they are policed first so that they act in an informed and appropriate manner. If paper reports are correct, the adult police service does a lot of harm to the juveniles. Most frustratingly, neither the government nor the police administration understands the necessity of policing the police to deal with the children who need the State's special care. The international community vociferously says that special police units would be indispensable for administering juvenile justice and for improving the prevention and control of juvenile crimes and the handling of juvenile offenders. Gender justice was unknown to the British law-makers during 1861 when they created a male police force to deal with women and girls. Of course, the sex is biological and the gender is socio-cultural and the concept of gender justice is of recent origin. Are the police in India policed enough to maintain gender decency in their work? Custodial molestation and custody-rapes are reported in the press, punished by the courts and compensated for by the Human Rights Commission. Are the police sufficiently policed to respect human rights and the worth of a human person ? The reports of the National Human Rights Commission bear testimony to the fact that the police in India need to be policed to administer justice in a human rights friendly way. The police are yet to know that criminal justice is just an aspect of justice administration. People today demand of an Equal Justice System and they want just justice to the crime-doers, to the victims of crime including the victims of abuse of power/misuse of authority, to the society and to the justice system. The police is a subsystem in the Equal Justice System and they need to administer justice to all who need it. For this, the police ought to be policed first. The third millennium wishes to have such a police service and the nation cries for such a police system. Indians suffered long enough from the suppressive and oppressive police force for centuries and they cannot bear the pain any longer.

I thank my wife Mary and daughters Neethu and Neethie for their support and encouragement to write this book. The views and opinions expressed in this book are personal and do not reflect the views and opinions of the Government of India, State Governments, Home Offices and police departments. Dr. James Vadackumchery affirms that he has the moral rights to be identified as the author if this title *'Policing the Police: A Nation's Cry!*

Dr. James Vadackumchery
Criminologist

August 15, 2002
Thiruvananthapuram

1

Policing a Society

"Policing a society is easy; policing the police is difficult" - said a criminologist in a private conversation. Why did he say so? The reason was that there was the police to police the society, but there was no such agency to police the police. Who would or could police the police? Organized policing was of recent origin and it came out as a result of the society's felt need to police the society. The society wanted the police to police the society and at that time when the society created organized policing, no one thought seriously about policing the police. The police certainly represented a cross section of the society and precisely, therefore, the good and the evil seen in society were seen in equal measures - a little more or a little less - among the police functionaries. There was no agency created for policing the police, for, then the question was: "who would police that agency which is to police the police?" If an agency to police the police were created, then would arise another question: "Who would police that agency?" The problem extended endlessly.

As years went by after the creation of organized policing in the world, the society found out that the police themselves were involved in the violation of the laws and human rights violations. This necessitated the society to create a Vigilance Department,which kept a watchful eye on the activities and mostly it concentrated on corruption and corrupt practices. As a result, policing the police beyond the area of corruption such as torture in police custody, enforcement crimes, informal arrests, illegal detentions, manipulation of records, etc., which were reported in police functioning became matters of serious concern from 1855 when Torture Commission filed their report and even before. Society enacted many provisions of laws and incorporated them in the Indian Penal Code-1860, Code of Criminal Procedure - 1861 and the Indian Evidence Act - 1872. Nevertheless, something lacked in policing the police even after the enactment of the special provisions, and the Indian Police Commission enumerated many crimes committed by the Indian Police during 1860-1900 and lack of policing. The Indian Police Commission: 1902-03 wanted to correct the police and made many recommendations. The Commission felt that the recommendations would cost a lot of money, but they ought to be spent. However, the National Police Commission: 1977-1981 reiterated many of the observations noted by the Indian Police Commission: 1902-03. No doubt, there has been a lack of policing in the police and even when it was the condition, the police continued to police the society. The society spent lavishly on the police and, as it is today, the annual expenditure on the police in the country is found to be around Rs.9000 crores of rupees. The society seems to be happy to spend more money on the police as it wants *policing* the society. There is a feeling that it is not the society that is found to be reluctant to spend money on the police, rather it is the police and political administration which often have a second thought on police expenditure. After each budget in the Centre or State, no one has so far made any negative criticisms on the police expenditure. People want to invest any amount on the police to police the society. But the same people make a lot of hue and cry when they find lack of policing in the police department. Whenever a custodial death takes place in a police station, people rush to the police stations. Recently, a lawyer was alleged to have been manhandled by a police subinspector. More than 2000 lawyers boycotted the court proceedings and proceeded to the police station. They created a scene and the same was telecasted repeatedly in the media. Ultimately, the Commissioner of Police came to the spot and had negotiations with the representatives of the Bar. The lawyers were not prepared to have a compromise until and at last the police officer was placed under suspension pending a departmental inquiry. A criminal case was registered against the police officer alleged to have manhandled the lawyer. What is more? When lack of policing is seen in a police department, people hold demonstrations and conduct *"dharnas"* in police stations.... Public litigation societies and lawyers' forums file suits against the police and they show that the people are not prepared to tolerate lack of policing in the police department. The National Police Commission: 1977-81 made recommendations for initiating special procedures against police functionaries when custodial deaths would take place and the National Human Rights Commission has issued specific directives to the police in case of custodial deaths. The postmortem of the dead in police custody is videographed for scrutiny by the National Human Rights Commission. In cases of custodial deaths, a heavy amount of compensation is allowed to the next of kin of the deceased in police custody. All said and done, a lot of news against the police and about the lack of policing in the police appears in the print and electronic media. Where is the matter going wrong?

Why to Police the Society and Police?

It was a felt need of the people in all societies and cultures to police the society - to maintain social solidarity. The laws of the society must be enforced. According to Emile Durkheim, the society must maintain the social cohesion intact. Detection of law violators and awarding punishments to them were found to be necessary to keep people law abiding. In order to do so, the society felt the necessity to have an organized policing, the society was policed by some system of policing and the objective was to punish the wrong-doers.

Policing by the State is a concept of recent origin. From experience, the society learnt a lesson that the people taking private revenge on wrong-doers ought to be stopped. Some people who did not have a superior strength than the crime-doers could not take private revenge against the law violators. Likewise, those who did have superior strength inflicted punishment which was disproportionate to the gravity of the crime they committed. The society wanted to see that adequate, correct, fair and just action was initiated against the State by its corporate capacity. The result was the setting up of organized policing.

To begin with, the police was created as a Force to police the society. Today, the police work more as a service than as a Force. "The police ought to be deterrent and the more the police force would be deterrent, the more the general public would desist from the commission of crime". Whether or not this belief has any empirical validity is not the issue here, rather many people including some well meaning police officers believe so even today. A senior police officer told me recently that the police ought to be deterrent in order that the people do not commit crimes. I did not argue with him as I knew very well that he was an "argument proof" and more over, he had little or very little information on the theory of deterrence and administration of justice in the modern world.

Historically, the police in India did many things - including atrocities on human beings - to cause deterrence among the people. Police Commissions in India attested the view that causing deterrence in public was a strategy for the Indian Police during the British Raj and later. In causing deterrence, the police sometimes resorted to the means and methods which showed to the people that there was lack of proper policing among the policemen/officers. The arguments that police strategies do or do not deter all types of people are generally based on conjecture, emotions and unsubstantiated research findings. In front of the police, some people commit crimes and the underworld criminals establish nexuses with the police to commit crimes. Deterrence from police may be effective in preventing a petty thief from pocketpicking, but not necessarily a person from committing naxalite crimes, organized crimes, terrorism and nexus criminality. It means that certain types of people are deterred by the police while others are not.

Police are sometimes blamed for informal arrests, illegal detention,use of torture and inhuman treatment. If the allegations are true, then there is no policing in the police. Why? It is not correct to presume that all people are deterred by the informal arrests or the employment of torture. There are recidivists and hardened criminals who are not usually deterred by the police. Police strategies do not necessarily and often deter all kinds of people.

The police have to police the society, and the society looks at the police to see how policed they are. If the police are not policed, then the police cannot and will not be able to police any society. The police have to ensure the welfare of the people and in so doing the police have to show to the people that they are more policed than the people in society. It is unwise to show lack of policing in the police (namely, use of torture, registration of false cases, manipulation of records, concoction of evidence, production of touts, etc.) solely for the purpose of creating deterrence among the people. A society can never be truly policed by any police strategies that do not deal justly and wisely with its people.

In my life, I have listened to many well meaning people talking against the police and about the inhuman and degrading treatments which the police offer to the people on many occasions. Many of them say: "police the police first before policing the society". Somehow or other, many people in society seem to have developed such a feeling against the police and certainly their attitude against the police can be changed only if the police change their behaviour - only if the police make a conscious attempt to convince the people that they are more policed than the society they serve. The police force is a service - a public facility and not a force that needs policing. Why do the police behave the way they do? I do not want to attribute any good or bad motives to the police behaviours as they are seen today. Nevertheless, the fact remains that the people make a lot of accusations against the police and research studies endorse many of the views/opinions of the people to be true. Some of the views/opinions are of bad taste and indicate a lack of policing in the police service. The international community has noted the police violating thc human rights of the people and deprive people of their freedom and subject them to humiliation, shame and degrading treatment. The Convention against Torture and many other Conventions of the United Nations deal with the lack of policing in the police service and provisions for policing the police. Policing a society violating the human rights of people - with good intentions to ensure welfare and solidarity - may be worse than tyranny and oppression.

Retribution: Policing Society and Police

Revenge/vengeance to criminals had historically been one of the widely seen reactions of the public. The *Eye for the Eye; a tooth for a tooth* doctrine for law violators is traced back to the Bible and Hammurabi's Code. Even when organized policing was not in existence, the society inflicted retributive justice to police the people. When the State took up the responsibility of punishing the offenders, it followed the old methods of retribution. The State inflicted cruel, inhuman and barbarous punishments on law violators and the policemen were utilized for the purpose. In 1704, Pope Clement XI erected the Papal Prison of San Michele in Rome and the intention was to inflict less severe punishment on the offenders. Imprisonment came to be thus a form of penalty and many States in Europe followed the new approach. This shift in the retributive approach to criminals paved the way for the States to become more humanitarian in their attitude towards the crime-doers. As the States became more humanitarian, the police too had to adopt a humanitarian approach to the criminals. Did or could the police become humanitarian towards the criminals while they dealt with them?

Retribution was/is a public reaction against the offenders. No doubt, it is an unrefined expression of human energy in a negative and aggressive way. Through socialization and value formation, the aggressive instincts can be controlled; it is virtually not possible to effect adequate control on people's instinctive expressions. In order to do so, the police become necessary. The policeman is trained to acquire adequate ego and instinctual control. He is professionally trained to deal with criminals with adequate ego controls. This does not take place if he expresses his revengeful attitude towards the crime-doers. Whenever he tortures a crime-doer or violates his human rights, he behaves like an unrefined person without adequate ego controls. Historically, it has been brought to light that the policeman too behaved in an unbecoming way expressing his instinctive energy with retributive spirit. If it happens, it is a lawless law-enforcement and as a result it is an expression of lack of policing in the police. Crimes have to be detected and the criminals ought to be punished. The punishment must be inflicted by a court of law and only after following the procedure established by the law. Whenever a policeman behaves with retributive spirit towards the criminal by inflicting torture or by expressing aggression, then he violates the law and assumes the duty of the court. The police in such situations encourage more violence and precisely therefore it manifests lack of policing. The victims of the abuse of power/misuse of authority by the police are the victims of the lack of policing in the police service. Once a policeman brutally manhandled a suspect in a crime and, seeing the brutality, the complainant said: "Don't hurt him any more". The retributive approach to the criminals is always discouraged and punished in modern police work.

Incapacitation through corporal punishment was not favoured by the society. The society found that 'making a criminal physically impossible for him to commit crimes' was meaningless. The cutting of the legs, plucking of the eyes, chopping of the sex-organs, etc., are not commonly endorsed today in civilized societies. But, the police historically is found to have employed many methods to incapacitate a person from making an honest living. It has been alleged that some people handled by the police had become complete wrecks in the sea of life. Though they had the legs, eyes, hands and tongues, they were found to suffer the cruel effects of brutal treatment in police stations. Allegations were raised that some such unfortunates of police manhandling died within a short period after their treatment in police custody. Certainly, the society felt that such an incapacitation was not necessary and was indicative of the lack of policing of the policemen. Criminologists find that the police cruelty to the suspects in crime/arrestees/criminals has its root in the natural impulse of revenge expressed by unrefined people. The police do not enjoy any right of retaliation and, if they assume that they have such a right, it shows lack of refinement in police service. Attempts have been made by many at different levels to humanize the police and it itself shows that the police need to be policed for ensuring justice to society.

Physician: Cure Thyself First!

It is a common argument that one must be all right before one makes attempts to make others all right. It therefore follows that the police must be policed before they police the society. "If the average working man is bigoted, that is his business; but if a policeman's bigoted, that is everyone's business. Policemen may simply be very ordinary people who happen to be extraordinarily visible", observed Robert W. Bulch. If so, it means that any lack of policing among the policemen becomes highly visible and the society does not/cannot approve of such situations. In a law-and-order situation, the police may be responding to the concepts of their role as defined by the law and their intention may be to maintain law and order.For that, they may have to take a stand against the demonstrators. The demonstrators generally look at the police in a critical way and any law violations on the part of the police may be attacked with critical comments. Everything the police do legally and illegally is very conspicuous and the criticism will be against the lawless law enforcement by the police. The lawless people may violate the laws during a demonstration, but they do not want the police to violate the laws even at very provoking situations. The police may legally fire at an unruly mob, but the society expects the police not to fire at the citizens. Any wrong committed by the police during their firing will be cashed by the vested interests. It goes without saying that the society expects the police to be legal and honest in their work whereas the same society does not expect the people to be law-abiding during a law-and-order situation. The society expects perfect policing in the police whereas it does not put such demands on the people in the society. Hence the argument: "Physician, cure thyself first". If the police are not law-abiding, the irritating press may publicize any misconduct by the policemen with their views and interpretations. Necessarily, it carves out a poor image of the police as the violators of the law and justice. As a result, the police lose their public acceptance. The press, the people and politicians slap the police with criticisms when they see a lack of policing in any police function. Law-violating policemen are faced by abuses, lack of respect for what they do and threats against their survival in the police department.

Law violations by the police have been studied by many in foreign countries. But, the researchers did not look at the law violations by the police as crimes; rather they studied them under various captions like police violence, police excesses, police brutality, etc., and many studies suggested that they were as old as the police, but have become more obvious in recent years. The visibility of police crimes and misbehaviour has now attracted human right activists to raise their voice against the police. A police misbehaviour involves an intention to employ excessive force on the people or to resort to means and methods which are nothing but abuse of power/misuse of authority.

Justifications for Lack of Policing in Police

Why are you corrupt? - a question was asked to many policemen and a good majority of them answered: "poor pay and perks". Is it a justification for lawlessness in the police service? More than 100 policemen/officers were asked to give their responses to some questions which related to the lack of policing in the police department. The answers which the majority offered (more than 50 per cent of the Sample) are given below:

Questions/Answers

Ques 1 : Why are you registering a false F.I.R.?

Ans : The pressures from many sources are heavy.

Ques 2 : Why are you resorting to informal arrests?

Ans : Arresting a person as per the law is difficult and time-consuming.

Ques 3 : Why are you keeping a person in illegal custody?

Ans : The collection of evidence through interrogation is time-consuming.

Ques 4 : Why are you not providing adequate food for the detainees?

Ans : There is inadequacy of funds at our disposal.

Ques 5 : Why are you reluctant to provide adequate facilities for the detinues?

Ans : There exist no facilities in police stations.

Ques 6 : Why do you torture people in custody?

Ans : This is done to elicit information in a quick way.

Ques 7 : Why do you humiliate the people in the police custody?

Ans : The society wants such treatment to the people dealt with by police.

Ques 8 : Why do you accept corruption money?

Ans : Poor pay and perks.

Ques 9 : Why do you resort to corrupt practices?

Ans : To make a living and to go along with others who are corrupt.

Ques 10 : Why do you speak filthy language?

Ans : The people often do not understand sober expressions and language.

Ques 11 : Why do you harass people?

Ans : Harassment is a part of law enforcement.

Que 12 : Why do you call people epithets during a V.I.P.'s visit or a law-and-order situation?

Ans : They have quick responses from people in a desired direction.

Ques 13 : Why do you produce false witnesses?

Ans : To satisfy the requirements of law.

Ques 14 : Why do you concoct evidence?

Ans : To obtain a conviction in criminal cases.

Ques 15 : Why do you produce touts in courts?

Ans : It is easy to do so in cases where witnesses are not available.

Ques 16 : Why do you violate human rights?

Ans : Lack of knowledge on human rights.

Ques 17 : Why do you become susceptible to political pressures?

Ans : There is no option other than yielding to politician's wishes.

Ques 18 : Why do you ill-treat people?

Ans : It is not ill-treatment; rather it is a feeling that they are ill-treated.

Ques 19 : Why do you become disinterested in your work?

Ans : Workload and lack of leisure time.

Ques 20 : Why are you not showing due respect to witnesses?

Ans : Respect is shown, but the witnesses feel otherwise.

Ques 21 : Why are you not gender-decent to women?

Ans : Gender decency is shown,but the women feel otherwise.

Ques 22 : Why do you drink intoxicating liquors?

Ans : To release the tension of the job.

Ques 23 : Why do you show differential treatment to various types of people?

Ans : It is their feeling only and not real.

Ques 24 : Why do you manipulate records?

Ans : There will be only conscientious manipulations?

Que 25 : Why do you violate laws?

Ans : There is no option, but to violate them.

One may ask any question to a policeman/officer, he may have a justification/rationalization for everything he does. Criminologists will say further that no one has desisted from committing crimes just because he has no reason to justify his action. This is true not only with regard to crime-doers, but also with regard to any person doing any act. Hence, I did not want to ask more questions to more policemen/officers. Therefore, I asked the some questions to the members of the public. Their reasons were different from what the policemen/ officers offered. For examples :

Questions/Answers

Ques 1 : Why do the police resort to informal arrests?

Ans : They think that they can afford to do so without any evil consequences.

Ques 2 : Why do the police keep a person in illegal custody?

Ans : There is no one to question the police on such illegalities.

Ques 3 : Why do the police torture people in their custody?

Ans : The poor people suffer the police and the police express their aggressiveness as they do not fear anybody.

Ques 4 : Why do the police accept corruption money?

Ans : They want to live a luxurious life.

And thus, the people have formed their views/opinions against the police although the police may give any justifications for what they do. The police do not/cannot convince the people or are not able to do so. The people too are as intelligent as or more intelligent than the policemen/officers and therefore they make their own evaluations, views and opinions. Non-policing in the police will not be tolerated at any cost. Once a director general of police was directed to arrest a political leader for the commission of an offence. The director general was unhappy to do so. He thought that arresting a person for having committed an offence was not the duty/responsibility of the director general of police. It could be done by a subinspector of police. He objected to the suggestion which came from above, but he went at last to do the unpleasant job and the political leader was finally arrested in his presence. This happened about 12 years ago and then the people said "Look, there is differential treatment in law enforcement and arrest". Who must be blamed? - the police or the people?

Policing the police is a police job and the people must see it. There is only one Constitution in India and the laws are the same everywhere. The police are bound to enforce the same law in a manner accepted by the law. If adulteration is seen in the enforcement of law or differential enforcement is noticed, the people blame the policeman/officer responsible for the same and will accuse the police for the non-policing amidst them. Any amount of justification will not/can not convince the people and approve of police actions.

William Westley once argued that the social reactions to a job ought to be taken into account. If the social reactions to the police doings, actions and omissions are not praiseworthy, then there is something wrong in that. He also said that the self-concept each man has when he performed the job mattered a lot. What is the self-esteem of a police officer who tortures a suspect? - who accepts corruption money? - who yields to political whims? - who wants to retain his chair at any cost? - who is unethical in his approaches?

Some policemen/officers have a misconception that they employ different scales to evaluate the policing of the society and the policing of the police service. They do not have two different scales. They employ one and the same scale to evaluate both. "Don't fight against a person, but against the passion" - this is a normative scale which the society applies to both man and policeman. Hence, whenever, a policeman employs torture on a fellow citizen, the society accuses him saying that he is not fighting against his passions and confirms the fact that there is lack of policing in him.

Scales to Decide the Lack of Policing in Police

There is no effective or useful scale to decide the extent and intensity of policing in the police. The policemen employ legal scales (laws) to police the society. In other words, whenever a person commits a violation of the law, he is caught by the police. But, when a policeman violates the law, then the people in society cannot catch him. For example, smoking in public is a violation of the law. Whenever a member of the public smokes, he is caught; but whenever a policeman does the same thing he is not caught. It being so, it is not easy to decide the extent or lack of policing in the police whereas it is very easy to decide the same among the public. The statistics on crimes gives details of crimes committed by the public and nothing about the same committed by police. The National Police Commission : 1977-81 found no justification for 60 per cent of the arrests the police made and certainly no case was registered against many police functionaries who made such illegal/unjustifiable arrests. Was it a symptom of non-policing within the police?

The individualistic, normative, socio-cultural, statistical and diagnostic scales which the people have for assessing human behaviour to be normal or abnormal are the ones which they use to assess police behaviour as well. If the people find that the police behave abnormally when they apply the scales, then they say that there is lack of policing in the police. For example, registering a false case against a person is a mean act and the people evaluate it as "mean" and they are right in doing so. Certainly, it indicates lack of policing. For, a conscientious man will not do any such acts. In such situations, a police officer deviates from his legal duties and he exercises his authority in an absolute and tyrannical way. Laws can be interpreted and one can take it upon himself to interpret the "spirit of the law" to suit to his objectives. A noncognizable crime can be registered as a cognizable one by putting cognizable sections. A simple hurt can be interpreted as an attempt to murder and such misdoings lead to a lack of conscience and impartiality, which, as a rule, means that the helpless and the less influential people receive the blunt end of justice. Laws are then unequally applied to citizens and the procedure causes widespread criticism against the police. The due process of law and equality before law are not honoured and, in such a state of affairs, policing the society becomes an impossible task.

There has been little or no transparency in police work and it could cause suspicion among the people. Incommunicado detentions were in vogue and there have been several instances that the courts interfered to set matters right. Allegations were plenty that the detinues were treated with brutality in police custody. A journalist told me recently that "some policemen/ officers are arbitrary and even sadistic in their treatment of detinues in their custody. Such people express emotions and are often suffer from a virtually pathological emotional complex".

Disparity in Treatment and Policing the Police

Can the police, or better, do the police treat everyone equal? The immediate answer is "no" - they can't; they don't. The Acts give the laws; they do not talk anything about the manner in which the laws are to be enforced. The same law can be enforced in different ways. For example, the laws on arrest do not say anything about when to arrest a person. In some cases, people may be arrested during night hours and kept in police lockup and, in some other cases, the arrestees are produced before the courts immediately after the arrests. A lot of discretion is given to police officers in taking decisions and there can be disparity in the treatment. If the disparity is intolerable, then criticism comes into being. Some disparity must exist - say criminologists - or the system cannot work. No system works/can work in ideal situations. But, certainly and clearly, that disparity should not be based on poverty, lack of influence, politics, money power, corruption, etc., rather it must be based on the grounds which are justified morally and legally. There must be a "treatment philosophy" for the police. What must be that "treatment philosophy?" There comes human rights and respect for human dignity. The police is a minority group in the larger society, but they have developed the self-concepts which are not approved by the dominant culture. There is a strong feeling in a section of the public that the self-concepts developed by the police suffer from a lack of respect to others, their dignity and human rights. This may be a reason for the differential treatment in police service. They see some people as enemies of the police and to them they behave in an aggressive manner - or if at all not enemies, they think that they can behave in any manner they like.

This may have a historical background. Disparity in the treatment of the people was in vogue during the British rule and the Indian police inherited it in spite of a change in governmental ideology and societal needs after independence. The police force in British India was more hated than respected as it was more repressive in its character. The police in India after independence could not succeed in making the people show their respect to them. They could not do so because they did not show any enviable change in their behaviour. Giriraj Shah, an officer of the Indian Police service writes: "...the existing fear of the police is not out of respect but is born out of the disrespect because most of us are accustomed to breaking laws in one or other forms"[3]. "Breaking laws in one or other forms" means a lot in policing the police. Giriraj Shah continues: "This ruthless machinery *(police)* was primarily used to crush the freedom struggle. It is from here that it picked up the existing attitude, behaviour and use of third degree methods. Many of the freedom fighters who bore the brunt of brutal force are still alive to tell the tale of police atrocities. The ruthless machinery was passed on to their successors who did not properly attend to the task of introducing timely administrative reforms". In other words, the police in independent India did not police the police first to serve the people in a democratic country. He enumerates increasing indiscipline, belief in third degree methods, fabrication of evidence, rude behaviour, etc., as some of the symptoms of lack of policing in independent India.

Social Justice and Policing the Police

Will Durant in his *The Pleasures of Philosophy* wrote: "The Thrasymachus of the Republic proclaimed to the world that 'might is right' and justice merely the interest of the stronger". Do the police in India believe in what is written above? If policing is not seen in the police, certainly it means that the police do believe what Will Durant says in his book. If might is right, then social justice may have no meaning in a democracy. The helpless, the downtrodden, the weak, the handicapped, the fragile, the defenceless and so on approach the police for services. Doubtlessly a policed police service only will be able to render service to the people in an enviable way. Police justice must not challenge social justice. The police might/ought not conquer human conscience and social justice. Adulterated police justice, if it exists, is a symptom of lack of policing in the police. *Justice in the police and justice by the police* - both have to be equitably spread for human happiness and social welfare. The slum-dwellers and pavement dwellers need police justice - policed police justice just like the upper classes in society get it from the police. The poor, the helpless and the defenceless are the largest in Indian society and precisely therefore justice done to them is justice done to society. Their access to the policed police justice is a measure to show the justness in police service. Sensitive policemen - constables and the directors general of police - conscientised into policed police justice will meet the challenges, but the allegation is that such conscientious policemen are not many today. A sense of accountability on the part of the police may be dead or lacking. Policed police justice is people's justice where the tyranny of power is transformed into the democracy of social good. To quote Blaise Pascal: "Justice without power is inefficient; power without justice, tyranny. Justice without power is opposed, because there are always wicked men. Power without justice is soon questioned. Justice and power must, therefore, be brought together, so that whatever is just may be powerful, and whatever is powerful may be just". Only a policed police service can think the way Pascal says and only the police with a sense of social justice thinks or can think the way stated above. Lack of policing in the police service is apt to distort the official integrity of the department. The police is what the police do in society.

Police is What the Police Do Here and Now

Take today's news paper and read the news about the police and policing; study what the police do here and now; assess thc policing in the police and that is the police today. If the people read that the police have become a law unto themselves, then it goes without saying that the police need policing. A suspect tortured, a false case registered, an arrestee detained for long hours - all these may show how the police exercise their authority and pseudo-authority. Some call it "institutional injustice" and others say that they are the symptoms of lack of policing. They see a lawless law-in-action with no police philosophy. Delay necessarily breeds corruption and what is the delay in police work and performance? How many cases are pending investigation? - and how long? The destructive delay in police actions indicates police irresponsibility, involves heavy expenses and invites political interferences. The culpable irresponsibility needs investigation, inquiry and punishment - say the victims of police delay. If speedy justice is a human right, inordinate delay is a violation of that human right. The pathology of police injustice must be diagnosed, if that is found necessary. Might must not crush the right of the people - the right being the right to get speedier justice. Justice V.R. Krishna Iyer wrote: "In India, some judges are stated to be notoriously communal, openly biased, foster favourites and have close relatives at the Bar which factor leads to many improper practices. There are factions among judges which inflict mortal wounds on Justice". Is this observation valid in the case of police functionaries too? Many people answer the question with "yes", but are unable to raise their voice against the lack of policing in police service. If a member in the police service commits a crime, he is liable under law and there is no vacillation against prosecution of police functionaries even if they are in police uniform. No policeman is above the law.

"Why do you observe the splinter in your brother's eye and never notice the plank in your own? How can you say to your brother, "Brother, let me take out the splinter that is in your eye" when you cannot see the plank in your own? Hypocrite! Take the plank out of your own eye first, and then you will see clearly enough to take out the splinter that is in your brother's eye". Jesus Christ told so about 2000 years ago and the same question is asked to the policemen who want to police the society without policing them. Some Indian writers, often themselves members of the police fraternity, justify police actions under rationalized interpretations. Any amount of rationalization cannot make lack of policing a virtue in the police service. People condemn such explanations and interpretations as deserving no consideration. Dr. David Arnold[5], a researcher in History at the University of Lancaster in England wrote: "The creation of the police by the State to serve its own needs and the lack of public accountability contributed to a further characteristic of India's emergent police raj - the coercive strength and disposition of the colonial police. Since it was not made to feel responsible to the public and since its officers almost invariably enjoyed, thanks to the government, immunity from prosecution, the police were free to use violence, including the use of firearms to an extent that would have been unacceptable in a police system like that of England". The Englishmen themselves take note of non-policing in the Indian police system. They observe that the changes that resulted from the transfer of power on 15 August 1947 could not alter the behaviour and strategies of an already non-policed police force in India. They continued to behave the same way they did in the pre-independence period. To quote David Arnold again: "The forty years since independence have done nothing to enhance the overall prestige of the police nor free them from the taint of brutality and corruption. If anything, the reputation of the police is worse now than it was at the time of 1902 Police

Commission or during the Civil Disobedience Movement of the early 1930s. While becoming no more answerable to the public than in the past, the police have fallen increasingly under the politicians' sway. The politicians are the new masters, to whom the police show deference and obey"[6]. The next chapter therefore is on politicization of the police.

References

1. Robert W. Bulch, *The Police Personality: Fact or Fiction,* Journal of Criminology, Criminal Law and Police Science, 63 March 1972
2. William A Westley, *Violence and the Police*, American Journal of Sociology, 49 July, 1963
3. Giriraj Shah, *Indian Police: A Retrospect,* Police and Emerging Challenges, B.R. Publishing Corporation, Delhi, 1988
4. V.R. Krishna Iyer, *Justice at Crossroads,* Deep and Deep, Delhi, 1992
5. David Arnold, *Police Power and Colonial Rule: Madras 1859-1947,* Oxford University Press, Madras, 1986
6. David Arnold, *ibid.*

2

Politicization of Police and Authority

There is a view that some policemen/officers always have involved themselves in politics some way or other. Some canvass votes for a particular party and historically it is seen that they become the blue-eyed sons of politicians when they come into power. If the policemen/officers behave like political partymen, then policing will become politicized policing. In such a policing, there will be lack of proper policing and the policemen/officers will be divided into many groups depending upon their political affiliations. When police associations came into existence in some States, some political parties came forward to sponsor them. It could help to create divisions among the policemen and ultimately led to chaos and confusions. In India, the police have gone for strikes in some States and in the para-military forces. In the United States, owing to the politicization of the police, it has been noticed that there were police riots there. Rodney Stark writes about the police riots in United States and about a new phenomenon that has developed there: "...the emergence of the police as a self-conscious, organized, and militant political constituency, bidding for far reaching political power in their own right"[1]. If the police are politicized, then they will no longer be controlled by the law, procedure established by the law or by the rules and regulations enacted to control their behaviour. Rodney Stark gives a case of police politicization in New York city. Once a civilian-dominated police Review Board was established in New York City. The police did not want such a Board. Hence the police harassed many people who supported the Board and they were successful in seeing that the Board was wound up.

The police have a lot of power vested in them and a well-policed police service can do wonders. But, a politicized police service may respond only to the private code of a political party and not at all to the law and Constitution of a country. Political parties and individual politicians may abuse the police to satisfy their self interests, and many things the police may do then will reflect the lack of policing in a uniformed service having people with muscles, guns, pistols, lathies, etc.

Quis Custodiet Ipsos Custodes?

The above Latin dictum means: "Who guard is the guardians"? If the ruling political party and the police join together, they may do many things which they will not do otherwise. If the police are politicized, then all people will not get just responses from the police when they are approached. Only the politicians of the ruling party and their followers will get police help in a manner that may satisfy them. That is not at all policing a democracy or a society. It is policing a society by the politicized policemen/officers. Today many policemen/officers are accused of having unholy relations with the political parties. In a south Indian State, violence erupted recently between a political party in the ruling front and another political party in the opposition. The head of the district police was a confirmed political party worker from his school days and he took partisan decisions supporting the followers of the political party in which he was a worker. Bombs, murders, stabbings, arson, agitation, etc., were daily occurrences there so much so that the Government in power was forced to transfer the superintendent of police. No policeman/officer with his political attachment can work justly, fairly and honestly among the people who have different political interests. Caesar's wife must be above suspicion and likewise the policeman must be above the politics and reproach of the public on political grounds and affiliations. If the policemen are neutral in politics, the hostility which people have for the "politician policemen" will be eliminated and the criticism against the lack of policing in the police will be minimized.

Looking at the working of the police in the United States, W.C. Reckless said: "Police have been unusually susceptible to being influenced by corrupt politicians, underworld interests, and organized crime. When police department operates under corrupt conditions, law enforcement suffers and police service becomes a defensive manoeuvre rather than an alert striking force to combat crime"[2]. The politicians and their followers judge police efficiency from the way they perform their duties in accordance with their vested interests. This sort of evaluation of the police service by politicians and their Governments has tended to perpetuate the policemen having unholy *nexus* with them to do anything in the way the politicians want them to do. Conscientious policemen/officers are not necessary for the politicians if they want to make use of the police to satisfy their vested interests. They do not allow the policemen/officers to deal justly and honestly with the conditions and situations as they find them. If they do anything as per their conscience, they are transferred out or harassed in many ways. The politicians make use of the higher-ups to trouble the policemen/officers who are not their "yes men". Necessarily, this leads to a lack of policing in the police service.

Some policemen/officers in India purposefully avoid interaction with politicians of the party in opposition. They are literally afraid of the evil consequences if they interact with them. In many instances, the politicians want their opponents to be arrested by the police under some violations of the law and want them to be put in police lock-ups. Many police lock-ups are unfit for human dwelling. They are unsanitary without adequate lighting, ventilation or bathrooms. The detinues in police custody sleep on the floor without mattresses or blankets. The politicians want to see it and enjoy the sadistic condition. In earlier days, the detinues were tortured in police lock-ups and the politicians knew it well. A night in a lock-ups means extreme humiliation for many people and some unscrupulous politicians want the police to do such atrocities on human beings.

I asked a State level politician once to tell me honestly the reasons for their misuse of the police for their vested interests. He was candid enough to tell me that they could get votes if they misused the police for their advantage. The people in general were afraid of the police and a small help to them in their helpless conditions would ensure many followers for them. They could become leaders immediately. They could misuse the police to harass their opponents.

Police and Political Interference

Politicians can create chaos everywhere and anywhere. In a feature film, once I saw a deputy inspector general of police running after a thief and I asked the director: "Why do you ask the D.I.G. to do so"? He replied that the people would appreciate the film if they would see a D.I.G. running after the criminal. I told him that he was picturing wrong things and his film would give wrong signals to the people. A head constable or a sub-inspector or a deputy superintendent of police would run after a criminal and a deputy inspector general of police would have to attend to other functions in police administration.

The most strange and interesting aspect of the story was that the role of the deputy inspector general of police was enacted by a police officer who had the rank of a deputy superintendent of police. He knew very well that the deputy inspector general of police was not supposed or legally bound to do such duties which the head constables/sub-inspectors would do. Yet he acted in that way. Why?

I asked the deputy superintendent of police to tell me why he acted in that way. Why did he not object to the wrong picturing of the police role and functions? His act in the film was helpful only to carve out a wrong image of the department. He then told me that he did everything as the director of the film told him to do. For, he got money for his acts and the police image did not offer any remuneration to him. O.K., he had his justifications and the film director had his justifications. In connection with a political-communal tension in a village, the chief Minister of a State made a statement to the press that he had given instructions to the director general of police to proceed to the trouble spot and to settle the issue. The elders in the police service then said that the director general of police in a State ought to sit at police headquarters and the issues ought to be negotiated by lower cadres. They had their arguments - i.e., the mere proceeding of the director general of police to a trouble spot would give wrong signals to the public that they would expect the director general of police to settle issues in similar situations. The post of the director general of police and the position he holds should not be made use of for obtaining political mileage to the party in power. The police force has a hierarchy and anything that can be done by a particular rank must be entrusted to such a rank in the police. The politicians have only one objective in mind and that is nothing but political power and people's votes. They use, misuse and abuse the police hierarchy for their political advantages. The director general of police and his position must not be made use of for obtaining political gains, and the director general of police ought not to yield to such political pressures. If he does so, he becomes one like the film actor - the deputy superintendent of police - who acted any role for making money for himself. The allegation against some police functionaries is that they sacrifice their principles and are inclined to do many things to please their political masters and to keep up their position (post) in service. The politicians and their higher-ups know the weaknesses of the police functionaries and more often than not they cash on it for political gains and votes. Studies, observations and media reports prove that political factors determine police decisions. Once I wanted to study the political affiliations of some police functionaries and I interviewed a few - seven in all - to know more about it. I could learn that all of them had a history of political activities prior to their entry to police service. They had close ties with politicians. Most of them did not have any enviable academic achievements. But, they were found to retain their close relations with the politicians even after their entry into police service. With their uniform, they could make considerable contributions for ensuring more votes for the political party with which they had earlier affiliations. Their behaviour was, to a great extent, shaped by their political backgrounds. For example, a policeman/officer who was a party worker prior to his entry into the police service used his discretion 'often' in favour of the suspect/arrestee/detinue if he was a member of the party to which the policeman/officer had affiliations.

When a person is taken into custody/arrested by the police, naturally a series of traumatic events follow and a policeman/officer can mitigate the severity of the experiences if he has a favourable attitude towards him. It has been found that a policeman/officer shows leniency to the suspect/detinue/arrestee if he belongs to the political party to which the policeman/officer has affiliations and attachments. In some instances, it has been observed that the detinue is not thrown into a police lock-up; instead he is requested to remain in police stations/premises with the secret understanding that he will not run away. The bail may be granted if that is possible. The same attitude/approach may not be shown to a person belonging to a political party to which the policeman/officer has no special attachment/interest. Probably, the most severe criticism against the police involves the disparity in their treatment of the people belonging to different political parties. People say that there is politicization of the police and that creates lack of proper policing of the police.

Giriraj Shah conducted a study on the police to know the various aspects of political interference in police work.

The survey was conducted in the Delhi metropolis. He classified the strategies taken by politicians to force the police to do things in the way they wanted. They were:

(1) If the complainant belonged to the political party in the opposition, the politician of the ruling front would say that he would not take interest in the case. He would advise them to approach other political leaders.

(2) He used to interfere in cases in which he had a special interest. In such instances, he would speak to the officer in-charge of a police station or to his superiors. He would express his concern and special interest in the matter.

(3) He would write a letter to the police officer insisting on the nature of the action to be taken in the matter. He might say that the action ought to be taken.

(4) He would send the complainants to the senior police officers known to him with a letter of introduction/recommendation.

(5) He would even accompany the complainants in some cases and speak to the Officer in-charge of the police station or to the senior officers directly.

(6) In special cases, he would tell the Minister, Home Affairs or the Chief Minister. He might even take them to the police chief or any other officer who could do things in their favour.[3]

For a politician, his political influence, power and authority are just means for his political advantage. He wants more followers and like them to accept his leadership. The police officers who want to get contacts with politicians may delay action to see that political interference comes. When political interference comes to play a role, the police officers make use of their contacts with the politicians for their own benefits and advantages. According to the politicians and some police officers, the help is reciprocal.

What is the effect of the political interference? According Giriraj Shah, the effects are many which are :

(1) Crisis of conscience for police functionaries. They cannot do anything as their conscience dictates to them. They become incapable of acting according to their conscience and fair justice.

(2) Police officers become reluctant to initiate appropriate action. For, they are forced to conduct investigation in an improper and inadequate way. They need political support to do anything in such instances.
(3) When the police become susceptible to political interference, the public lose their confidence in the fairness of the police and justness of police actions.
(4) Political interference causes deterioration in the quality of police work.

Political interference in the police work means that thc laws have no relevance. The police then become a weapon in the hands of politicians to get things done as they like. The people therefore approach politicians for any work they have with the police. What about the police approach and susceptibility to political interference?

Police Approach and Susceptibility to Political Interference

Policing the police - politicizing the police - policing the politics - these have different meanings. The police can police the police only by enforcing, implementing and abiding by the laws and not by politics or politicization. Nevertheless, observations on police functioning indicate that some police functionaries want politics and politicization in police work. If they want so, it is for their advantage. How? A historical retrospect may explain the facts.

It is known to everybody that thc Indian police was organized by the British regime in India. The British organised a civil police that would be "politically more useful" for them. When India became independent in 1947, the "politically more useful" police functioned exactly in the same way as it did during the British rule. Instead of the British administration, democratic India had a political administration with politicians to rule the public. The police started to serve the politicians just as they served the British administrators during their regime. The expectations of the politicians and the people's expectations of the police functions were not the same. The police were to exercise their functions within the limits of the law, but often they could not do so owing to political interference. Historically, the hierarchy failed to exercise their powers over the subordinates as they too were forced by the powerful politicians to perform their duties according to the instructions given by the political executives. Even today, the same state of affairs continues. A director general of police was transferred out just because he did not listen to the politicians' orders. In the place of the director general of police, an additional director general was appointed. Both the additional director general newly posted and the political hierarchy felt happy at the transfer and postings. This sort of transfers and postings gave an impression among the members of the police service that they could occupy a post only if they performed their duties as per the wishes of the political hierarchy.

Many politicians in a democracy do not enjoy power and authority in themselves. Nevertheless, they become powerful if they get police support. They try to misuse/abuse police power for their advantage and the submissive policemen/officers yield to the political interference so much so that they - the politicians and the police - together exercise, use, misuse, abuse police power and authority. Many studies and news paper reports show the unholy *nexus* between the police and politicians. Some policemen/officers purposefully create situations to establish an unholy police-politician *nexus*. Some policemen/officers are candid enough to say that their *nexus* with the politicians is a safeguard against official harassment and a protection during a crisis situation. Sometimes, the departmental higher-ups may disown them when the politicians come forward with their wholehearted support. The politicians in India were intelligent enough to understand the weaknesses of the police personnel and therefore they regarded the police as a task force to execute their decisions rightly or wrongly. They wanted allegiance and absolute loyalty from the police to them. As such, whenever a new government came into force, the policemen/officers were transferred out to see that the blue-eyed sons of the ruling politicians occupied strategic positions in the police. The policemen/officers knew the desire of the politicians and therefore they extended their full support and faithful loyalty to them during the time of elections and subsequently when they came into power. They wanted not policing, but a politicized policing. Policing the police was not their concern, rather politicizing the police was their aim during and after the elections.

Political Surveillance and Lack of Policing

Politicians or the political party in power make use of the police for conducting political surveillance on the parties in the opposition. The ruling political party which has the Home portfolio wants the police to collect political intelligence and to provide the information about everything to the government. This makes the politicians and the police to come closer and closer. As it is today, a policeman/officer can work in any branch of the police and therefore the closeness which the politicians establish with the police may be misused/abused as and when required.

An 'Intelligence Wing' known as the Police *Special Branch* was formed in 1888 in Madras and what was the Special Branch doing? Their duty was collection of intelligence on political movements which had political significance. Thus, a portion of the police always worked for the ruling political party and often against the political parties in the opposition. The policemen/officers in the intelligence (Special Branch) wing had to establish special liaison with the people belonging to the various political parties and necessarily the relationship thus developed might be used, misused or abused as the case might be. P. Griffiths says that the Criminal Intelligence Department established in 1904 in Simla was later converted to the Intelligence Bureau for collecting political intelligence. The transformation which took place at the Centre had its provincial parallels. The Criminal Investigation Department in the Provinces was converted into a Special Branch and the police were thus entrusted to political functions. Naturally, a policeman/officer who works in the Special Branch develops consciously or unconsciously some liking to the political party in power - comes closer and closer to the politicians of the ruling party. When the policeman/officer is transferred out of the Special Branch, he continues to maintain his relationship with the politicians of his liking. Naturally, he becomes susceptible to political interference. So long as the Special Branch works the way it does today, it is difficult to take away political interference in the police work. Every political party which comes into power wants to see that their men/officers are posted in the Special Branch and in police stations.

What is seen today may be that the policemen are recruited and the allegation is that there is political interference in the recruitment. True or false the allegation, the new recruits to the police can play havoc if they have political affiliations to a political party. The political parties in the opposition always accuse the police of their affiliation to the political party in power. The accusations are not altogether baseless. The opposition speaks of 'Police Raj' and they mean that the police are misused/abused by the political party in power for obtaining political advantage for them. The history of free India shows that every government that came into power from time to time in various States abused/misused the police for their political gains. When I joined the Faculty of the Police Training College in 1976, I have heard many senior police officers telling that the police was the coercive weapon of the government in power. The government in power often means the political party in power. If the police officers thought that they were the coercive weapons of the government in power, necessarily they could feel happy about the political interference in the police work. The police, history reveals, used violence and excessive violence including the use of fire arms to protect the political interests of the ruling party in power.

The political parties - the governments in power - always wanted the police to be their coercive weapon not only for their existence and survival, but also for the promotion of their political ideologies. The police have armed/paramilitary sections and the coercive potential and political utility of the police become more and more evident in these days. The police act as the coercive arm of the Government (political party in power) in the suppression of demonstrations, disturbances and attacks against the *rule of* the government. As pointed out in the introduction of this book, it may be reiterated what David Arnold in his book (1986) has written. He writes: "The forty years since Independence have done nothing to enhance the overall prestige of the police nor free them from the taint of brutality and corruption. If anything, the reputation of the police is worse now than it was at the time of the 1902 Police Commission or during the Civil Disobedience Movement of the early 1930s. While becoming no more answerable to the public than in the past, the police have fallen increasingly under the politicians' sway. The politicians are the new masters to whom the police show deference and obey".[4] If this is the reality, there will be no policing within the police.

Police Association, Politicization and Policing

After the National Police Commission's recommendation to allow the police to form associations for different ranks, rankwise associations were formed with *no political affiliations*. Before that, the policemen expressed their protests in an individualistic, disorganized and personal way. The politicians were aware of their problems and weaknesses. They knew that the policemen/officers could not raise their voice jointly. Studies during the pre-National Police Commission period show that the dissatisfied policemen/officers did resign, take frequent sick leave or perform their duties in an indifferent or disinterested way. After the formation of police associations, the policemen/officers established secret (even open) understanding with politicians and started to seek redress for their grievances over pay, allowances, welfare, housing and other conditions through political patronage. They started to voice their demands collectively through their association leaders.

The politicians and the ministers listened to them patiently. They came to address the policemen/officers during the annual conventions. They publicly offered full support to the policemen/officers. The notices printed in connection with the State Level Conventions of police association contained the names of politicians in the ruling front and opposition. The clear linkage between the politicians and police personnel thus becomes clear and the news papers publish the *nexus* between police associations and political patronage. According to the news papers, there exist divisions in policemen/officers on the basis of their political affiliations. Of course, the politicians and policemen/officers do not openly admit their affiliations to politicians; nevertheless, the general public have a feeling that there is a positive political influence on police association/ union activities. Their feeling may not be entirely groundless. It follows necessarily that the more the policemen/officers have their attachment and affiliation with the politicians, the more will be the political interference in the police work. The more is the political interference in the police work, the more will be the lack of policing in the police service.

Political Patronage and Policing

The policemen/officers at the lower levels and middle levels have a lot of problems which the hierarchy often ignores. The policemen/officers know well that they can get things done with political patronage and politicians' good will. The politicians know well that the lower levels in police are their vote bank. They are the people working at the cutting edge of police administration and so to say their support to a political party can and will ensure more votes for them. There is a reciprocal advantage and therefore it is in the interest of the politicians to keep the constabulary and lower level police functionaries in good spirit. No doubt, the policemen/officers do approach the politicians to get their patronage, and likewise the politicians approach the policemen/officers for ensuring to plead for the policemen and in disciplinary inquiries, the politicians are found to extend support to the delinquent personnel. The delinquents find politicians as their saviours in distress and this tie-up with the politicians make them become susceptible to political interference. The gun men, the security staff of the politicians and so on are police personnel. Consciously or unconsciously, they come closer and closer. To sever links between the politicians and police is indeed very difficult in a democratic set-up. Many politicians are related by blood, friendship and marriage with policeman/officers. In such a situation, how can the link between them be cut off?

In a democracy, agitations against the ruling government and its policies by the political parties in the opposition may be seen. In all such strikes, processions and agitations, the police experience a dilemma and come to their wit's end. Anything the police does in such situations may be criticized by vested interests. Then, the burden of supporting the police falls on the shoulders of the politicians in the ruling front. Some politicians justify police actions while others may not. This too makes the police to come closer to the politicians. The police are not allowed to speak then as it may affect their discipline and morale. They need the support of public men, the press and politicians. The police retain their ties, visibly or otherwise, with the politicians which no force in a democracy can hope to sever. The police today cannot isolate themselves from the clutches of the politicians.

Owing to the political patronage and support, naturally the hierarchy loses its control over the subordinate ranks. Despite the acceptance of human rights and individual's liberty/dignity in the police service, there remains in official circles a basic contempt for the work of the subordinate ranks. This necessitates the subordinate ranks to establish links with the politicians for showing their affiliations to the police hierarchy. For them, it is a means to exert control over the hierarchy. So long as the subordinate ranks retain their political connections, interference by the politicians becomes an inevitable necessity in the police work. As long as the subordinate ranks can exercise discretion in their work, they can use, misuse, abuse their power and authority in favour of or against the politicians. Partiality, favouritism and prejudices against or in favour of a particular politician/political party becomes most evident then.

When STD telephone facilities were made easier, wider and less expensive, the telephone charges of the police department went up. Police officers then received many telephone calls purported to have been from distant places. The caller of the telephone used to claim that he was the district chief or taluka chief of a particular political party having the Home portfolio in Government. On further scrutiny, it could be unearthed that the callers were resorting to impersonation. Some police officers who were afraid of politicians yielded to the pressures of the distant political leaders (?) while others did not. How? They invariably requested them to tell them the telephone numbers and they used to call them back to the number they thus received. More often than not, the politician purported to be the district/taluka Chief would not be there. They were found to be false telephone calls and the politicians used to exploit the police *phobia* towards political pressures and politicians. I don't think that the police have politician *phobia* which is an irrational fear. They have a sort of *pretended fear*. In psychiatry, fear of bad men is seen. It is called *"pavor sceleris* or *scelerophobia"*. People are afraid of burglars, kidnappers, *goondas* and likewise the politicians of bad character are feared. The policemen/officers fear the politicians as the ones who can do a lot of harm to them. They may be transferred to distant places causing discomforts or to unimportant posts having no public contacts. Sometimes, the politicians may see that some disciplinary actions are initiated against the policemen/officers who are deaf to their pressures. Policemen/officers who do not have an upright conscience or commit atrocities or are corrupt are really afraid of the ill effects of political interventions. There are officers who respectfully ignore political pressures and politicians' interferences. Generally, they are men of character and of upright conscience.

Hypengyophobia is known as fear of responsibility. Police work is a responsible job and responsibility means fairness, justness, honesty, concern and many other human qualities. Some policemen/officers who experience the fear of responsibility become easily susceptible to political pressures and politicians' interferences. They want support and the political support may be the best support in a democratic rule. Politicians become godfathers to policemen/officers who do not want to share police responsibility in a responsible way. Politicization of police comes into being if many in the police are not prepared to shoulder the responsibility entrusted to them by law.

Earlier I said that many policemen/officers are not suffering from politicians' phobia, rather, they show a pretended fear. Phobia is a morbid fear associated with morbid anxiety. In policemen/officers, I do not find such morbid fear or anxiety of political interference. They hate political interference and one of the reasons for their hatred is that they cannot do anything as they want whenever political interference comes into being. Politicians inspire fear only in policemen/officers who are not straight and upright in character. Such policemen/officers experience anxiety when they think of politicians and political intervention in police work. They feel that they are powerless before the powerful politicians. Certainly, the police have powers conferred on them by law and the politicians do not have any such statutorily conferred power and authority. Nevertheless, the policemen/officers are afraid of politicians/political interferences. Fear, psychiatrists say, is a reaction to a real or threatened danger, anxiety, and according to them, it is more typically a relation to an unreal or imagined danger. Do the policemen/officers have fear or anxiety towards politicians? Some policemen/officers have personally told me that they play a lot of "psychological games" to please the politicians and they do so for their existence and survival. If a policeman/officer has no vested interests, he can administer justice to people and in such situations, the politicians and politics have no relevance in the police work.

Policemen/officers go after politicians and the politicians go after the police. There exist some reciprocal relationship. Both have power and assumed powers. Both want to exercise authority and pseudo-authority. It has been observed that both police and politicians, irrespective of their status and position in the police and political hierarchy, suffer from a neurotic craving for power. They want to show their power and command over other people and sometimes they want to exercise their power, authority, pseudo-power/authority in a manner contrary to reason, logic and justification. If the police and politicians join together, they can do it in an easy way. They do it under political blessings and police muscles. The exercise of authority may be rational or irrational. If the police and politicians go hand in hand for exercising authority/pseudo-authority, they may find their power having magic-forces.

There is the story of the great painter Apelles (330 B.C.) who used to hide behind his paintings and the intention was to listen to the observations and critical remarks made by the common folk about his paintings. One day, a passing shoe-maker made a comment and found fault with one sandal-loop being smaller than the other. Apelles redrew it later on the next day. On the following morning, the same shoe-maker made another comment. He began to jeer about the leg. Apelles could not tolerate him. Hence, he came out from his hiding place and squelched the glib critic with crushing: "A cobbler should not judge above the sandal". I have carefully studied some police officers who work at Thana levels, circle officers, sub-divisional officers and district police officers. Immediately after taking charge, they do something and hide behind the curtain to listen to what the politicians in the ruling front speak about them. If they speak good about the police officers, then they do more things in their favour and then further more and more until at last they may say that a "politician should not judge above politics". What does it mean? It means that the police work has been so much politicized that some conscientious policemen/officers cannot but react to the politicians' interferences. A particular political party has a news paper published. Whenever that political party comes into power, people go to police stations with the copy of that day's news paper with them. They keep the paper in their hand in such a way that the sub-inspector, circle inspector, inspector general of police can read the name of the news paper in their hand. It means that even a news paper run by a political party in hand has political influence with some policemen/officers. Another political party has a television channel and the police officer discusses the contents of the T.V. serials shown in that channel. He wants to test whether or not his subordinates too enjoy the same channel. The officer in charge of the police station/circle office/sub divisional office sees that his reviews and discussions about the 'serials' in the channel reach the political party in power. It shows that some policemen/officers want to politicize the police and their working environments. Politicization for them includes policization, and policization includes politicization as well.

Politicians go to the police stations, because they get reception there. The policemen/officers go to the politicians, for they get reception there. The allegation is that the police and politicians have an unholy *nexus* and so long as the unholy *nexus* exists between the police and politicians, policing the police becomes a difficult task.

As early as 1920, or even before, the politicians and the police in India had established *nexuses*. For example, the colonial constabulary established a police union on March 12, 1920 in Madras city with a Muslim head constable, Ibrahim Khan as its president. They had the patronage of Congress Party politicians. The grievances and demands of the policemen were brought to the notice of the authorities through the support of politicians. Thus the politicisation of the police has a history of over 80 years and, when India became independent in 1947, the police-politician relations became conspicuously visible. If one political party in power ignored the police demands, then another political party attended to them when it came to power in the democracy. The politicians have their eye on the constables' vote bank and precisely therefore politicisation of the police becomes necessary in police work. With political support, the policemen refused to accept their pay at the end of 1920 and threatened to go on strikes. Just a few days ago, the policemen in a north Indian State declared strikes with political support and patronage. The British used the Indian constables to beat Indians under the direction of European officers. Likewise, today the ruling political parties make use of or at least attempt to make use of police muscles to subdue the members of the political party in opposition. Once a policeman said that he misused his authority to harass politicians in the opposition when he was pressed by the political party in authority and later he served the politicians whom he harassed earlier when they came into power and afterwards he abused his authority to harass the politicians who were in power earlier. The cyclic process continues and the politicians who support the police when they are in power become the arch-enemies of the police when they are in the opposition in a democracy. The police have a crushing and serving role and politicisation of the police is the method by which the political parties usc/misuse/abuse the police. The policemen/officers, by the very nature of their work, are condemned to serve more their political masters than the public today. The allegation made against the police now is that their political functions overshadow their other functions including the dwarfing of investigating, preventing and controlling of crimes and public relations. So long as the police have the intelligence wing with them, the political party in power thinks that it is the responsibility of the police to retain the Government in power. Once an inspector general is posted to head the intelligence wing, he is branded as a man of the Government (political party) in power. When an inspector is transferred to the Special Branch (Intelligence), he collects information to aid the Government to continue in power. A constable in the Special branch is said to be the Government's (political party's) field man.

If anyone of them is found to be unfit to work for the political party in power, he is transferred out to other units. Hence, some policemen/officers become more loyal - more royal - than the King himself. Some work as partymen and establish all sorts of relations/ties with all kinds of politicians from the ground level to the top level in the political party. How can these policemen/offices cut off their contacts/relations with the political partymen even when they go out of power? The affinity-conscious and unconscious - continues to decide the relationship between the police and political parties.

Is the collection of political intelligence a police function in a democracy? There is a history behind it. In 1860, the Police Commission did not see the need to establish an intelligence wing in the police. In 1887, i.e., two years after the Indian National Congress came into existence (was founded), the then Government of India felt the necessity of creating an intelligence wing for the collection of information relating to anti-colonial rule. Political surveillance was the main objective for the creation of such a separate wing and the *Thugi* and *Dakaiti* department was entrusted with the responsibility. The special and main duty was political surveillance and collection of political information so that the colonial rule could be maintained. At the provincial level, in 1888, a "Special Branch" in the police was created for the political surveillance and collection of intelligence. The police thus kept constant watch over political leaders, political movements, seditious publications, etc. Anything which has some political significance was an item of importance for the police.

The politicians at that time were the politicians of the Indian National Congress who fought against the British rule. The British then made use of their police to collect political intelligence as they were government servants. Today, there are many political parties and one party fights against another. The Government in a democracy means the government formed by a political party/political parties. The Government in power makes use of the police (Intelligence Wing) to collect political intelligence and information about politicians which may be of bad taste. Why? The policemen/officers today are, unlike the British Indian police, public servants and they have, or should have, no special interest to retain a particular political party in power/out of power. The collection of political intelligence must be a work of the political parties and the public exchequer must not be misused for the purpose. The British did it under different circumstances and the democracy cannot or should not afford to do so. If the democratic governments do so, it is nothing but misuse of police power/abuse of police authority for political advantages. Politicisation of the police necessarily comes into being. Police duties become politicians' duties and the police manpower is misused for obtaining political mileage for the politicians in power. It is high time that a system which was devised by the colonial government is abolished and the police must not be entrusted with political duties.

As the political movement against the colonial rule in India became stronger and stronger, the British had no option but to strengthen the intelligence wing of the police to have political surveillance and for the collection of political information. The Indian Police Commission: 1902-03 and Lord Curzon who appointed the Commission felt so. They wanted the police to be used as their men for political advantages. The Thugi and Dakaiti Department was replaced by a Central Intelligence Department which was established at Simla in 1904. When Swadeshi movements and anti-partition activities were found spreading in the Country, the British made use of the Central Intelligence Department fully and wholly for the collection of political intelligence, surveillance of political leaders and relaying political information to other provinces. The Central Intelligence Department earlier collected criminal intelligence relating to wandering gangs and criminals operating across provincial boundaries. As the Government realized that the collection of political intelligence was more important for them than the collection of criminal intelligence, the duties relating to collection of criminal intelligence were taken away from the Central Intelligence Department and the department was renamed as Intelligence Bureau. In a way, the British made the Intelligence Bureau their political wing to collect political intelligence and information on political leaders.

When India became independent, the Country was ruled by a single political party for many decades. Naturally, the political party which came into power became almost like the British Government in the pre-independence period. The intelligence wing of the Government continued their political surveillance against political parties in the opposition. Thus, a section of the police became a politicised wing of the police. That wing along with other units of the police did many things to retain the political party in power. When the political parties in the opposition later became the ruling political party at the centre, the policemen/officers who worked earlier for the political party in power started political surveillance over the political members of the earlier governments. Thus a new politicisation of the police came into existence. Afterwards, different political parties assumed powers in Central Government so much so that politicisation of the police by a single political party became impossible.

When it happened at the Centre, the story was different in many States. After India became independent, many political parties - sometimes regional parties - formed the governments. The policemen/officers who worked in the police Special Branches were pressured to collect political intelligence and to conduct political surveillance over politicians with an objective to retain the governments in power. The new governments did not have trust or confidence in the Special Branch (Intelligence) of the State police. Hence, as soon as a new government came into power, the administration shuffled the existing Special Branch of the police and posted their well-wishers, adherents and *'partymen'* in the Special Branches. They did so for collecting political intelligence and to keep political surveillance over the politicians of the opposition parties. The police became thus an agency to retain governments in power. Politicisation of police thus became a necessity.

As a corollary to the politicisation of the police, many policemen/officers who were working for the political parties in power earlier were posted to other units of the police. Though they were posted to other units, they continued to maintain their affinity and relationship with individual politicians and the political parties whom they served earlier. The conscious and unconscious affinity and contacts in a way helped to strengthen the politicisation of the police in the different branches of the police department. The impact has been such that policemen/officers of all political parties now work in police the department. Some become overenthusiastic in their political activities in a particular party so much so that they become unapproachable to other political parties in the State. Thus, every policeman/officer is identified either as desirable or undesirable for a particular political party. The data relating to each policeman/officer is kept alive in the computer in political party offices so much so that the politicians get in touch with a policeman/officer after studying his political affiliations. Some policemen work for the political party to which they have affiliations and against the political party to which they do not maintain any cordial relationship. There is a view now that the police cannot get away from politicisation so long as they are entrusted with the collection of political intelligence and surveillance of political leaders and their activities. The police are expected to collect only criminal intelligence and not political intelligence. The collection of political intelligence is not a police work and politicization of the police will continue to be in force so long as the police are utilized, misused or abused for political advantages for the ruling political party in government. The news paper section, district special branch, State Special Branch are functioning today for the political interests of the ruling front/political parties in government so much so that they are in a way the politicised police wings. In such a system, the policemen/officers work as political agents. The policemen/officers during the British regime were trained in shorthand for the accurate transcripts of political speeches. Even today, such short hand bureaus are functioning in the police special branch and in several occasions political parties raise their objections to the presence of special branch policemen/officers in their meetings. They go in mufty and report to the government many things which are not palatable to the political parties. The presence of the special branch policemen/officers in political meetings have a deterrent effect and the police functionaries are pictured as the political partymen of the ruling government.

The police department has *paid informers* for the collection of political intelligence. This too has a historical background. The presence of the policemen was objected to by the politicians in the British past. The British therefore made use of police spies and informants for the collection of political intelligence. For paying, they sanctioned a special secret fund. It was all right during the British period. But, during the democracy, why should the police be utilized for the political interests of the ruling government? Why does the police spend money from the public exchequer to maintain a political party in power? Maintaining a political party is not a police job. They have other works and the present system of utilizing the police for the political gains of the ruling political parties can help only to politicise the police and not to police the police. The next chapter deals with political powers and police empowerment.

References

1. Rodney Stark, *Police Riots: Collective Violence and Law Enforcement,* Focus Books, Belmont, Calif, 1972
2. Walter C Reckless, *The Crime Problem,* Vakils, Feffer and Simons Private Ltd., Bombay, 1967
3. Giriraj Shah, *Indian Police: A Retrospect, from Police and Emerging Challenges* by S K Chaturvedi, B.R. Publishing Corporation, Delhi, 1988
4. David Arnold, *Police Power and Colonial Rule: Madras 1859-1947,* Oxford University Press, Delhi, 1986.

3

Political Powers and Police Empowerment

After India became independent in 1947, the politicians became very important and became rulers and decision-makers. They enjoyed a lot of powers and authority. Law and order management became the main function of the newly formed democratic governments in the Centre and in the States. The police was a State subject in the Indian Constitution and as such the administration of the police became a State affair. Every State had a number of the political parties and each had its own vested interests and parochial achievements.

The right to form associations and to conduct demonstrations, etc., was a guaranteed fundamental right under the Indian Constitution. The political parties in many States held several protest meetings and demonstrations against the ruling governments and, sometimes, they became violent and uncontrollable. The politicians were wholly powerless to control and prevent political demonstrations without the help of the police. The ruling politicians could exercise their powers only if they were supported by the police strength. Necessarily, the political powers in the States had to empower the police to maintain their political rule and governments. The police thus became a powerful machinery to protect the interests of the politicians and the ruling governments.

During the British raj, the police could work for the government in power. It was not a democracy and as such the same government continued to rule the country until freedom was given. In a democracy, today's ruling party becomes tomorrow's opposition party and therefore the police cannot use their authority/power for ensuring political gains for the ruling party. The police actions are minutely watched and scrutinized by the people and the political parties and the police become a target of political attacks by the parties in opposition. The ruling party may have to support the police activities and sometimes to endorse everything the police do. Police empowerment to do anything as the situation demands then becomes essential. The police become accountable to the people, and the government in power become accountable to the public. This was not the situation in the British past. The police are always criticized as politicized by the political party in the ruling government and alleging so, the political parties in the opposition cash on it.

The police may have to use force sometimes against the agitating members of the political party in the opposition. The use of force by the police may become necessary, but interpreting it to be politicization may not be always true. The political parties in the opposition may be unethical to accuse the police as politicized whenever they resort to force. "Lawlessness" by the political parties in the opposition must be controlled by the use of force as per the law and procedure established by the law. "Lawlessness" can not be justified and control of lawlessness by the use of force by the police is not politicization. The political parties have energy, manpower, destructive mentality and they can be brought down and controlled only by a superior might and the police alone have the power and authority to do so in a democracy. If the police do not use their superior might, then their inertia and lethargy may result in greater insecurity to the life and property of the people. A police lathi-charge on an aggressive crowd is to create a general impression among the people that the police are active and they are safe. In many instances, police lathi-charge, firing or use of other forms of force may be fully justified for an impartial assessor of police acts. Nevertheless, some over-enthusiastic and politically motivated policemen/officers apply excessive force, cruelty and violence on people for obtaining political advantages for the ruling party. This puts the police into bad shape and results in inviting adverse criticisms against the police. The police may be caricatured as anti-people and fully politicized in such situations. The impartial people who evaluate the police actions in an objective way may blame the police as vicious and atrocious. There may be anti-police emotions and the people may see even the good works done by the police in bad light. The political parties in the opposition often desire to turn the police action into police brutality and the intention is to convert the police action for anti-government propaganda. During election campaigns, the politicians cash on the police actions - excessive actions - inactions - abuse of power and authority, etc., and they turn everything against the ruling political parties. A few lathi-charges, policing firings, police overactions may create an anti-government feeling in many people. People, rightly or wrongly, are inclined to think that the police are politicized and often behave as the coercive power of the ruling politicians in power. Violence in any form used by the police is not favoured by the people. They think that it is used by the police as desired by the politicians of the ruling government. Any police violence has a repressive and deterrent effect and, if it is merciless, then the people are against the police and the ruling politicians in the government. They attribute motives and make attempts to find out the politicization of police in such situations.

In a democracy, no member of the police is an untouchable for a political party. There is no permanent friend or enemy in politics. The politicians of the ruling government usually do not want to displease the people by a repressive or oppressive police force. Hence, many a time, the ruling government and their politicians insist on the police to have recourse to a minimum use of force during public agitations.

Even when the people are violent, the public wants the police to keep a remarkable restraint in expressing violence. Nevertheless, some overenthusiastic policemen/officers may behave in an excessively aggressive way. Sometimes, in connection with *bandhs, hartals,* strikes, etc., many preventive arrests are made by the police under instructions from the government. Often, wholesale arrests may not have satisfactory or desirable effects and, on many occasions, they have proved to be less deterrent. Nevertheless, the police may be pressured to do it and, in such situations, it is necessary to see that the arrests are made keeping strict decency in a human rights friendly way. Often the police are criticized and attacked by the press and politicians if they are not people friendly. Even the British police were very careful when they carried out preventive arrests.

Police coercion is not a State polity in any democracy and it must not be so. If the police coercion becomes a vital instrument of State policy in a democracy, there will be vehement public criticisms of police "excesses" and that was what was seen during the internal emergency (1975-1976) in India. There were police excesses and the police behaved as they were directed by the politicians then. But the prize which the ruling politicians had to pay for the police excesses was too heavy for them. Afterwards, there was a change in governments both at the Centre and in the States. A number of cases was registered against the police and Commissions of Inquiry were instituted. A politicized police is not accepted by democracies and fulsome praise for the politicized activities of the police is not given by the people. During the colonial regime in India, the British Indian Government assured the police that any violent activities taken by the police in good faith in the discharge of their duties in connection with the Civil Disobedience Movement would be supported by the Government. But whenever the police used excessive force to suppress the movement, the people condemned their actions and reacted violently. If that was the way people responded to the colonial police then, the reactions would be very severe in our democracy. During the British raj, the Government was forced to instruct the police to keep remarkable restraint when the police resorted to force. If that was so, the police in a democracy will not be pardoned if they are found to employ excessive violence on people. Commissions of Inquiry will be instituted to probe into any instance in which the police force is found to have used excessive force and violence. If the police are found guilty, then prosecution procedures may be initiated against the guilty. The argument that "once the police applies force, it cannot always regulate its use" does not hold good to convince the commissions of inquiry. A politicized police force is a tyrant. It is cruel and insolent. It harasses political opponents for the ruling political parties in power and behaves in an offensive way. A policed police service does not do so.

Attack on Politicized Police Force

After India became independent, the press, the people and politicians alleged politicization of the police. They made use of the print media, street corner meetings, public statements, etc., for the purpose. The police helplessness, incompetence, loyalty and susceptibility to political pressures, etc., were exposed freely in free India. A number of films, T.V. serials and dramas brought out the politicization of the police and thus the criticisms against the police became sharper and more sustained in the recent past. After the passing of the Protection of Human Rights Act - 1993, the politicized police used to be in the media quite frequently. A police department is necessary for detecting criminals, investigating crimes and administering fair justice. But, a politicized police is not what the people want. Instead of concentrating on crime work and law-and-order management, the police devote a lot of man power, resources, energy and fund for shadowing politicians, annoying them, keeping a surveillance on political opponents of the ruling party and, if possible, harassing people who hold opinions against the political party in power. People do not expect such political activities from the police although the politicians want the police to do such political work for them with no expenditure for them and their party. The collection of political intelligence through the police may be the cheapest way to remain in power and the political party spends money from the public exchequer for political advantages for them. Who is happy about it? Only the politicians in the ruling government may be happy. The British Government spent money on collecting political intelligence through their police and it was for retaining their rule in India. How can a political party in democratic India spend money from public exchequer to see that they retain their government? Retaining a political party in power is not a police job and that is the precise reason why the politicized police become a target of public criticism and hostility. Policemen/officers are misused to work as secret agents to collect political intelligence and to keep surveillance on the politicians of the opposition and many people think that it is not policing.

During the colonial rule, the police worked as government servants and they were accountable only to the white administration. Once, the police fired and killed/injured many people, the politicians demanded an inquiry into the matter and the white administration simply refused to order for an inquiry. The British administration said that the "Government cannot allow officers who have done their duty to be pilloried". This is not possible in a democracy. In a democracy, governments come and governments go, but the police continue to exist. If one government refused to initiate action on police activities, another government may do it. Any number of examples can be quoted and after the internal emergency (1975-76), many inquiries were ordered against police functionaries and some of them were prosecuted and punished. A politicized police force is not tolerated by the people in many parts of the world and no policed police will permit such abuses of power by the politicians in the ruling/opposition parties. Whenever the police behave as politicized police, people condemn them as vicious and brutal agents of the politicians. The policemen are attacked by the people and angry crowds may not allow the policemen/officers to work as party men during a law-and-order situation. In Madras city, before independence, the policemen once fired at the people and the Madras Government praised the policemen for the "splendid loyalty" shown to the British rule. The people of Madras abused the policemen with words such as "traitors to India" and "Myrmidons of India's tyrants". The people insulted them in public, spat upon them and thus expressed their hostility. Likewise, whenever the public see politicized policemen/officers, they hate them and sometimes cajole others to desert their services. The people want a policed police service and not a politicized police service. The politicized police service is a service to the political parties and not to the people who maintain the police in a democracy.

Yesterday, the opposition political parties organized a general hartal and the mike announcement had the words like "political *goondas* and policemen". They compare political *goondas* with policemen. The interesting aspect is that the same politicians who blame the police today will support the police tomorrow when they come into power. Sometimes anonymous wall-posts may be seen in the city against the politicized police. The politicians make remarks that the police have more loyalty towards the political party in power than to the people. Political opinions swing in favour of and against the police. The same politicians who castigate and condemn police actions when they are in the opposition will certainly support and encourage police actions when they are in power. They blame the police for beating people and speak against lathy charges. The circumstances which compelled the police to have recourse to such violent tactics and methods are purposefully suppressed and the ignorant people become hostile to the police. The police may be pictured as the aggressors and the people may be coloured as peace lovers. When many T.V. channels come forward to show how the situations forcing the police to resort to lathy charges/violence have come into being, the politicians find it extremely difficult to convince the people that the police is always wrong and the people are always right and peace-loving.

Photographs which often appear in the print media depict the police as aggressors who always are prone to adopt violent and arbitrary methods. They give the news with their views and an impartial evaluator of the news media often doubts about the sincerity and ethics of news reporting. The journalists' versions are that the news favouring the police may not be sold easily as they understand that the people want the police to be blamed more than the public. Consciously or unconsciously, the people have developed an anti-police attitude and they always see the policemen/officers as the people of the ruling political parties. Thc public are yet to be convinced that the police work more for the people than for the political parties in power. The police beat the people unjustifiably and the people ask why they should be beaten like dogs. The police have to establish the needed rapport with the people. Frustratingly enough, the police could not get the public trust and confidence even after 50 years of democratic rule. They consider the police as the police of the colonial past - always doing many things as the coercive weapon of the ruling political party and government.

The Government in power sometimes order judicial inquiries on police atrocities or appoint commissions of inquiries. Of late, some politicians, intellectuals, social workers, writers and public men appoint their own commissions to conduct inquiries independently. They bring out their own inquiry reports and try to convince the people that the policemen behave violently to support the political parties in the government. In such situations, it becomes extremely difficult for the official commissions to convince the people with their findings if they are against the findings of the people's commission. Some human rights activists hold their own inquiries and publish their findings in the press. In some of their reports, they blame the police and politicians alike. People are found to believe more the contents of an impartial non-official commission than the same of an official commission. Usually, retired judges may be appointed to head the commission by the ruling government, and the integrity of such commissions are suspicious to the political parties in the opposition. A feeling had developed among the people that the "yes-men judges" of the ruling government may be appointed often to inquire into police atrocities and violence. These retired judges are viewed with suspicion so much so that the political parties frequently demand for the appointment of serving judges to conduct the inquiry. Whatever that may be, a politicized police service or a seemingly politicized police service cannot achieve public trust and approval. The attitude which the people in pre-independent India had towards the British Indian police continues to rule the people even today. If the police then were the Myrmidons of the British rulers, the police today is viewed as the Myrmidons of the law of the ruling political parties by the people. Is it true to think so? About the police in the British India, David Arnold writes: "Despite the introduction of the Police (Incitement to Disaffection) Act on 13 May 1930 and tightened control over the press, the nationalists took every opportunity - on public platforms, in the provincial legislature, in cyclostyled leaflets and news-sheets as well as through the newspapers themselves - to give the fullest possible publicity to police violence".[1] Even today, the political parties, the media and cultural programmes take the same strategies in a wider and deeper way. They bring police violence into the electronic media, in print, in novels and dramas, in films and T.V. serials, in street corner meetings and foot-path dramas, in audio and video-cassets, in legislatures, in public speeches and platform addresses, in whispering conversations and parks etc. David Arnold found: "The police were accused of 'running amok', their customary malevolence and cruelty unrestrained, and even encouraged, by their European Officers".[2] Today, the politicians accuse the police and the politicization of the police as the principal cause of police violence. According to the politicians of the opposition in democratic India, the politicians of the ruling front misuse and make use of police power and authority to do things - to refrain from doing things according to their arbitrary fancy and whim. The politicians organize rallies and processions with anti-police and anti-government slogans like: "Don't beat us, Don't kill us; Don't beat to kill us" and they carry evidence to convince the people of police brutality. They blame the "police raj" in a democracy and express their bitterness and resentment against police strategies and political encouragements.

The ruling political parties may be able to repress public agitations by police strategies, but the people react violently to such government policies and police atrocities. Knowing fully well that the police will employ repressive forces and brutal strategies to suppress the public agitations against government policies, the politicians of the opposition organize protest meetings, jadhas and picketings. The intention here may be to give maximum publicity to police excesses and thereby to activate the people against the ruling front. Sometimes, they become successful in their attempts. The politicians thus keep alive the spirit of opposition to the government and the police. They may cash on it during the next election to the State/Centre.

Individual Policeman, Individual Politician and Police-Politician Nexus

'This police officer is the man of that political party. He has good relations with so and so politicians - That policeman has close ties with so and so politicians'. These remarks are often heard in police circles. It means that there takes place politicization at individual levels. Such policemen/officers may cause havoc in police administration and in the administration of fair justice. A Deputy Inspector General of Police who of late became the director general of police was the blue-eyed son of a very senior veteran political leader. He got always the support of politicians. More than many things, it is through politicization that individual policemen/officers and politicians work together. Count the telephone calls reaching a police office- from police station to police headquarters - and take a decision about the extent of the politicization in police work. Look at the number of politicians visiting police offices and see how closely the politicians and the police work. One day, a sub-inspector saw a politician smoking a cigarette in front of his superintendent of police at the district police headquarters. Such interactions speak louder than words about police - politician *nexuses*. Why think so? There may be open interactions. The police officers and politicians are seen in hotels, motels and restaurants together eating and drinking or making merry. People observe their merry-making and talking in restaurants, railway stations, bus stands and home kitchens. "Tell me the name of a police officer, and I shall tell you to which political party he belongs" - said a journalist once. Every person in a democracy may have his political ideologies and affiliations. But, identifying with a political party is different from having political affinities with a party. A policeman is not, and ought not be, a party-man and the moment he becomes a party-man, his credibility is lost and his integrity is doubted. No policeman/officer can be trusted fully. For, they have secret and open relationship with a political party in general and individual politicians in particular. They cannot see people by their naked eyes, for they see people only through their "political eyes". If that is a reality, politicization plays an important and decisive role in policing the society in India.

The policemen/officers who are politicized may create environments which may ensure political advantages for the party which politicize them. The atmosphere may be such that :

(1) The politicians of the ruling party get a more favoured treatment than the politicians of the opposition in a democracy. The "pleasure of politicians" becomes the sole motive of the functionaries.

(2) Recommendations and introductions from the politicians of the ruling front become essential to get criminal cases registered, to get the cases investigated; to get the case referred to; to get the case charge-sheeted, etc. The police functionaries show special considerations to such cases sponsored by the politicians.

(3) The policemen/officers who are politicized become favoured functionaries to the political leadership. They can become corrupt and practise corruption to which the departmental and governmental administration takes a tolerating attitude.

(4) A politicized policeman/officer is protected by his political godfathers. Together they make a living. Just like the politicized policeman/officer becomes corrupt, the politicians too become corrupt through police support. The help is mutual and the utility is reciprocal for the police and politicians.

(5) The people lose confidence in police integrity and they go after the politicians to get their support. Police justice and politicians' justice become one and the same. The laws made by the people may not hold good without political support.

Political power becomes the power for police empowerment. The police force without political support has no meaning and the political powers without the support and empowerment of the police have no value now. In the eyes of the politicized policeman/officer, the politicians are a dangerous class and therefore some of them do anything to please the politicians. There are many research studies to show and instances to prove that the police are susceptible to political interference. Politicians are very visible and their interference with police works too are very conspicuous. Policemen/officers are very visible and their susceptibility to political interference too is very conspicuous. The police uniform, the interaction with politicians, their mutual helps become a topic of interest among the people and other political parties.

Policing the Politicians and Politicizing the Police

Policing the politicians may be a difficult and a rather impossible task. For some are politicians, some are political workers and some survive by politics. In a country of unemployment, there are political labourers as well. If political interference in the police is stopped, some political labourers and the so-named politicians may lose their income and starve themselves to death. Police behaviour so far has created - rightly or wrongly - an image due to which people cannot freely walk into a police station. Hence the people go after the politicians for recommendations and introductions. Some low level politicians come to police stations at the expense of the ones who need their help. After the help, all of them go together to a hotel for lunch and afterwards accept some service money to be split between them and the police functionaries. The politicians emerge from chaos, live and survive in chaos and therefore it may not be possible to police the politicians. On the other hand, it is easier to politicize the police.

Allegations are heard about police-politicians-businessmen *nexuses*. They establish unholy *nexuses* to make money. My book on *Indian Police and Nexus Crime* discusses them in detail. It means that the politicization of police is not only to make political advantages for the ruling party in government, but also to make individual fortunes for the police and politicians. The police-politician *nexus* with businessmen can help to commit organized crimes and corruption.

Politicians make use of and misuse the police to collect party funds and sometimes to canvass votes for the political parties. Political power plus police power can make wonders in a democracy. A conspiracy of mutual help and encouragement may yield good results to practise corruption in a democracy. If a policeman/officer has the support of two or three MsLA, then the entire hierarchy seems to be afraid of him. He may politicize the police activities to make some extra-earnings or to have some political advantages for him. Occupying a post in the operational field with the help of some politicians can ensure some income for the work he does. But, a policeman/officer with an upright conscience correctly formed may not allow the politicization of police work. A politicized constable is a strong man-stronger than the non-politicized superior ranks.

"British the police" for me means make the police oppressive and repressive. A "Britished" policeman was not misused for collection of money for the Englishman. But a politicized policeman is misused for making political advantage, monetary gains, party fund, corruption money and for committing organized crimes, profiteering, enforcement criminality, etc. In that sense, a Britshed policeman was less harmful than a politicized policeman. I do not see a politicized policeman ever punished. If someone ventures to punish a politicized policeman, he is doomed and is treated as an arch-enemy of the political party in the government. His asylum will be some god-forsaken post in the department. No one generally wants to be a political orphan and therefore there is competition to become the favoured sons of some politicians. The *survival of the fittest* principle works here and the more politicized policeman is preferred to a less politicized policeman. The National Police Commission has made some recommendations to establish a State Security Commission to eliminate political interference, influence and rule in the police department. The governments which have come into power from time to time have just rejected the recommendation. It means that the politicians want to politicize the police? - or they want to police the police through their political interference? Of course, keeping away the politicians from the police may not be a good proposal in a democracy, yet politicization of the police is a harmful process for fair administration of justice.

1979-80 witnessed police strikes all throughout the country. Historians may say that the police strikes were the outbursts of the accumulated fury in policemen against their superior ranks and their oppressive tactics. Whatever that be, the general election during 1967 resulted in a change in governments in a dozen States in India. From 1947 to 1967, all States except one (or two), had the governments formed by a single political party. When a change in the government came into being in 1967, the political parties who were in the opposition till then could know the advantages of politicizing the police to their favour. The new political administration in some States allowed the policemen/officers to form their association. Afterwards, the National Police Commission: 1977-81 had recommended the formation of police associations and the change in governments during 1967 helped a lot to form the police associations. Police associations were formed subsequently in Uttar Pradesh, Bihar, Orissa, West Bengal, Manipur, Delhi, etc. By 1969 the police associations thus formed were either prohibited or made sterile and it was due to the changes in political leadership and change of governments. Nevertheless, there was a police strike in the PAC in Uttar Pradesh during April, 1973. The strike was suppressed with iron hands and 22 policemen died in the strike. In May 1979, the Punjab police demonstrated and declared a strike. Subsequently, it was spread to other States. Repressive actions were taken to suppress the police strikes in Punjab, but the policemen were supported by the politicians of the opposition. The entry of the politicians into the police affairs might have its roots in the oppressive, suppressive and human-rights-unfriendly attitude and approaches of the superior ranks to the subordinates, especially to the constabulary. When the politicians come forward to help the policemen to achieve their needs and demands, it is easy for them to politicize the police to their advantage. The negative and sometimes offensive attitudes taken by the higher ranks in the police is found to be a powerful cause for the acceptance and development of politicization in police departments. Disciplinary actions are sometimes initiated without any justification and many a time politicians come forward to aid the policeman/officer in distress. An inspector general of police personally met many political leaders of the ruling party to see that he was not punished in a disciplinary inquiry which, according to him, was unjustly initiated. Besides meeting political leaders personally, he had to contact several of them by telephone over and over again. How can he cut off his relations with politicians when he is reinstated? Many policemen who are suspended go to political party offices to see that they are reinstated in service. If one goes to the office of the Home Minister, he can see many constables/officers with the politicians and most of them have service problems or disciplinary actions pending against them. The politicians come as their saviours in distress situations and how can the policemen/officers show a negative or hostile attitude to them when they come with a problem. The politicization of the police takes place consciously or unconsciously in such situations. The politicians are not untouchables and the police lavishly make use/misuse of them for their advantage just like the politicians make use/misuse of police functionaries for their advantage. Some policemen/ officers have lost their trust in their superior ranks and such people heavily depend upon political support and godfatherly treatment. There are instances in which superior ranks have disowned the subordinates, and in such distress situations, the politicians have come forward with their whole-hearted support. How can the police take away politicization if they themselves are not honest to their superiors, associates and subordinates?

Politicization in Police: A Study

I wanted to study the causes of the politicization in the police. I asked 92 policemen/officers and 487 members of the public including politicians, political party workers and political labourers about the causes of politicization in police work. Their responses are give below. Of course, more responses were collected, but only the most prominent ones are listed below.

The responses from the policemen/officers regarding the causes of the politicization in the police (only the prominent ones are listed):

(1) Policemen/officers want to establish special relations with politicians who are powerful.

(2) Politicians want to establish special relations with policemen/ officials who are powerful.

(3) Police - politician *nexus* is a great strength. They can make use of it for their mutual advantages. They can misuse it/abuse it for mutual benefits.

(4) Police support enhances the political influence of the politicians among his followers. Political support ensures the stability, fortunes and authority of police functionaries.

(5) If they stand together, they gain a lot. If they become divided, both stand to lose.

(6) The survival of the fittest works in the department. If one policeman is not inclined to become susceptible to political interference, there are any number of policemen who go after it. The politicians know it well and, therefore, they exploit the situation to their advantage/mutual benefits.

(7) The higher ranks in the police are politicized. The lower ranks cannot but yield to them. A politicized superior is worse than a politician.

(8) A politicized policeman/officer can afford to become corrupt, commit crimes including *nexus* and enforcement criminality. A non-politicized policeman/officer cannot do even legal things in a just way. For, he has enemies and he is always attacked by vested interests. The "Better to yield than fight" policy may be more advantageous to police functionaries.

The responses from the members of the public including politicians, political party workers and political labourers regarding the causes of the politicization in police work (Only the prominent ones are listed):

(1) The police force is a strong source of energy for politicians. The politicians can enjoy police power/authority only through politicization.

(2) The politicians have political power and man-power. They can use/misuse them against the police and the police are afraid of politicians' influence, power and authority. They welcome the politicians and want to be friendly. Politicization comes automatically in police work.

(3) Policemen/officers who come to a new jurisdiction are newcomers. They cannot but depend upon the local politicians/leaders to start working there. Necessarily, they become closer to and friendly with the politicians.

(4) Some local level politicians make a living by their contacts with the police. A smile from a police officer, a word from a head constable, a good gesture from the station staff, etc., are money and business for a small scale politician. They may even work as agents for the police. They can destroy a police officer if they want too. Their importance cannot be underestimated. *The "Keep them in good humour"* - policy is found to be more beneficial for the police. Hence, they are encouraged and entertained. Politicization is the end-result.

(5) In a democracy, the politicization of the police is natural, necessary and inevitable for the smooth survival of the policemen/officials and the politician. The system works well and let it continue as it is seen.

(6) The politician-police-businessman *nexus* is highly remunerative. The administration of justice in an ideal condition is not possible. The administration of justice in a politicized atmosphere may bring about advantages to the police and politicians. Adopt the more beneficial strategies and avoid the difficult ones. This seems to be the police approach to the issue.

There are many reasons for the politicization of the police work. In a politicized atmosphere, policization is difficult, if not impossible. A policed policeman will be a misfit in such a politicization surcharged police atmosphere.

Police-Politician Relations

During the British rule, the politicians approached the police to obtain their support to overthrow the Englishmen from India. The politicians tried their level best to win the support of the subordinate police functionaries. When police unions were formed in 1920, the politicians sponsored and supported the police to be firm in their activities. The Congress at its Calcutta Special Session in September 1920 adopted a programme to request the Indians to withdraw from the police. The then government counterattacked the politicians' move to get police support for the Non-Cooperation movements. Ultimately, the Government of India introduced a Police (Incitement to Disaffection) Act in 1922. Today, there are many political parties and, in every State, there are regional political parties as well. Getting police support for political advantages becomes the objective of many political parties They try their best for the purpose. They resort to punitive transfers and other pressuring tactics and the intention is to bring the police functionaries under their political umbrella and patronage. When politicians come to rule the police, the functional independence of the police is lost. Unless the police functionaries behave with an upright conscience against the high-handed aggression on the justness of police work, the administration of justice by the police becomes an unachievable task in a democracy. A non-politicized police is a basic condition for fair administration of justice and the management of law and order. But, what is seen today is that the politicians and their politicized police functionaries violate the principles of police jurisprudence in a democracy. Fairness in a police job can no longer be bought or sold as a commodity for political patronage.

Political Powers and Police Empowerment

Police powers in law and *police powers* in actual practice-both are poles apart. The law empowers the police to enforce the law, but in practice they cannot, because the political powers do not allow them to execute the laws. This is a dilemma faced by the police in the present day democracy. The law says that the police can use necessary force to maintain peace or to manage a law and order situation. But the politicians say that no force must be employed if the employment of force is to their political disadvantage. The politicians tell the police to use excessive force if the victims belong to a political party which is in the opposition. If the police cannot enforce law as per the law and procedure established by the law, then they are criticized. In such instances, they have more loyalty to the politicians who rule the people. As the police are not free to enforce law in the present day society, there is a growing feeling among the people that the political powers ensure police empowerment. The police look at the political hierarchy several times before they enforce the law in a lawful manner. This is not policing, it rather is politicized policing. During the British raj, the police looked at the white men to get orders and likewise, the police look at the political executives to get orders. No law empowers the politicians and political executives to direct the police in their work, but in practice, they are found to drive the vehicle keeping the statutorily created police functionaries at the front. "Back-seat" driving is undesirable, but a system has come into existence that the "back-seat" driving is accepted by many in society. The law in principle is not the law in practice. A policeman in the statute is not the policeman in the field. A man becomes a politicized policemen in due course and in some cases a party man in police uniform.

This is what the people talk about the policeman according to the law and the same man in practice. Police empowerment has nothing much to do with political powers and likewise political powers have nothing much to do with police empowerment. The police can be empowered only through constitutionally enacted laws and procedures. But deviations are seen and that is the reason why the people speak about policing the police before policing the society. So long as the people see politicized policing, the police cannot get the willing cooperation and participation of the people. A policed police service will have the full support and good will of the people irrespective of their political affiliations. If the police become politicized, then they become the party men of a political party and precisely therefore they cannot work for the entire people. An impartial, non-politicized, just, fair-minded, human rights friendly policeman is a friend of everybody in a democracy. He is a policed policeman and is empowered to administer justice with a human conscience and justness.

References

1. David Arnold, *Police Power and Colonial Rule - Madras: 1859-1947*, Oxford University Press, Madras, 1986.
2. *Ibid.*

4

Susceptibility and Policing the Police

"A dog does not eat its own flesh" - this is an old saying, but the British wanted the Indians to eat their own flesh. They recruited illiterate Indians to their police and asked them to fight against their own countrymen. The British succeeded in their attempts and they could do so just by offering peanuts as their salary or wages for repressing the Indians who raised their voice against the British imperialism. The Indians were susceptible to British tactics and temptations. They made the police as the first line of internal defence and the Indians did their duty by repressing and oppressing the Indians. For doing so, the British allowed the wages of unskilled labourers for the lowest rank in the police. The small pay given to the constables was found to be a powerful motivating force to become corrupt. In 1880, 200 policemen were convicted for their corrupt connivance with dacoits among the *Bheels*. The concept of *nexus crimes* was not known to them then. At the same time, they became susceptible to temptations to make money by conniving with the dacoits. The low pay given to the constables might be one of the precipitating causes for their connivance with the dacoits. The police functionaries drawing high and very fat salaries are now accused of involving themselves in *nexus* transactions with organized criminals, crime syndicates, underworld bandits and so on. Why? Susceptibility or proneness to commit crimes has been in existence for centuries among the police in India. The same tendency is found among the policemen/officers in other countries and cultures as well and all throughout the history of police. The criminal in police uniform connives with other criminals.

Susceptibility to commit crimes shows a lack of policing in the police service. During 1875-1880, the policemen (in Gaya) registered false cases against innocent people and implicated them in the commission of dacoities. Researches show that the policemen themselves committed the dacoities and they caught hold of innocent people to prove their detective efficiency. Incredible indeed! Nevertheless, even today the police are blamed for registering false cases and implicating innocent people. Why? Sometimes, criminal cases are acquitted by courts as they are found to be false, Why? The allegation, if it is true, shows that the very objectives of the police service are defeated by such criminal activities by the police themselves. Crime-doers become crime-investigators! A sense of accountability on the part of the police is dead in such instances. The integrity and justice-mindedness of the police service get lost. Do the people pay salaries for the police to do such things? More policemen, more police officers, more salaries, more perks, more vehicles, more science and technology, more psychological techniques are the panaceas proposed for the decline in convictions. If false cases were registered and investigators were found to be susceptible to such acts for centuries, then the real causes for such criminal acts must be identified. The fidelity and the ability to bear true allegiance to the values of policing must not be put to test. Why do the police have such an attitude?

Attitude is described as a "a readiness" of the psyche to act or react in a certain direction.[1] Why do the police act in the way they do now? Psychologists speak about the *collective attitude* which is an "an attitude that is peculiar not to one individual, but to many, at the same time - i.e., either to a society, a people or to mankind in general".[2] Is it the collective attitude of the police to become susceptible to registration of false cases and manipulation of records?

The Supreme Court of India interpreting Article 21 of the Indian Constitution spoke about human dignity. The Supreme Court held: "We think that the right to life includes the right to live with basic human dignity and all that goes along with it". A false case against an individual means that his right to live with human dignity is questioned and challenged. No doubt, it is a human right violation and an indicator of the non-policing of the police service. It is a disgrace to any civilized police in the world. Unfortunately, the police conscience is said to be coarsened and their sensitivity blunted in such circumstances of human rights violations.

Susceptibility to Torture, Inhuman and Degrading Treatment

Human life has a dignity and a divinity. The Supreme Court of India held: "When we talk of the right to life as a basic human right, it is intended to be a legal safeguard not only against violent aggression but also against the creeping, gradually effective encroachment on vital conditions of life, conditions without which it is impossible to survive as a human being". Nevertheless, the report of the Torture Commission - 1855 and the bitter experiences of the people with the police before and after the said report show that the police have exhibited their susceptibility to torture. There is no accurate account of death by torture in police custody, yet allegations and instances are plenty even today that the police continue to torture people. The report of the Torture Commission speaks about the widespread use of intimidation and physical cruelty to extract confessions. The report says that torture was employed to force the payment of bribes as well. What happened in India during the period of internal emergency (1975-76) ? Senior/ very senior police officers were accused of causing custodial deaths. When people die in police custody, it is usual to say that the death is suicidal.

Psychologists speak about *phenothiazine* deaths and they describe them as sudden deaths or a sudden cardiovascular collapse without physical or autopsy findings that explain the death.[3] The *phenothiazine deaths* are sudden, unexplained and autopsy-negative and there are many such cases of sudden deaths reported from police stations.

The Statement of the Police Committee on the Administration of Madras city reads (1902): "...petty annoyance to the poor and illiterate by means of threat, petty assaults, vexatious complaints, blackmailing, etc.," were abundant in police work. The report of the Police Committee reads further: "It has been forcibly pointed out to us in almost every district we visited that instead of looking on the police as their protectors, the people regard them as their enemies and oppressors and that they are generally afraid to complain of police malpractices". The National Police Commission: 1977-81 saw the same things in a deeper and wider way and the people have been experiencing the same things for centuries. Nearly one and half centuries are now over since the Torture Commission of 1855 wanted to put an end to police torture, nevertheless one sees coercion, intimidation and corruption in police subculture.

Why do the police resort totorture? A policed police service is not expected to show aggressiveness to the people, especially to the ignorant and timid peasantry or to the helpless and defenceless people. Sociologists are of the view that one of the causes for the police to employ torture is social and cultural. It may be true to some extent but the same can be checked and corrected if the police want so. They must realize the fact that torture in police custody is a disgrace to civilized policing. In a democratic set-up, the police are accountable to the same people whom they torture or treat in an inhuman and degrading way.

Susceptibility to harassing people and humiliating them may be seen in police subculture. Why? Some people say that the policemen are generally sadists. I do not and cannot agree with such a sweeping statement. There may be sadists in the police service. As the word sadism (After Marquis de Sade, 1740-1814) means a sexual pleasure derived by a person upon inflicting cruelty upon others, I think that the word has only a limited application to the police susceptibility to torture, harassment and humiliation to the people in police custody. The ignorant or little educated policeman during the British raj had no psychological tool with him to question the suspect in the crime. He had his muscle power and crude sense of administering justice. Today's police officer who possesses a master's degree in Information Technology or a doctorate in English literature too is as ignorant or little educated as the colonial policeman. Both - the colonial policeman and the democracy's police officer - may misuse his muscle power, out of helplessness, to extort a confession from the suspects in a crime. Susceptibility to inhuman and degrading treatment is more a psychological reaction than a socially or culturally inherited behavioural pattern. Police the police with knowledge and moral sense may be the only option to protect the people from police harassment, humiliation and torture.

Susceptibility to Aggression and Cruelty

To whom are the police becoming cruel and aggressive? - to their own patrons in a democracy? The idea that the people are the patrons of the police could not, somehow or other, influence the police in uniform. There might be historical reasons for it. How could the police who found the people hostile to British imperialism might respect the people as patrons over-night when India became independent? It is just not possible. The British found the crude and rude nature of the military policing. They created the police as a principal means of state control. They created a civilian force, under direct magisterial control, to protect the people and their property. When India became independent, the police were made to serve the people as the people were not the enemies of the State. They were the strength and force of the State. They became the patrons of the police. Nevertheless, reports and studies on police-people relations show that something is wrong somewhere.

The British wanted a repressive and oppressive police force in India. The same people later had to enact laws to control the police in their repressive activities. They made special provisions in the penal, procedural and evidence laws for the purpose. The provisions were intended to police the police. When India became independent, constitutional safeguards were made against aggression and cruelty by the police. The founding fathers of the Constitution did not want the people to suffer the abuse of power/misuse of authority by the police. They wanted a people-oriented police service. The republic wanted human justice to the people and not a sort of justice pregnant with retribution, aggression and torture. They did not want the police to become a law unto themselves. If the police become a law unto themselves, then the poor and the weak will become the victims and such a victimized administration of justice by the police will be deplorable. In such a situation, the police become a lawless law-in-action with no meaning and philosophy. Violence to anyone in police custody is a human right violation and no civilized police will resort to aggression to administer justice in criminal cases. The wilful physical harm inflicted by the police on a person in their custody is not policing. *Anger, hate* and *rage* are the internal, emotional concomitants of aggression. Ethnology may view man as a killer-ape, but genetic anthropology sees him as a noble savage characterized by cooperation with other men. They are moot issues not to be discussed by the policemen. The policemen empowered to administer justice are neither killer apes nor noble savages. The law is what the law does and the police is not the law, but an agency to enforce law in a lawful and human rights friendly way.

All throughout the history of the police in India, one sees the police resorting to aggression and cruelty towards the people on many occasions. They have become a recurring reality. The destructive delay in the investigation of criminal cases is a cruelty. The unbearable expenses caused to the accused is certainly a cruelty particularly when he is honourably acquitted by a court of law. Any delay in investigation breeds corruption and ensures miscarriage of justice.

Susceptibility to Corruption and Corrupt Practices

The police "is generally regarded as corrupt and oppressive" - wrote the Police Commission: 1902-03. What is justice administration if the people entrusted with the duty are corrupt? The people are able to understand the integrity and susceptibility of a system to corrupt practices. During 1902-03, the Indian Police Commission wrote, "...everywhere they went, the Commission heard the most bitter complaints of corruption of the police". Corruption presupposes abuse of power and misuse of authority. If the system permits corruption, then it must be seen at every level and in every stage of work. But the 1902-03 Police Commission could notice corruption among station-house officers throughout the country and certainly in every stage of work in police stations. If corruption is seen in the police stations, it means that the same is prevalent in police headquarters and among the police constabulary. This is what researches show and therefore the susceptibility to corruption is seen in many in the entire hierarchy. The National Police Commission: 1977-81 found corruption wider, deeper and stronger than what the 1902-03 Police Commission observed. Just a few days ago, the Governor of a South Indian State released a study report prepared by a non-governmental organization which contained an observation that corruption was highest in police departments. I do not want to comment on the validity of the study, yet I observe that the allegation is not without basis. One is shocked to read everyday the news in the media. The ministers in government, chief secretaries, directors general of police, chairmen of Boards down to the peon are caught and convicted for corruption in democratic India. It reveals a fact that the entire administration is blamed for corruption and corrupt practices. The dictionary meaning of corruption - i.e., guilty of dishonest practices as bribery - is no more valid or relevant now. Bribery means anything promised or given as illicit payment and the corruption practised or perpetuated in these days go beyond the meanings seen in dictionaries. Long ago, Lord Macaulay wrote: "What is administered is not law but a kind of rule and capricious equity. I asked an able and excellent judge lately returned from India how one of our zilla courts would decide several legal questions of great importance - questions not involving consideration of religion or caste - mere questions of commercial law. He told me that it was a mere lottery". Is the writing of Lord Macaulay valid in criminal justice administration? In an atmosphere pregnant with *nexus* crimes, corruption Mafia, enforcement criminality, crime syndicates, etc., do the people get or expect to get justice worth its meaning from the enforcement agencies?

Susceptibility to corruption is seen from time immemorial. "So I am old and do not know when I may die. Now take your weapons, your quiver and bow; go out into the country and hunt me some game. Make me the kind of savoury I like and bring it to me, so that I may eat and give you my blessing before I die" said Isaac to his son Esau. Rebekah overheard the conversation and managed to get the blessings of Isaac to her son Jacob by cunning.[4] Like this, the people around the police are able to know each policeman's/officer's weakness and susceptibility to corruption and corrupt practices which may be anything from womanizing to amassment of wealth. "What are you prepared to give me if I hand him over to you. They paid him thirty silver pieces, and from that moment he looked for an opportunity to betray him".[5] If the people are prepared to corrupt the police, then the policemen/officers ask them "what are you prepared to give me?" and they give cash, car, flats, bank accounts, articles, gadgets, positions, promises, fortunes, etc. The susceptibility to offer temptations, to accept offers, to insist on offers etc., is seen in people and the police is no exception. Nevertheless, the misuse of power/abuse of authority by the police with corrupt motives causes extensive damage and severe harm to the people and to the justice system. The Police Committee of 1838 said: "The Darogahs and their subordinate officers are corrupt" and the same thing is repeated by the news papers today and the study reports on the police in these days. Only Cornwallis, Minto, Hastings, Auckland, Napier, Clerk and Grant knew it well then; but today, kindergarten children know it through the media and from the films and T.V. serials. The National Police Commission made some recommendations for checking corruption in the police service. If corruption in the police is checked effectively, then policing the police becomes easy. Many of the complaints against the police are connected with corruption and corrupt practices, According to the National Police Commission: 1977-81, the percentage of substantiated complaints of police torture is highest in judicial inquiries, lower in magisterial inquiries and lowest in inquiries conducted by the police department or other agencies. The conclusions to be drawn may be disturbing to many police functionaries - i.e., there is corruption even in disciplinary inquiries conducted by departmental officers. It may be a Xmas cake, an Indian bottle, a Scotch, a gold coin, an electric fan or a modern gadget or some rupee notes having Mahatma Gandhi's fine picture. Allegations are there that disciplinary inquiries are not effective enough to police the police as the inquiries are sometimes conducted under corrupt conditions by corrupt police officials. The hierarchy loses its credibility and the officers at the apex level do not enjoy the full confidence of the lower levels. Many who are at the lower levels of the police approach the High Courts and Administrative Tribunals to get disciplinary justice. In some States, the appointment of the directors general of police is made on political considerations. If the political affiliation is not acceptable, then the director general will have to leave his chair to an additional director general of police to occupy-to administer justice to the people in the State. Will he be able to police the police if the policemen think that their director general occupies the post not out of his merit, but out of the grace of a political party in power? In a south Indian State, some policemen claim that their Service Association has a *decisive say* in the posting of the director general of police. If it is true, then policing the police will be a very difficult task. When the appointment to the position of the director general of police in a State is decided by politics and political affiliations, then police performance ceases to be impartial; policing the police will be very hard. Just justice is the value people seek through the institution of the police and such a politically favoured director general will not be able to administer fair justice to himself, his men and the people.

Susceptibility to Women and Liquor

In a seminar on Women Empowerment, I went to present a paper on *women* and *violence against women*. There was a retired professor who was the wife of a retired police officer. She too presented a paper. On our return in a car, she told me: "I suffered enough in my life. My husband was a police officer and he occupied very high positions. He was a drunkard and we had to suffer him. He was not policed enough to police him". Yes, she narrated her life story fully and was candid enough to say that her husband got more bottles than the number of rupee notes he received from the public exchequer. He was an alcoholic and she asked: "How can an alcoholic *police* the society"? It might be an isolated case or we wish it to be so. Nevertheless, a few questions :

(1) How many policemen have died of alcohol addiction?
(2) How many policemen are alcohol dependent and serve in the police department?
(3) How many middle level functionaries in the police suffer from alcohol dependence/addiction?
(4) What about the senior and top level in the police?

The answers to these questions in an honest way will show the extent and intensity of policing the police department. Once in a film I saw a police officer 'drinking' in his office and I felt angry with the cine actor, script writer and the producer. After leaving the theatre, I found two policemen misbehaving in public in an intoxicated mood. I blamed me for feeling angry with the cine actor, script writer and the producer. A liquor addict can never become a policeman and he cannot police the society. A lot of stories are heard about many police officers in the hierarchy and they are about their drinking habits and womanizing tendencies. True or false, the stories about police functionaries thus told and propagated by police officers and policemen draw an unenviable picture of the police and of the policing within the police. Susceptibility to women and liquor has always been a traditional enemy of policing.

'Custodial rape' is a serious offence under the Indian Penal Code - but custodial rapes take place in India. The Crime in India published by the Ministry of Home Affairs, Government of India, gives the statistics on custodial rapes in the police. If custodial rapes are reported in 2000 A.D., it means that the institution of the police lacks moral sense and legal responsibility. A deaf and dumb girl was alleged to have been raped by a policeman in a police van in a court compound. The girl was a prisoner remanded to judicial custody. The press and the people made it a big issue and a criminal case was registered against the rapist. But who can save the department from the damage caused by such a sexopath?

The police is a male-dominated, or better, all-men organization. Necessarily, they must be gender-decent and fair-sex friendly. When the police was organized in India, women offenders were not there. Today, women come to police stations in large numbers - in various capacities. There are rules and regulations specifying the manner in which women are to be interacted in police offices/custody. Often, women may be alone - in a helpless and defenceless position when they are interrogated. True or false, allegations are raised against policemen/officers of sex-indecency and gender unfriendly attitude. Some psychologists say that women in police custody sexualize some policemen/officers. Some policemen may crack sexual jokes which may sexualize others. Thoughts too can be sexualized. The psychic energy connected with sensual and somatic satisfaction is said to be the sexual energy. When women are in police custody, it may sexualize some and precisely, therefore, the rules have been framed to interact with women in the presence of another woman.

"Organ pleasure" at the sight of a woman in her desperate condition is quite possible. Unless the policeman/officer is not well policed, he may become organ-erotic. Organ-erotic means "relating to or characterized by the attachment of the erotic instinctual component to an organ of the body". A policeman may be organ-erotic to a particular body-part of a lady (e.g. lips, buttocks, hair, breast, etc.) and if he becomes so, it is possible that he behaves in a sex-indecent way. A policeman who is a fetish may behave abnormally when he interacts with a girl in his custody. The most common fetishes are long hair, ear-rings, undergarments, feet etc., and it may sexualize a policeman/officer. In India, many commissions of inquiry have been appointed to investigate custodial rapes and some have brought out surprising facts behind custodial rapes. Nevertheless, these commissions generally do not inquire into the psychological and psychiatric aspects of custodial rapes. In connection with a raid organized by the police in a south Indian State, severe allegations of molestation of women by the police were raised. The people accused the police of raping women and ultimately the Government appointed a commission of inquiry which brought out a report confirming sexual abuses, harassment and indecency by the police on women. Certainly, it is not policing. The psychological aspects of sexual indecency by policemen in uniform may reveal strange facts and factors behind sexually indecent behaviour by policemen.

Drunkenness, it may be admitted in fairness, is a problem that affects adversely the policing of the police. One may become drunk without being an alcoholic. I have interviewed some policemen/officers who were noted for drunkenness. I understand that they became alcoholic as they had many opportunities to get free liquor from many sources. Some resorted to drinking as an escape mechanism from their burden and responsibilities. Some who found difficulties to adjust with their tensions may have recourse to alcoholic beverages. People who were suspended from service and not reinstated even after a long period found asylum in drinks. What was more? They had a weak ego structure and they made vain attempts to flee from their worries by drinking. Policemen who were insecure were found to be more alcohol prone. Whatever might be the causes of drunkenness, they could carve out a poor image of the police in the eye of the public. They were not morally justified to apprehend people who were drunkards.

Susceptibility to Political Whims

Transfers and postings of police officers in strategic positions are done politically. They can be replaced as the political winds shift and therefore susceptibility to the political wishes, whims and desires becomes necessary for survival in certain posts. The Government in power and the politicians who rule the government want information from the bottom of the police hierarchy. In order to get information which may help the Government to remain in power, each government wants their own people. In such a situation, susceptibility to political directions becomes essential for many policemen/officers. The police brutality, prejudices, cynicism and displeasure to politicians and party-men in the opposition to the ruling political parties are adversely criticized. Studies show that the politicians in the opposition are often negative in their evaluation of police performance. The policemen/officers who have political godfathers become more authoritarian in their approaches than those who do not have political patronage. Those who enjoy political support may even behave in an unbecoming way - in a non-policed manner. The authoritarian policeman/officer may express pseudo-authority and wants to show his power, muscle, toughness and hatred to people. They may collect money for the party fund and may become corrupt to please the corrupt politicians who support them when they are in trouble.

During the British raj, the politicians tried to exert their influence on the police. During 1920, when Police Union was formed in Madras city, the politicians urged the policemen to be firm on their demands for better salary and working conditions. The British did not like the police establishing linkage with the politicians. Therefore, the British rejected the police demand for improved conditions and wages for the police. The British Indian Government said that they would not accept and recognize any union which had political influence. A politician-free police force was what the British wanted. They knew well that the police susceptibility to political intervention would affect adversely their rule in India. When they left India and democracy was established, the ruling Government in power wanted the police force with them. It being the objective, the ruling political party in Government did every thing to see that the politicians of the opposition did not come anywhere near to the policemen/officers. Hence, they saw to it that the policemen/officers who were politically close to them were appointed at important posts and positions. They wanted a total susceptibility to their political interest from the police.

Every policeman/officer had a political background before he joined the police. Hence, they were picked and posted by the governments which came into power from time to time. Politicians became more powerful through their policemen/officers and the policemen/officers became more powerful through their politicians. This *nexus* between the police and the ruling politicians paved the way for the politicization of the police after independence. Sometimes, the *nexus* became unholy, but the unholy *nexus* helped them to make fortunes in many ways.

Susceptibility to Human Rights Unfriendly Approaches

The oppressive and repressive police force of the British in India could never become human rights friendly. The principles contained in the Magna Carta were then unknown to the ignorant and illiterate policeman. General Dyer's savage use of troops at Jallianwala Bagh in Amritsar in April 1919 was an instance of how the police could be misused for human rights violations. In independent India, the police were to uphold the constitutional values and human rights of the people. "It is easier said than done" and the policemen/officers found it extremely difficult to be human rights friendly to the people in the newly established democracy. The susceptibility to the socio-cultural values inherited by the police from their British past made them behave rudely and in a non-police manner.

More than a civil police, the British wanted a paramilitary force; more than human rights, they wanted bayonet training for the policemen; more than the dignity of man, they wanted cheap muscle power with grossly inadequate pay; more than justice administration, they wanted to retain their reign in India; more than investigation of crime, they wanted the police to quell riots and garrison disturbed areas. In such a set-up, human rights and the protection of human rights had no value or *locus standi*.

The 1861 Police Act had the provision for the creation of district armed reserves. All constables were given a paramilitary training and had to pass through a period of training and service with the armed reserves before they came to police stations. Even today, the same procedure of recruitment and entry to the General Executive via the armed reserve/armed battalion is the rule for constables. Thus the civil police constables have an armed police background and a paramilitary training. Can they become human rights friendly is a moot issue discussed among human rights activists. A force that has been trained to quell riots, drilled and disciplined to fight against the people with lathies and arms, taught mob control operations and garrisoning techniques at disturbed areas by show of force and muscle power cannot become human rights friendly all on a sudden - over-night - one day, too soon when they are transferred from the armed reserve to the general executive branch of the civil police. The susceptibility to their arms, lathies, muscle power, boots, paramilitary looks, military voices, crushing attitudes, etc., continues to be in many even when they frog-jump from the armed reserve to the local police. Take for instance the Malabar Special Police sanctioned on 30, September, 1921. They were equipped with magazine Lee-Enfield rifles and with Lewis guns when the force was formed. When India became independent, these men from the M.S.P. (Malabar Special Police) too opted for serving the people as civil police and the system of constables entering into the para-military (police) battalions and from there entering to the civil police to serve the people in a "human rights friendly" way continues to follow even today. After the enactment of the Protection of Human Rights Act in 1993, massive campaigns were organized throughout the country to inculcate the finer points in human rights to the police including the members of the constabulary. Nevertheless, there was some resistance exerted by the policemen to absorb the concepts of human rights in their day-to-day work. One reason for it was the ignorance of the policemen in the scientific investigation of crimes and the psychological approaches to the people in a human rights friendly way. The tragic impact of it has been that more and more policemen were detected to be human rights violators and dealt with accordingly by the National or State Human Rights Commissions, courts of law and the media. A paramilitary strategy to deal with the civilian population has been found to be objectionable and, as a result, demands were put by the police functionaries to bifurcate the police into two separate wings - namely, the police for law and order and the police for investigation of crimes. But the governments seem to be taking no interest in forming such a set-up for the police. The policemen are found to be unhappy about it. The negative attitude of the governments certainly affects adversely the morale of the police service. The hierarchy is helpless to enforce their plans if the governments are not favouring their new proposals. In 1973, there was a PAC revolt and the hierarchy suggested many strategies which the authorities ignored. In 1979, one found police agitation. K.F. Rustamji said: "The demands of the constabulary were voiced again and again for a decade. No one paid any heed. And now, the moment a few in the constabulary shouted a few slogans, all sorts of favours have been announced. If these demands are legitimate today, why were they not examined and conceded day before yesterday?" At present, the police do not have suicide-proof lock-ups, no fund for feeding the detinues, no furniture, no facilities for providing minimum human comforts in a human rights friendly manner, etc., in police stations. They do not have proper interrogation rooms, no scientific aids for investigation, no trained police interrogator, no psychological assistance, etc., when they are pressured to be human rights friendly. They demand them over and over again and their demands gather dust in Secretariats while their grievances accumulate in a severe way. Susceptibility to protect human rights cannot be ensured unless and until a human rights friendly environment is provided.

Susceptibility to Miscarriage of Justice

We have a notorious history of policemen committing crimes and accusing innocent people as criminals during 1877-78 in Gaya district. They did so to prove their detective efficiency. There is no dearth of literature and research studies to show how the police manipulate records, concoct evidence, produce tutored witnesses and touts, file false statements before the courts to see that the courts convict the accused in crimes. The Central Committee on Police Training appointed by the Government of India in 1971 has enumerated the various ways the police administered wounded justice or miscarriage of justice. The committee wanted to police the police through meaningful training and inculcation of human values. The police susceptibility to miscarriage of justice has a history of its own. Why did the police become susceptible to miscarriage of justice? The reasons found out by the police commissions, administrators and individual researchers are numerous. Some of them are :

(1) Want of the detective ability of the police in general was found to be a cause of fewer arrest during 1867 in Oudh by the then administration. This was certainly a miscarriage of justice to the society.

(2) The constable's pay was Rs.5, head constables - Rs.8$^{3/4}$; chief constable - Rs.20, European constable - Rs.50 and inspector - Rs.65 during 1862. The low pay of the police was a cause of corruption, abuse of power, misuse of authority in police work - noted by the then administration.

(3) Want of intelligent and well educated constables/chief constables was an important cause of poor detection and investigation of cases during 1869 - observed by the then police authorities.

(4) Lack of training and education in police officers was a serious cause for large-scale acquittals of criminal cases - found by police commissions, police authorities, research scholars and individual police officers from time to time - over and over again - all over the country for the last two centuries and the story continues ensuring miscarriage of justice. The percentage of convictions comes down and of acquittals goes up year after year. The subsystems in justice administration blames one another and the solution is not seen by anyone. The result is miscarriage of justice. In a system which tolerates miscarriage of justice or which shows a Nelson's eye to it or encourages it, the susceptibility to the miscarriage of justice is likely to be stronger than what it would be in a system that discourages any miscarriage of justice. For nearly a century and a half, for instance, the courts have been remanding suspects in crimes to police custody or to judicial custody. No law or judicial officer wanted to know whether or not the detinue in police custody was looked after properly by the State!

A court remands a suspect to police custody. But no court in India asks the questions: "When can the detainee go to bed in police custodial facility?", "at what time can the detinue take his meals in police custody?" In prisons in India, there is a time schedule and in police stations, there is no time schedule for anything. "At what time can a detainee rise up?, can he pray?, can he read a paper?" - there exists no rule and if the detainee happens to be an innocent person, then he suffers and suffers the miscarriage of justice committed on detainees in police custodial facility for centuries in this land of Dharma. Is it not a punishment to do so to a person in custody? The nineteenth century laws and procedures are great scandals for the modern concepts of justice. In a world which accepts correction of the crime-doer as the objectives of the justice system, the age-old and museum piece legislation are of no use. They are a powerful source for the policeman to become susceptible to miscarriage of justice. The sufferers of the miscarriage of justice in police custody, court procedures and prisons take naturally violent revenge upon the aggressors. A custodial death is seen to be a horrible crime by all, but it is repeated in cold blood. Why? People look at it as brutality, blame the aggressors and condemn such acts in the strongest words. Likewise, denial of food, water, human comforts, sleep, etc., in police custody is condemned by the people and society. They are seen as miscarriage of justice.

Susceptibility to Public Demands

The general public have a lot of demands to their police. First of all, they want a policed police and secondly they want peace and harmony. Earlier, the people looked at the police from a distance from police stations as they were afraid of police muscles. Today, people keep a watch on the policemen and police stations. In some places in India, they keep a mobile (cellular) phone and communicate to the human rights activists/ press, etc., if they listen to human cries when they are tortured in police stations. They keep a watch/vigil even during night hours and make press conference, conduct jadhas, *dharnas*, public meetings and street corner gatherings to make publicity over the activities of the police. Recently, in connection with a political clash between two political parties, a number of people were murdered. The political party produced the culprits purported to have committed the murder. The people in the locality knew well that they were innocent people who had nothing to do with the murders. Nevertheless, they were strong adherents of the political party which produced them before the police. The people and human rights activists gave great publicity about the political drama and exposed the police-politician *nexus* in the matter. Wall-posters were seen and press-releases were given. The police cut a sorry figure if they connive with politicians in such situations. Instances have been reported that the people came to the police stations to get the innocent people released from police custody. The people in the locality know the real culprits in many cases and, therefore, they raise their protests when innocent people are arrested by the police. In British India, the police used to do so, and in the democratic India, the police continue to do so. But, now the general public do not allow such malpractices to take place in some instances. The trend is likely to be strengthened in the years to come. In one instance, a political party produced some innocent people-political adherents - before the police and they admitted that they committed the offence. They were produced before the Magistrate who simply refused to grant bail to them. They were remanded to judicial custody and the political party which produced the innocent people was accused of having cheated their political adherents by offering false promises. The courts are also aware of the foul play by the political parties with the connivance of the police as alleged by the public. When the public become vibrant and sensitive to the illegalities committed by the powerful, the police have no option but to become susceptible to public demands. The public do not have any sustained demands so much so that they refrain from their persistence in due course. This is being exploited by vested interests.

The public do not mean the total population or the entire people in an area. It means the vocal public - may be a minority that can mould the public opinion. They may be able to create a confusion if they cannot convince the people. Police do not have a media with them or vocal influence among the people. What they can do is to enforce the law in a fair and legal way - with public appreciation and approval. Police uniform, police vehicle, police activities, police performance, police stations, police weapons, police walk, talk and behaviour, etc., are conspicuously visible to the public who discuss them at many levels in different fora. Earlier, the police could afford to ignore the public opinions about their activities and performances. But today, there is the public auditing of police performance and the audited accounts will be placed before the public during election campaigns. Legal literacy is promoted by many agencies including the National Literacy Mission. Seminars, Symposia and work shops on the police, police laws, police-citizen interactions are organized at village/panchayath levels. The policeman is threatened with public actions and agitations, so much so that ignoring of people's opinion on police performance is a virtual impossibility. People know the policemen today and they may isolate them from social intercourse if they do not honour the public views and opinions. The family of the policeman and his children may have to suffer social isolation and public avoidance. A retired director general of police once told me: "I feel that I am rejected by the public. They make complaints that I did not do anything good for them when I was in service and had enough powers. I feel lonely and condemned". Certainly, the public are a force to be reckoned with by the police. There is an old saying: "If the king hates a man, he can live in a forest; if the public hate a man, he cannot live even in a forest". The public is a reality and not a faceless mass. Precisely therefore the police have to become susceptible to them. A policed police service have to become susceptible to them. It service will do everything in a decent way so much so that they will get public acceptance, recognition and approval.

The policemen claim sometimes that they are the members of the public and likewise the people in society often say that they are members of the police service. I think that both are right in their own ways and what we require today is a mutual acceptance of that reality/fact. The police become susceptible to the public and the public become susceptible to the police. Even if they want to become otherwise, they cannot. The police want to police the society and the society wants to police the police.

Police justice means public justice and public justice means social justice. If the police become susceptible to pressures which do not ensure social justice, then the purpose of policing is defeated. When abuses of police power and authority are noted, the people become dissatisfied. In a liberal democracy, the dissatisfaction is expressed in many ways. For example, the poor people detained in police custody have a right to remain in police custody with dignity. The law says that they must be provided with necessary wearing apparel and the police have the discretion to decide the type or nature of the wearing apparel. In any case, they must have their dress more than their underwear or short loin clothes. But, allegations are heard that the poor people are pressured to remain naked, half-naked or their private parts covered with news papers in the custodial facility. If the allegations are true to the least, then the police discretion is violative of what the Supreme Court has upheld: "We think that the right to live include the right to live with basic human dignity and all that goes along with it, namely, the bare necessities of life such as adequate nutrition, clothing and shelter over the head and facilities for reading, writing and expressing oneself in diverse forms". If this is what is held by the Supreme Court of India, a question is raised: "Do the detinues in police custody get the needed facilities to spend their time there with human dignity if they are not provided with adequate food, clothes and human comforts?" If the State does not provide them, will it not be an encroachment on the basic prerequisite of the life of the detainees in police custody? So far, no one has raised this question and therefore even the policed police officers are not inclined to consider any degrading and humiliating treatment in police custody to be a violation of the most basic right to life. If the State power - the police - does not execute the constitutional pledge of justice in favour of the suspects, arrestees, detinues and so on, then it is a disgrace to the very concept of social justice. The detinues too form a part of the Republic and social justice is the justice done to the Republic. The tyranny of power must not murder people's justice and no policed police service will tolerate any such tyranny. For, the policed police service recognizes the fact that any power without justice is tyranny and the police service which is maintained to protect the democracy's social good must not be instrumental to promote tyranny and oppression on the people who are socially, economically, politically and otherwise handicapped.

Susceptibility to Animal Instincts in Man

A policed police officer is one who has a self-esteem. He has self-control and control over his animal instincts. He has no identity crisis. He has values and an upright conscience. He is not susceptible to temptations, positions and promotions. He has limited desires and knows fully well that he has limitations. He accepts the fact that he is limited in time and space - is it true to think so?

During the early periods of democracy in India - may be two decades or more - some policemen/officers were notoriously nicknamed as *Lions, Tigers, Vultures,* etc. They took pride in being called so. Some psychologists, long ago, wanted to explain human behaviour on the basis of instincts. They tried to prove that all forms of human activity was instinctive. But later researches proved that human behaviour varied widely from culture to culture - from individual to individual. Hence, the concept of instinct has received little or no attention from the psychologists of the recent past. When I joined the police department in 1976, many policemen/officers were found to have a lot of appreciation for the theory of instincts to explain police behaviour. I have listened to them telling that police behaviour ought to be instinctive. They lacked scientific information on instincts and human behaviour. Instincts have value in studying the behaviour of animals and not man. Psychologists show that animal behaviours which were thought to be instinctive once were later proved to be not so when the same were studied scientifically. They proved their theory by showing the mice-killing behaviour of the Norway rat (the common brown rat). Psychologists found that some rats killed mice while others did not. Why? We are not interested in studying more about the mice killing nature of rats. We could see many lions, vultures, tigers in police earlier and they were called so by the people by seeing their animal like behaviours which were instinctual in nature. In other words, their susceptibility to instincts was highly projected. A recent study on the nicknames of policemen/officers shows that the tigers, lions and vultures in police have vanished into the thin air in large numbers. Why? Their susceptibility to animal behaviour-instinctual behaviour - has come down owing to the human rights movements. It shows that behavioural modification is quite possible in the police provided that they encourage the policing of the police. Susceptibility to aggression, to pleasure, to pain avoidance, etc., may be seen and any such susceptibilities will damage the policing. Torture may be due to one's susceptibility to aggression and certainly it can be controlled. The control mechanisms in the police must be activated to control the police. Non-policing or lack of policing in the police may be due to defective supervision. There is no substitute for effective supervision. The supervisors must be the role models, but lack of such role models will be a cause of non-policing in the police service. The officers suffering from vices and bad character are threats to good policing. Susceptibility to drinks, women, food, luxuries, fortunes, etc., have ruined the department and any defects among the man-power resources are defects in the policing of the police. The police in pre-independent India suffered from illiteracy and lack of education. The British, time and again, acknowledged the fact that the police in India could appreciate human values and sober behaviour. The humanization of the police started and any attempts made to humanize the police were attempts made to police the police. The British developed only the rudimentary, biological and primitive forms of behaviour in Indian police functionaries. Indian democracy did not make any attempts to develop the human qualities in early police functionaries. Proper police training did not receive any attention and as such the police could not develop their social motives. Attitudinal changes were necessary to make a policed police service. But, no efforts were made to have any such attitudinal change among the police functionaries. The Gore Committee made many suggestions to effect attitudinal changes and behavioural modifications in the police. But their suggestions and recommendations were indifferently accepted and enforced. The result has been that the police attitude, behaviour, susceptibility, values, etc., remained as they were in the remote past even when the police celebrated their 50 years of independence.

Susceptibility to British-Indian Police Values

The contemporary policeman faces many problems of living together harmoniously with the people in society. There exist adjustment problems and failures in adjustment in police-citizen interactions. Why? The social values and standards of life of the people are rapidly changing and still the police want the people to be afraid of the police. No, the people do not want it. I find that the difficulties for establishing a harmonious emotional adjustment between the police and the people become a problem even today. So long as the problem remains, policing the police remains and will remain as a problem. For example, when Isaac Alexander, the sub-inspector saw that the counter-petitioner did not come to him when he was called by his constable, he thought that he deserved muscle treatment. He took him into custody and manhandled him for disobeying the sub-inspector's order. The poor sub-inspector could not understand that he did a wrong thing, for, he enjoyed no statutory authority to inquire into petitions, to send for the counter petitioner, to take him into custody and to manhandle him. Time has changed and so have values, yet the sub-inspector adhered to the British-Indian police values. He was not prepared to make harmonious adjustment with the changes in society, people, values and outlooks. This is a problem - a problem that makes the police to behave in a non-policed way.

I met Isaac Alexander and asked him: "Why did you behave the way you did?" He told me: "Sir, I know that I did wrong - I did an illegal act. But, I just could not but do so. For, he did not respect the uniform I wore". See, how does he stick to the British Indian Police values? He thought that he could afford to behave the way he did. He thought that he was not accountable to anybody. 50 years are over since the British

Indian police left the country, but their behaviour, attitude, approaches and values have been in existence even afterwards.

The concepts of justice have undergone drastic changes during the last fifty years and the police are still kept in blissful ignorance of the same. Criminal justice was known to the British Indian police and the criminal suffered a lot as a consequence. Today, victim justice, human rights justice, gender justice, juvenile justice, social justice, equal justice, administrative justice, disciplinary justice, etc., have come into being and the police want to administer criminal justice under antiquated criminal laws, procedure code and Evidence Act. Under the existing laws, the police can never administer equal justice to the people and the police can never be policed.

The concepts of policing have undergone drastic changes. The same policeman - be he the officer of the Indian Police Service or the bottom level policeman - policing the juveniles, women, traffic offenders, politicians, criminals organized racketeers and so on may employ an unscientific approach. The British needed a paramilitary force or a militarized police force in India and they had enough of them. But, democratic India needs specialists in the police to serve the people. There is no meaning in having a "Jack of All Trades" policy adopted in policing the society. A policeman who undergoes a few months training and acquires some elementary information about law, police administration, parade or drill must not be entrusted with the task of policing the society. Likewise, an officer who is enlisted at the middle level and who undergoes a year's institutional training in law, police science, criminology, etc., should not be entrusted with policing juveniles to terrorists. What about the officers in the Indian Police Service? In a world of specialists and professionals, India needs police professionals and specialists to police the society. Investigation of crime is different from prevention of crime which is different from management of law and order or insurgency operations. Even in the area of investigation of crimes, the police need specialists to investigate murder cases- Mafia cases - *nexus* crimes - drug trafficking and crimes having interstate or international ramifications. As it is today, one and the same police officer assumes all the roles and acts as the "master of none". He is not a film actor who can act in any role. He is a policeman/officer and he faces real life situations. If professionalism does not come into the police, the police will not be able to police themselves and society. If the police do not specialise in specific areas of police work, then they will not be able to do specialized duties. Specialization in police work is offered in many foreign countries and the policemen/ officers must be sent to specialize in police work. If an aeroplane is hijacked, then the policeman trained in managing a law-and-order situation will not be able to do anything in the airport. A police officer trained in the investigation of anti-corruption cases will be nobody if he is asked to provide V.I.P. security to the Prime Minister of India. A police officer professionally trained to be a specialist interrogator will not be able to deal with juvenile delinquents. Detecting delinquents, investigating delinquency cases, planning preventive strategies and control mechanisms in a delinquency prone area is different from collecting intelligence for special branch work. When senior and very senior officers talk, they express their inability to do many specialist jobs in the police. A senior police officer who was a computer illiterate was once asked to give a lecture on cyber crimes. After some time, he was asked to investigate a cyber crime and certainly, it is nothing but a mockery of police work. The police administration and the Government ought to recognize the fact that policing is a professional work which any Dick, Tom and Harry cannot do. In an era of information technology and internet communications, bullock cart transports, museum piece laws, parade ground policemen and antiquated methods of policing will pay no dividends.

A Criminologist's Reflections on Indian Police

Everyday, one sees at least one criminal shown in the T.V. news. Sometimes, many criminals are shown. They are big persons in politics, business, share-markets, bureaucracy, underworld, cinema world, Mafia and the police do arrest them, produce them in courts, get them remanded, interrogate them and it takes a lot of time to know the result of the investigation. In the news papers, I notice 40-60% space spent on crime news, views and what not. A country where robbery, dacoity, riots, murders, etc., were seen during the British regime is now full of most modern crimes which are novel in many respects. How far are the police capable of investigating them? How much research is undertaken to investigate them? How competent are the police? Investment rackets, communal riots, political clashes, terrorism, insurgency, hijacking of aeroplanes, sabotage of trains, bombing, suicide squads, etc., are plenty and the police come to their wit's end as to what to do - how to go about. They have to investigate the crimes keeping in view the most modern views in human rights justice, gender justice, equal justice, fair and total justice in a people friendly way. Can they do so? Are the communication systems adequate enough to meet the challenges? Are the crime laboratories and forensic institutions sufficiently equipped to deal effectively with the emerging and emerged challenges in crime investigation? What about the professional expertise of police officers? Is the political climate favourable to conduct a fair and impartial investigation? How can the police susceptibility to temptations be put down? The questions are many and the answers are limited - are inadequate and far away from being satisfactory. Then how can we police the police?

References

1. Robert J Campbell, *Psychiatric Dictionary* (fifth edition), Oxford University Press, New York, 1981
2. *Ibid.*
3. See, R. Peele and I.S. Von Loetzen, American Journal of Psychiatry, 130; 1973) and Robert J Campbell, *ibid.*
4. Holy Bible, *Old Testament,* Genesis, Chapt. 27, 1-45
5. Holy Bible, *New Testament,* Mathew, 26, 15-16
6. Robert J Campbell, *op.cit.*.

5

Police Discipline and Policing

'Let major and minor penalties be regulated and proportioned to delinquencies and misconduct, let dismissal be passed only on those found guilty of having committed very serious delinquencies and let harassment, humiliation, mental torture, suspensions, victimization, vindictiveness, hostility, ego-clashes that revolt humanity be abolished for ever in disciplinary inquiries' - I said so in my lecture to a group of officers who attended a course on departmental inquiries organized by the State Vigilance and Anti-corruption Bureau at the Institute of Management in Government, Thiruvananthapuram. Why did I say so? I could understand that some higher authorities held the view that policing is possible only through punishments via disciplinary inquiries. In the police, for centuries, this belief ruled the thinking of the administrators. Police history might show any number of such instances. The cruel pleasure taken in punishing the Indian illiterate constables who received a salary of Rs. 5/- was a British way of disciplining the bottom level of the police pyramid. The whites by the colour of their skin did not see the despair in their victims even when they dismissed hundreds of policemen for minor misconduct or interpreted misconduct. The nineteenth century attitude continues to rule some higher authorities in the police even today and they misuse their power or abuse their authority on the glamour of stars, emblems, swords and batons on their shoulders - say some constables. Is it policing the police? I do not know how far the allegation is true today! Nevertheless, I know that some senior levels are excessively punishment-prone in disciplinary inquiries. They have an idea that they can maintain discipline only through punishment in departmental inquiries. The "Scratch him, if you can not kill him" attitude is proved to be harmful in disciplining subordinates. "Punishment" in any form - anywhere - in any area must have "humanity" as its measure and the principle is applicable to disciplinary inquiries as well. The classical criminologists advocated this principle during eighteenth century, but the British police authorities could not understand it. Some of the higher authorities in the white police administration in India were as ignorant, illiterate and uneducated as the Indian policemen. Many in the Indian police honestly felt that they were harassed men, ill-paid, neglected, not respected, ignored and still they served their English masters with fear and anxiety. Discipline on one side and despair on the other side! This British climate dominated the police even after India became independent. The policemen enimical to their white superiors came under the Indian masters and the enemity came out in many police strikes after the Independence of India. In 1979, the policemen shouted slogans and went on strikes in almost all States and the disciplinarians started to redefine the concept of discipline in the police service. Police Associations were formed and afterwards, the definition of discipline in the police underwent further revision. The authorities and subordinates could realize that new approaches, attitudes, management styles, leadership principles, definitions, etc., were essential to police the police in the changed socio-political milieu. But a realization alone could not do much. Instead of an aggressively militant disciplinary control, some resorted to mitigated disciplinary approaches. They felt with Beccaria: "Let the idea of torture and execution be ever present in the heart of the weak man and dominate the feeling that drives him to crime". Disciplinary rules and penalties like dismissals, discharge, compulsory retirement, etc., could affect only the weak in the police service. Those who had political connections, affiliations and linkages are found to be not affected much by disciplinary rules, penalties and hard masters of discipline in the police department. Policing the police by the threat of initiating disciplinary inquiries seems to have little or no deterrent impact upon a section of the police service. Policing the police has become more or less an art. The police administration so far did not define in clear terms the concept of misconduct and precisely therefore the policemen/officers raise a number of questions relating to misconduct. They take the issues to the press/media and before the courts of law and, more often than not, they want transparency in disciplinary proceedings. Penalties for misconduct must come from the nature of the delinquency and not from the attitude, personality, will and whim of the punishing authority. This idea dominates police functionaries now. Strangely enough, the misconducts are not defined -no punishment is prescribed. Hence everything is left to the sweet discretion of the punishing authorities. The nature of the misconduct and the nature of punishment are to be specified if one wants to police the police in the present socio-political environment wherein the opinion of the constables is counted like the opinion of the director general of police. In a democracy, it is the people who decide the nature of the misconduct and the nature of punishment. A drunken constable was once dismissed while a drunken director general of police was honoured with salutes and present-arms! The news appeared in the media and the people said: "shame, shame!" If this is what happens today, the transparency and accountability in disciplinary proceedings become essential not only in the case of senior levels, but also in the case of bottom level functionaries in the police. Once a deputy inspector general of police was issued with a memo to explain how the secrecy in his office leaked out to the press. The memo as well as his reply to the memo came in print in news papers. Some people asked: "what is the transparency the administration speaks of if the deputy inspector general of police is harassed to this extent?" The police today is not the police of the British past. Most of the policemen/officers working today were born after India became independent in 1947. Hence, to imagine that the police can be disciplined as they were disciplined by the British will be just "day dreaming".

Adverse Effect of Disciplinary Penalties on Lower Level Functionaries

How many policemen/officers have committed suicide after the initiation of disciplinary inquiries? I don't have any account of the same. How many have taken to drinks/drugs after the initiation of disciplinary inquiries? I have no statistical data on the same. But, I know that some have done so. If they are well policed, why do they do so? If they are well disciplined men, then why do they resort to this sort of undesirable options? I have seen many police officers punishing their subordinates. All of them claim that they do so to police the police. I observe that they do not punish the same crimes in the same way or the same type of delinquents in the same way. Why? They are to police the police, but are they policed well to award punishment in a rational and just way? Are they 'scandals' to disciplinary justice? In the police, punitive drill is given. The punished one is taken to the hot sun and is asked to do the drill under the close supervision of a higher official. The drill in the hot sun is a public spectacle. People ignore it. Originally, it was thought by the British that such a public drill in the hot sun on the parade ground would be a deterrent to the potential delinquents. But, history has proved that the punishment had no deterrent value. It was treated more as a process of "humiliation" than as a corrective measure. When it has been demonstrated everybody on the parade ground, the humiliation effect too has been lost. It had become a routine affair in the British past and even today, the same punitive parade in the hot sun has no meaning than a routine ritual in police camps. It has no correctional content and the policemen comment: "It is an ugly punishment of the illiterate white police regime in India. There is no glory in punishing the policemen under the hot sun if he is not convinced of the need for correction". Every punishment awarded in departmental inquirers must be activated by a desire to correct, reclaim and cure the erring or erred policemen/ officers. Nevertheless, it is not seen even today - even after 50 years of democratic rule in India. Benjamin Rush once said in his address to the society for Promoting Political Inquiries: "I can only hope that the time is not far away when gallows, pillory, scaffold, flogging and wheel will, in the history of punishment, be regarded as the marks of the barbarity of centuries and as proofs of the feeble influence of reason and religion over the human mind". His wish has been actualized long ago. Likewise, the punitive parade, drill, fatigue, fine, etc., now awarded to the lower level police functionaries - which are not awarded to the higher levels for reasons unknown to many - will have a natural death in the years to come. The discrimination in dealing with different categories of police personnel will or ought to have its adverse effect on disciplining the police. The National Police Commission: 1977-81, it seems, did not think in this line. Zeal in punishing a subordinate must not go to the extent of shaming the principles established till now. The double standard in punishing different categories of police personnel may have to be done away with. The 'physical penalties' - parade, drill, punitive fatigue, etc., directly affect the body of the policemen. Corporal punishments are discouraged everywhere and in Europe, at the beginning of the nineteenth century, corporal punishments disappeared. Even in prisons, no corporal punishment is given and, if that is the trend, punishing the policeman with corporal punishment on the parade ground can be a sort of horrible cruelty committed on the weaker segments in the police service. The ethics of disciplinary justice does not accept a sort of public demonstration of the corporal punishment on parade grounds. As a penal measure, confinement to barracks is awarded and it is a form of torture. The disciplinary punishment must not be centred on torture which violates human freedom and rights. Confinement to barracks is a form of imprisonment and certainly it will have its adverse effects on the punished. Imprisonment involves a certain degree of physical pain and loss of human freedom. The punished policeman feels as one condemned to suffer the pain associated with imprisonment which does not have a correctional content and therefore it will not and cannot police the police. Mably says: "Punishment, if I may so put it, should strike the soul rather than the body". If this is what is appreciated in the case of people who commit heinous offences, then cannot be otherwise in the case of policemen who exhibit misconduct or departmental delinquencies.

In certain States, there exist special Police Discipline Inquiries Punishment Appeal Rules for policemen/officers of the State service. No such rules exist for the officers of the Indian Police Service. Why? The National Police Commission: 1977-81 recommended the enactment of special rules for disciplinary inquiries for the police in all States, but did not feel so for the officers of the Indian Police Service. Why? The reasons for taking a double approach are known to the Commission and not for criminologists and penologists. Whatever that be, the British could afford double standards in disciplinary matters and it was certainly to favour the whites which belonged to their flock. The British concepts of a policeman's delinquency have considerably changed over the last 50-60 years as many delinquencies have ceased to be so now because, earlier, they were bound up with certain notions which the whites had about their skin superiority. Today, no such superiority exists, yet special favours are shown to the higher-ups. This upsets the policing principles in a democratic set-up. The people and the press look at the policeman not from the point of view of the rank he holds, but from the nature of the delinquency he commits. If a policeman tortures a suspect, the people look at him with contempt and the same people look at the director general of police with the same attitude when he tortures a suspect in police custody. People want the same disciplinary rules to apply to both of them, but they do not see it. Why? Policing the police then becomes an unachievable task. When a director general of police orders for conducting an inquiry on a policeman, the whole lot of policemen look at the decision of the director general and pass judgements on whether or not he is morally competent to order such an inquiry. If they do not feel favourable to the director general, all of them look at him with contempt and say vociferously that he cannot police the police, whatever may be his legal competency.

Total Person and Policing the Police

'Total Person' is more important than a "part person" in policing the society. A corrupt police superior cannot initiate a disciplinary inquiry against a corrupt subordinate. He also cannot initiate disciplinary inquiry against a police subordinate who shows insubordination. Why? He has no moral justification to do so, for, his total personality is defective. A person's past and present are counted and the subordinates ask: "what can be expected from him?" A perverted or maladjusted superior can offer only a perverted and maladjusted leadership. Such a person can not punish a delinquent, supervise a subordinate, neutralize the delinquent tendencies, alter the delinquent mind and continue in his office with dignity and decorum. He is a misfit and is not a 'total person'. Knowledge of one's position, one's authority, one's character and one's moral sense - all these contribute much to the making of a total personality - a total person who has a soul - an upright conscience to police the police. Could the police administrators claim this in the past? Can they claim this at present? Disciplinary penalties are not simply negative mechanisms which help to eliminate delinquencies, but are positive and useful mechanisms to serve the people better. The departmental punishments brand the victim with infamy and precisely therefore it must be awarded with honesty and justness. Otherwise, it will be counter-productive for maintaining discipline within the department. Allegations are often heard that hostility, vengeance, ego-clashes, vindictiveness, etc., work as the motivating forces for initiating departmental inquiries. I do not think that the allegation is always true; yet, behind the untruth there is a lot of truth. The victims of disciplinary inquiries complain often that the punishment is arbitrarily awarded. There is some truth in such allegations. The penalty must be sensible and must not show the vindictive or retributive mind of the punishing authorities. To quote Rush: "...so, in order to decide on punishments, one will require some knowledge of the principles of sensation, and of the sympathies which occur in the nervous system". During the British rule, the white police officer was concerned only with the English rule in India. He was not at all interested in making a policeman a human person to serve the people of India. The repressive and oppressive policeman could be treated retributively by him and he was not accountable to anybody in India. But now? The police officer who suffers the punishment and who inflicts the penalty have the same colour of skin and are a part of the society where people having the same colour of the skin live and survive. Hence, the police officer of democratic India cannot become harsh to his subordinates. Preventive, corrective, utilitarian conceptions must rule his thinking. He punishes his subordinates not to repress and oppress the Indians, but to help him serve the people better. During the English regime, the penalty was to make the policeman more oppressive and repressive. The British wanted to terrorize and rule and they wanted cruel and animal-like policemen. In a democratic set-up, a policeman is departmentally punished to make him more human and to help him serve the people better.

Discipline and Policing

A muscle-man is not always a policed policeman. But, in the police it was thought that a muscle man could become a better policeman. Montgommery speaks about the ideal figure of an early seventeenth century soldier. He writes: "The signs for recognizing those most suited to this profession are a lovely, alert manner, an erect head, a taut stomach, broad shoulders, long arms, strong fingers, a small belly, thick thighs, slender legs and dry feet, because a man of such a figure could not fail to be agile and strong". According to F. de la Noue, a soldier must learn "how to handle horses, to practise with the dagger, with and without shield, to fence, to perform on horseback, to jump; if swimming and wrestling were added, it would be to the good, for all this makes the person robust and more subtle". This seventeeth century European notion about a soldier dominated the English rulers when they created the Indian police force to fight against the Indians. The policemen for the British were soldiers and they policed the police as they disciplined the soldiers. They found in India human clay at a cheap price and they moulded the clay as they wanted. Thus, the police recruits became accustomed to holding their heads high and erect. They became animal-like and anyone who could not stand against a wall in such a way that his heels, the thighs, the waist and shoulders touch it was punished mercilessly by the British. The training was not intended for human formation and even when India became independent, the same training continued to be the best training for the policemen. Any recruit who did not remain motionless until the order is given could undergo a punishment. Even today the police instructors insist that the members of the civil police must hold their head high and erect on the parade ground - must stand upright - must not bend the back - must not throw out the chest - must not throw back the shoulders - must not fix their eyes on the ground - must look always straight at those when they pass - must march with a bold step and what not? Do they impart training to soldiers to fight against the enemies? Do they require all these to investigate crimes, detect criminals, interrogate suspects, interview witnesses, interact with people, behave in a human rights friendly way? Do the police perform army or paramilitary functions? If they fail to do things as the soldiers do, then disciplinary inquiries may be initiated and they are punished. For what? Do they police the police by such punitive methods and tactics? I do not think they do, but I think that they are still ignorant about the concept of police discipline in a democracy. Do we still need to manipulate, shape and train human bodies just for obeying, responding and blindly executing orders like a soldier does in a war field? Do we need such a soldier's discipline for the democracy's policeman? Do the higher-ups need it? Do the higher-ups require a robust physique which a colonel may desire to have? I notice a lot of difference between the bodies of senior police officers and military officers. Do we require a Police Discipline Inquiries, Punishment and Appeal Rules for punishing the lower level functionaries in the police? If Civil Service Rules can be effectively used in the case of senior level police functionaries, the same can be used with effectiveness in the case of middle and lower level police personnel. If the body and mind of the senior officers are docile to civil service rules in disciplinary matters, the same will be applicable to the body and mind of the middle and lower level functionaries in the police.

Misconceived Ideas of Civil Police Discipline

A soldier for the Englishman was a policeman for Indian democracy. This created misconceived ideas of civil police discipline among the police authorities of Indian democracy. The body of the Indian policeman for the British was only an object through which they wanted to express their power and retain their rule. They shaped, manipulated, managed and trained the Indian Policeman's body just to obey their commands and accordingly the illiterate and robust Indian policeman shaped his body. The British called it discipline and the Indian democracy accepted the concept without questioning it for several decades until at last the constabulary in many States declared police strikes. Ultimately, a National Police Commission was appointed to make recommendations to convert the colonial police to a democracy's police. Somehow or other, the democratic Governments that came into power from time to time did not accept the recommendations of the

Commission and most of the recommendations were not implemented. However, the police could establish their right to form Associations and thus the concept of discipline in the police got changed, and today the British concept of police discipline is found to be not useful and effective to police the police. A monastery-like discipline, an army - like discipline, a trade union-like discipline, a political party - like discipline is not what the police want. The police in a democracy ought to have a police discipline - a civil police discipline and I think that the Indian police could not bring out such a discipline. The police in India developed a soldier - like police discipline and such a soldier-police mixture could not successfully police the police. It was not at all necessary for a soldier to come and discipline the civil police who were to police the society. If the director general of police took the attitude of the Chief of the Army to discipline his men in a democracy, the political leaders will come forward to discipline the director general of police. In a system of democratic rule where the director general of police and all officers down can be posted, transferred, harassed, victimized by political ill-will, a soldier-like disciplining is unimaginable, a soldier-police mixture of discipline is undesirable. Hence, what is required is a police discipline which will police the civil police in a democracy. However, such a system could not come into force even after 50 years of freedom in India. Even today, the soldier-police mixture of discipline works with unenviable success.

Soldier Discipline and Civil Police Discipline

Military discipline could bring the entire force under a word of command - could be used to fire at an angry mob - could repress an aggressive crowd - could increase the muscle power - could accelerate movements - could increase the capacity for resistance. Nevertheless, was it necessary to have such a military discipline to serve the people in a democracy? The discipline of a policeman during a V.I.P.'s visit, during crime-investigation, during the collection of intelligence, during patrolling, during police-human relations was unknown to the British soldier who wanted to repress and suppress the Indian people. The moral influence of the policeman had a better impact on the people in a democracy than his military or muscle influence.

Discipline was found necessary not only at the bottom of the police pyramid, but also to all from the bottom to the top. But one doubted whether or not such a discipline could be seen among the higher-ups. The nexus involvement of the police hierarchy, the transactions with underworld criminals and Mafia operators, the foul play with politicians, etc., strengthened the people's suspicion on the integrity and discipline of the hierarchy. The people and the press could notice the policemen/officers of all ranks in many places, but most unfortunately they observed them not eradicating the vices, rather tolerating, encouraging, conniving, promoting tobacco shops, hock sale, prostitution, gaming houses, public scandals, flesh-trade, and other disorders that disturb human conscience and spread criminality in society.

Hierarchy Control of Police Discipline

In India, after independence, the hierarchy's control over police discipline gradually came down. Of course, a part remained with them and by 2000 AD, a good part was taken over by the police associations and politicians who sponsored the activities of police associations/unions or individual policemen. The absolutism of the British police hierarchy lost all its grip and today the policing of the police becomes a matter of concern for the people, press, government, policemen and the politicians of the ruling front and opposition. The policemen have now to play a more positive role than merely repressive and oppressive roles. When the British established police training centres at Saugor, Phillaur or Vellore, they had mainly negative aims, but today the police training has a positive objective and function. In-service courses are organized to reorient the attitude of police personnel from the constables to the director general of police. All need to acquire information first to police themselves before they police the society. But one finds it extremely difficult to convince the higher-ups about the necessity of gathering information on policing the police. Most of them think that they are well policed. They have a wrong impression or opinion about disciplining and policing the police. The timetable is an old inheritance and perhaps the strict model was suggested by the monastic communities of the west. The English people wanted to police the police by making use of a time table. They had to rise up at a fixed time, had to report for parade at a fixed time, had to do the drill for a fixed time, etc. Any violation of a second in the time table was considered as a serious violation of the rules and punishments followed. Did the British police - soldiers (policemen) accept the strict adherence to the time table as a means of disciplining them? Did they follow the time table out of a genuine desire to become a disciplined police-soldier (constable)? Did the superior ranks in the police follow such a strict (monastic) time table? Did the top level in the police respect the time table? When India became independent, how did the superiors, supervisors and top level administration in the police follow the time table introduced and meticulously followed by the British policemen? The constables expected their higher ranks to come and inspect their inspection parades organized on certain days in a week, but they could not see them inspecting the parade at times. The "time-table" discipline was followed more in the armed battalions/armed reserve camps. Some policemen/officers of the general executive branch did not just think anything about a time table discipline and the superior ranks in general executive often forgot about a time table discipline in the police. Some policemen/officers from the General executive Branch were found to drink liquor, to dine in hotels, to enjoy films in theatres and to do many things which disciplined men were not supposed to do/could not do. The time table discipline in the police was limited only during the induction training period and afterwards the policemen/officers of the general executive were not concerned with any type of time table discipline. The rhythms of life during the period of police training could not be seen afterwards and it was more so in the case of members in the general executive branch of the police. Certainly, it affected and still affects the policing of the police in democratic India.

Discipline, Police Discipline, People's Discipline and Politicians' Discipline

Everyone wants the police to be disciplined. Even the worst (indisciplined) politician wants the policemen to be disciplined. The police hierarchy wants the policeman to be disciplined and the constables want the director general of police to be disciplined. All said and done, the media publishes news relating to indiscipline in the police from constables upwards.

Parade-ground discipline is what some policemen/ officers mean when they say discipline in the police. A collective response without questioning the word of command is what is meant by a parade ground discipline. "First obey" and then do what is told on the parade ground - "No questions back". Is this discipline? How do they obey the words of command? What is their attitude to the words of command? - all these are matters of serious concern when discipline is discussed. But, on the parade ground, the instructor is concerned only with the correlationship between body and gestures - the synchronizing of the word of command to the body action - a total submission and surrender to the words of command. Disciplinary controls do not consist simply in doing what is being commanded by the instructor. The best cadet who was awarded the first prize for the *paradeground training* was later caught for accepting corruption money. He was not a disciplined officer although he was very good on the parade ground when he underwent training. Hence discipline means many more things than becoming *docile bodies* to the superior's words of command. A person could become a well trained (skilled man) policeman on the parade ground, but could as well become the most hopelessly indisciplined person in police service. A good shooter is not necessarily a well disciplined man and so is a *well disciplined* man on the parade ground. A person who faithfully and smartly responds to the words of command - "attention, stand-at-case, double mark time" - is not always necessarily a well disciplined person. He may concoct evidence, manipulate records, produce touts and tutored witnesses, torture people and may commit atrocities on the people. The parade ground does not always and necessarily police a policeman - rather, the values and inner qualities do police the policeman. I have seen the policemen on guard duty offering smart salutes to officers - loose salutes to officers - indifferent salutes to officers and I used to think: "what type of discipline do they have?" Some officers/policemen who feel that they are born of a high caste background murmur when they have to salute officers who, they think, are born of a low caste background. The police are to protect human rights and all are equal before the law. Yet, a policeman feels mental objection to respect others and it shows his lack of proper refinement and self-policing. The eighteenth century English military theoreticians had a lot of obligatory syntax and *manoeuvres* and they developed them for their imperialistic achievements. They transplanted them to the Indian policc-soldiers and called them "police troops". The imperialistic definition of police discipline is not the definition of police discipline in a democracy. Indians could not/did not understand it when India got independence. Hence, the police applied a troop-like discipline to police the people and the police. The result has been that the police could not establish people friendly contacts. The police carved a bad image among the people. The police became more and more indisciplined and caught for a variety of nefarious activities. The entire hierarchy has been blamed for their people unfriendly approaches, indisciplined behaviour, corrupt dealings, and *nexus* transactions. The principles that underlaid the time table during the training period did not come for help to make a people friendly police service. A disciplined police could become friendly only if the police is inculcated with values in life.

To quote Michael Foucault in this context: "On entering most of our training schools, one sees all those unfortunate soldiers in constricting and forced attitudes, one sees all their muscles contracted, the circulation of their blood interrupted... If we studied the intention of nature and the construction of the human body, we would find the position and the bearing that nature clearly prescribes for the soldier. The head must be erect, standing out from the shoulders, sitting perpendicularly between them. It must be turned neither to left nor to right, because, in view of the correspondence between the vertebrae of the neck and the shoulder-blade to which they are attached, none of them may move in a circular manner without slightly bringing with it from the same side that it moves one of the shoulders and because, the body no longer being placed squarely, the soldier can no longer walk straight in front of him or serve as a point of alignment.... Since the hip-bone, which the ordinance indicates as the point against which the butt end should rest, is not situated the same in all men, the rifle must be placed more to the right for some, and more to the left for others. For the same reason of inequality of structure, the trigger-guard is more or less pressed against the body, depending on whether the outer parts of a man's shoulder is more or less fleshy".[1] No doubt it is a lengthy extract from Michel Foucault, nevertheless I find a lot of relevance in it. I study his observations with what I notice in police parade grounds, The policemen/officers are trained to serve the people in a democracy. Do the policemen require such stretching of their muscles to serve the people? If someone speaks about the needlessness of too many contractions of muscles, toughening of body, bayonet training, route-marches, etc., for civil police, the higher ups frown at him and make comments: "stupid", "non-sense". They think that discipline is closely linked with the parade ground. Why do the civil police require rifles? Will not a pistol serve the purpose? On how many occasions does a civil policeman/officers in his life make use of his rifle? Can they fire at the people as they want? Recently, a policeman made use of his rifle butt to beat at a man who later died. The policeman was convicted of murder and sentenced to life imprisonment. A civil policeman cannot do the things which a soldier in a battle field may do against his enemy. Every man in a democracy is a friend of the policeman and he does not require so much toughening and strengthening of his body to interact with people. A policeman's body today is trained to be docile to do many things which the soldiers in battle fields are supposed to do. This makes the policeman indisciplined in his job. He lacks self-policing.

In some police training schools, the constables have no bench to sit, no water to bath, no good toilet facilities, no good barracks to sleep, no play grounds, no good recreation rooms, no leisure-time activities, no canteens and certainly, they have too much of parade, drill, toughening, strengthening, stretching, etc. How can they become people friendly if at all they want to be so? Psychologically, they become anti-police and anti-people. They become anti-police because they see their superiors enjoying their lives with many human comforts which are denied to them. People find it extremely difficult to adjust and accommodate with such disparities and psychologists think that the disparities in different ranks in the police make some to become anti-police, anti-people and indisciplined.

It seems to me that both the administration and authorities in the police had wrong notions about policing the police. When Prof. M. S. Gore, as the Chairman of the Central Committee on Police Training, brought out the report in 1975 for updating the training of the police personnel of all ranks, a director general of police seriously made a comment: "It is like a person who has never been in the war field speaking about the battle that Prof. Gore writes about police training". I looked at his face and showed my disapproval of his comments, pitied his ignorance about imparting training to the police personnel in a democracy, disliked the way he made the comments. Prof. M.S. Gore had very brilliant ideas on police training and at that time the report was considered as a BIBLE for the police personnel. The evil effect of police ignorance on the excellent ideas on police training was that the implementation of the Central Committee's recommendation has been frustratingly slow. The police muscles and the hierarchy's antique concepts on police role could not but reject the modern views on police training. I used to say: "Let us destroy our old concepts and prejudices on police training" - the police in a democracy is not an army, but a public facility. But those who believe that it is an army want the policemen to have always with them lathies, pistols, rifles and muskets. The terms like *'section, platoon, regiment, unit, battalion'*, etc., are not applicable to the policemen in the general executive branch of the police. The people friendly policemen do not want fire power. Every citizen in a democracy is not a target for a policeman to fire at. A policeman among the people is not a soldier with a rifle. The patrolman is the uncle for all children in the locality and a son to every mother there and a brother for every girl in his jurisdiction. To establish a filial, a brotherly, a parental relationship with the people, the policeman does not require rifles and muskets. A policed policeman only can become people friendly and policing the police means people friendly policing in a democracy.

Correct Policing the Police

At the beginning of the last century, the Indian Police Commission: 1902-03 spoke of policing the police in India. For them, policing the police was an expensive affair, but they wanted the British Government to enforce and implement their recommendations. The British wanted strict discipline in the police and the police hierarchy wanted the same strict discipline in the police even when India became independent. Both the British and Indian administration believed that strict discipline could be infused into the policemen only through hard parade and drill, toughening and musketry. They did not think much about intellectual training and inculcation of human values in policemen/officers. The adverse impact was that the policemen who were very skilled in parade, drill, musketry, etc., came out in large numbers and they claimed themselves to be highly disciplined men. No one thought seriously about their moral upbringing, and in 1961 the inspectors general of police in their conference held in Delhi drafted a Code of Conduct to police the police. Nevertheless, the Code remained more as a Code on paper than in practice. It took nearly three decades for the Government to accept the Code. How could the police police the police without a proper Code of Conduct for them? Just recently, in a conference, a discussion on the Code of Conduct for the police came up and most unfortunately many senior level police functionaries were just ignorant of the very existence of a Code of Conduct for the Indian police. Certainly they have been policing the police and have been conducting investigations of simple hurt to Mafia operations, preventing, crimes from wayside gaming to large-scale drug trafficking, controlling criminal activities from smoking in cinema theatres to bootlegging syndicates, escorting pickpockets, discouraging flesh trade and detecting corruption and what not? They have been doing them without a Code of Conduct or without having an awareness about a Code of Conduct ! Though the police in India have travelled a long way after independence and have acquired a lot of modern gadgets from the simple magnifying glass to the latest computers and computer-based interrogation aids, the morality and moral principles of policing remain to be the same as they existed from the inception of the police in the world. The magnifying glass and atomizers which were an integral part of inspecting a scene of crime could not open the inner eyes of the police to see their moral conscience when they investigated crimes. The polygraph and luria techniques were good aids to the police interrogation, but were not of any use for a muscleman if he did not possess an upright conscience. Torture which started before 1855 Torture Commission Report has been continuing even when computer based Brain Finger Printing has come to aid the police. The "repression of the suspect, the rationalization of the interrogated, the regression of the detinue" are yet unknown areas of psychological interrogation not only to the lay - policeman in the police stations but also to the "veteran crime interrogator" in the crime investigation branch/bureau. The parade ground training, stand-at-ease position, double mark time, route-marches, mob-operation techniques, etc., were of little or no practical utility in the interrogation rooms or in the conduct of surveillance by the police in a democratic set-up. The activities of the policemen during their drill, unarmed combat, musketry, their skill, the way they set about their tasks during a jungle training, their promptness, their zeal, their behaviour, etc., are good, but not so good during the raid in a house, during the patrol, during the beat, during the surveillance, during the visit of a V.V.I.P. etc. In a democracy, people who are not policemen do them sometimes better than the trained policemen in musketry and unarmed combat. The British said in London that the people were the police and the police were the people even when they shaped police-troops in India. For them, the police in India were soldiers - illiterate and underpaid animal men to repress and oppress the Indian masses. They wanted "punitive police" and not "policed police". The moral qualities of the policemen/officers were not of any importance to the British. The examination conducted in police training schools/colleges/academies do not care for examining the moral conscience and moral sense of the police trainees. Their knowledge in every aspect of lathy drill to each word of command is examined and is allotted marks. Traditionally, the skills in parade ground were what were tested and the same tradition is followed even today. Examinations in indoor subjects are conducted by police officers themselves and the worth/value of the examination thus conducted is at best suspicious. The police enjoy a lot of power and authority. Precisely therefore, they require a lot of knowledge and values to function as honest police functionaries. When dead bodies are taken to the church, burial ground or crematorium, the members of the family, especially the womenfolk cry loudly. Likewise, when a person is taken into custody by the police from a house, the people in the family, particularly the women make loud cries and pray for help. Why? They think that the policemen may torture them in the name of policing the people/society. A raid in a house or an arrest from a family becomes a public spectacle and people talk more about non-policing than about policing a society. One can see signs of happiness, hatred, insults, satisfaction, threats, etc., on the face of the spectators. Why? People know that the policeman is executing the law when he does all these things nevertheless the people are not prepared to accept the ways the laws are executed. They find non-policed policing in police action. They notice an element of indiscipline in their so-called *disciplined acts*. Why should the members of the family make a loud cry if they know that the arrestee is in the safe hands of law-enforcement? This is seen not only in the houses of the petty thieves and pickpockets, but also in the houses of Mafia thieves and planned murderers. Humiliating the kith and kin of the arrested forms a part of the law enforcement exercises. Sometimes, the arrestees are beaten in front of their family members, kith and kin and afterwards are handcuffed just for humiliating them and others. Naturally, these cruel acts cause moral anger on the spectators and the people expose the non-policing of the police functionaries. The questions people ask are: "What is policing?; What exactly is correct policing?; What is policing the police?".

Policing and Deterrent Approaches

About 45 years ago, a police van was seen in my village. It was at 11 O'clock and all of us including my father did not go out of my house till we got the information that the police and their van left the village. We were literally afraid of the police. One of the cousins of my father was a sub-inspector when I was four or five years old. Once a year, he used to come to my house to see his old and infirm aunt. Whenever he visited my house, we never went out. He was deterrent not only to us but also to our neighbours. He had a deterrent appearance and he deterred many. He deterred many by his cruel approaches and all called him a police officer, but no one respected him as a policed police officer. I do not think even today that he was a disciplined man. His eyes were red coloured and he loved liquor very much. My father told me many things about him and I do not like to recollect them once again. For, they were symptoms of mental disorders, and not of policing the society. About 20-30 years ago, I have seen policemen/officers torturing people in public and even today we hear of such news and read about such torturing episodes. Today, people and policemen talk a lot - inflated rhetoric - about the "humanization" of the police. Now, the torture by the police is dying out and the people torture the police if they can. In today's newspaper, I read that eleven policemen were attacked by an unruly mob and the policemen fired in the air with rubber bullets. The police torturing individuals in public (as a spectacle) is disappearing. If the police cannot police the police, the people will start policing the police. The people can discipline the police if the police are not disciplined well. The people in a democracy think that policing is not to be centred on deterrent approaches, rather it must be based on people friendly attitudes and strategies. But, how many police officers will understand and can appreciate it ? The penal history gives enough proof that deterrent approaches could not succeed in policing any society; on the contrary, the people friendly approaches could always police the society. Today, policing with people's participation and community policing, etc., are highly appreciated ideas throughout the world. Death penalty could not and did not eradicate murders in any society. "Some prisoners may be condemned to be hanged, others to having their hands cut off or their tongues cut out or pierced and then to be hanged; others for more serious crimes, to be broken alive and to die on the wheel, after having their limbs broken; others to be broken until they die a natural death, others to be strangled and then broken, others to be burnt alive, others to be burnt after first being strangled; others to be drawn by four horses, others to have their heads cut off, and others to have their heads broken".[2] Michel Foucault writes so about death penalty and other writers elaborate the cruelties connected with capital punishment. Finally all of them ask the question: "Do the cruelties eradicate murders or curtail their extent?" Likewise, the authors on policing bring out many cruel strategies which the police adopt to police the society. They ask then another question: "Can the non-police strategies police the society?" Hence the fundamental question is: "How to police the police?".

References

1. Michel Foucault, *Discipline and Punish: The Birth of the Prison*, Penguin Books, 1977 (Translation by Alan Sheridan)
2. *Ibid.*

6

Police Functions and Policing the Police

"The functions of a police are either protective and repressive or detective" - This was told by the Police Commission appointed in August 1860. Protective, repressive, detective functions and what did they mean? Certainly it meant many things except a policed police service. How could a repressive police be a protective police? How could the police serve the people by repressing them? How could the police perform their detective functions by repressive tactics? Repressive functions might be military functions and certainly the police functions ought not to be military (repressive) in nature. In a democracy, the police is a public facility and precisely therefore it cannot become repressive. Nevertheless, the police force (2000 A.D.) in India works under a Police Act enacted in 1861 and therefore it works as protective, repressive or detective. The questions are three and they are :

(1) How do the police protect the people? Certainly, the police have devised some methods to protect the people and they range from simple patrolling to highly complex systems of surveillance. How do the police protect the people? In order to protect the road users, the traffic policeman is seen on the road. People feel happy at the sight of a traffic constable doing

his job, but frown at him when he accepts corruption money from drivers or shouts at people in filthy language. When they see a policeman misbehaving with a fellow passenger, they ask: "Is this a policeman? - a policed policeman?" Once an inspector general of police was found in the company of a notorious bootlegger; then the people asked: "How can he protect the people from the bootleggers?".

In the history of the development of penological thoughts, criminologists argued that deterrent punishments protected the people and society. "The sulphur was lit, but the flame was so poor that only the top skin of the hand was burnt, and that only slightly. Then the executioner, his sleeves rolled up, took the steel pincers, which had been especially made for the occasion, and which were about a foot and a half long, and pulled first at the calf of the right leg, then at the thing, and from there at the two fleshy parts of the right arm; then at the breasts. Though a strong, sturdy fellow, this executioner found it so difficult to tear away the pieces of flesh that he set about the same spot two or three times, twisting the pincers as he did so, and what he took away formed at each part a wound about the size of a six-pound crown piece".[1] This sort of narrations can be seen in any number of penological books. They did all these atrocities in the name of administering justice and for the protection of the people and society. Did they or could they protect the people and society by such inhuman and atrociously animal - like behaviour? They could not and precisely therefore the penologists today advocate the correction and reformation/ rehabilitation of the criminal as the objective of punishment.

Though the British loudly spoke about the protective functions of the police, they never meant anything by saying so. The narrations of torture employed by the police during the British raj could shame them and the report of the Police Commission: 1902-03 contained a lot about the police torture and atrocities. How could the policeman who exhibited animality and wild-animal instinct police the people? The British did not ask such a question to themselves, but rather allowed the brutal police to police and protect the people with their brutality and bayonets. The hunter-dogs protect the mild animals for the hunters to eat and enjoy. The British Indian police *'protected'* the people for the British to loot the country "with minimum expense", They wanted to ensure the effective administration of the country, with a repressive and oppressive police force, "with prompt suppression of all challenges to the British power and authority and the realization of the maximum revenues from all conceivable sources". When the British left India in 1947, the political parties which came into power from time to time in various States made use of and misused the police for their political advantages. Policing the police was not an item of priority for any political party, rather politicizing the police for their political advantage was an item of top priority for any political party which came into power for the last 50 years.

I quote Michel Foucault once again: "When the four limbs had been pulled away, the confessors came to speak to him; but his executioner told them that he was dead, though the truth was that I saw the man move, his lower jaw moving from side to side as if he were talking. One of the executioners even said shortly afterwards that when they had lifted the trunk to throw it on the stake, he was still alive. The four limbs were united from the ropes and thrown on the stake set up in the enclosure in line with the scaffold, then the trunk and the rest were covered with logs and faggots and the fire was put to the straw mixed with this wood". The narration was an oft-seen example of how criminal justice was administered during the eighteenth century in the west. Of course, it was done when the punishment was executed after a judicial pronouncement of the guilt of the accused. They did it for protecting the people and society from potential criminals!

The history of the police during the British raj - from Torture Commission: 1855, before and after - is a history of torture. I had some discussions with some freedom fighters and if their narrations of police torture are written here, they will be worse than what Michel Foucault exposed above. Why say so? My father who died at the age of 76 in 1988 told me about the torture stories of people during the British rule in India. My father was not a freedom fighter in the strict sense, but he had a lot of information about human suffering at police hands during the British regime in India. The protective functions of the British - Indian police were thus repressive in nature and that was what the Police Commission: 1860 was asked to keep in mind when they prepared the report - "...line which separates the protective and repressive functions of a civil police from functions purely military, may not always, in India be very clear". The Police Commission - 1860 prepared a Bill keeping those instructions in mind and the Police Act (V of 1861) was thus passed on 16th March, 1861 and came into force from 22 March, 1861. The same Act is in force on 31 July, 2002. The impact is that the line which separates the protective and repressive functions of the police are still not clear. The death in police custody, torture in police lock-ups, human rights violations, humiliating and degrading treatment, etc., reported in the media and inquired into by various commissions are examples of police atrocities and repressive tactics.

(2) How do the police repress the people? In democratic India, the repressive techniques/strategies are not as severe as they were during the British rule. For, the political parties in the opposition object to the repressive tactics/strategies. Today's political party in the opposition may/can be tomorrow's ruling political party and therefore the police are handicapped and handcuffed. For example, during the internal emergency period (1976), a number of stories of police excesses were reported in the media. The Shah Commission of Inquiry has brought out a number of police atrocities in the report and they showed to what extent the police could go to repress the people in free India. Now 25 years are over since the Shah Commission of Inquiry brought out the report. Has the situation improved for the better? Some studies reveal that the police cannot exhibit a policed behaviour if at all they want to be people friendly. Studies show that many police lock-ups are antiquated buildings unfit for human dwelling. They are insanitary and are without adequate lighting, ventilation or plumbing. The police lock-ups are used for keeping

all kinds of people taken into custody by the police and some of them are dirty and verminous. The detained sleep on the floor, sometimes without any mattresses, and at other times, they don't sleep at all. No blankets are provided and often mosquitoes feed on them. The bunks in some lock-ups are often verminous. Third degree may be practised and one sees no proper supervision of lock-ups by senior officers. The accusation is that many police lock-ups are left to the caprice and indifference of the police station staff. Even human rights activists pay little or no attention to police lock-ups. Police officers and policemen say vociferously that they can show a policed behaviour only if they are provided with adequate facilities to do so. I wanted to know the facilities which the policemen/officers want to police their behaviour during the detention of arrestees in police custody. Some of the suggestions they have made are :

(1) Proper sanitary and health control facilities in police lock-ups.

(2) Facilities to provide food and other human necessities.

(3) Provision to consult their lawyers, medical officers, etc.

(4) Professionally qualified police interrogators and personnel qualified in criminology, juvenile delinquency, gender justice, etc., to work in police stations. There must be trained professionals to deal with crime-doers, etc.

Policing the people is a State's affair. Likewise, policing the police is partly a State's affair. If the State is not keen to police the police, to police the police in a people friendly way, to police the police with human rights principles, then it is not easy to police the police in the proper way. Attempts were not made honestly to reduce police atrocities for the last one and half century in India - from the passing of the Police Act - 1861 and therefore the police historians do not talk much or anything about policing the police. People wanted less cruelty, less pain, more consideration, more kindness, more sympathy, more care, more respect, less degrading treatment, less humiliation, more humanity, more humanness from the police. Did they get them? No. They did not. Instead, they had a repressive and oppressive police force. Even today, *torture* is associated with the word *police* and I do not think that the police will be free from its association with 'torture' if it is to work under a Police Act which was enacted with the objective to oppress and repress the Indian masses. Hence, policing the police becomes a remote possibility in the existing socio-political scenario. What the British did with the police before India's independence, the political parties which come in power today do with the police or attempt to do with the police. Politicians, rightly or wrongly, think that police power, police muscle, police threats, police politician *nexus* can or do solve many of their problems. So long as they have such an impression about the police use/abuse of power, policing the police is a difficult or unattainable task. They want the repressive police force to oppress their political rivals and thereby they want to make political advantages for the party they represent. The *Fiat* policemen are prepared to do anything for the politicians if they get some advantages - career-wise, posting-wise or transfer-wise. What to do and how to police the police then?

(3) How do the police perform their detective functions? When the British spoke about the detective functions of the police, they were more concerned with the detection of the criminals who worked against their rule in India. The British had no moral right to speak against theft, for they themselves were thieving India. They were robbing India - were murdering Indians - were misappropriating property. Of course, the Indian Penal Code - 1860 had sections to deal with robbery, dacoity, criminal misappropriation of property, theft, extortion, murder, etc. Who were to detect them? The crimes and criminals were to be detected by the police functionaries who had little or no education and training in detective work. The policemen were illiterate and ignorant of the laws. The chapters included offences against the State, offences relating to the Army, Navy, offences against Public Tranquillity, relating to Public Servants, contempt of Lawful Authority of Public Servants, False Evidence and Offences against Public Justice, Relating to Coin, Government Stamps, Weights and Measures, Affecting the

Public Health, Safety, Conveniences, Decency and Morals and Relating to Religion, etc. A casual look at the arrangement of chapters in the Indian Penal Code-1860 might reveal the political context under which the Code was drafted and the special interest which the British had to protect their reign in India. When I was doing my LL.B. course, my Professor in Indian Penal Code, I think, did not devote much attention to many of the chapters given in the Penal Code. They are of no importance now. The question papers on crime for the LL.B. and LL.M. examinations down the decades in various universities would reveal that many sections in the Indian Penal Code-1860 were never asked at all. The British included a large number of illustrations under each section in the Indian Penal Code-1860 and that was intended to facilitate the magistrates, judges and leaders to understand the laws. They knew well that many judges, leaders and magistrates in India did not have any legal training and certainly the police were an ignorant lot. How could they detect crimes and criminals? They could detect through tortures and by the use of third degree methods. They did it lavishly and the British enjoyed it. They did not want to police the police and they successfully managed not to police the police. Some of the higher level officers were as ignorant as the illiterate constables and they were appointed to the superior cadres just because they had the white skin. Criminal cases were acquitted from courts in large numbers and one of the main reasons for the large scale acquittals of criminal cases was due to the ignorance of the police functionaries. Well policed functionaries were not policing the police so much so that one could never see proper policing in the police. Even today, criminal cases are acquitted in large numbers and police functionaries who know the causes of acquittals play a "deaf and dumb" game when they are asked to speak about the causes of the acquittals. The police is not properly policed and there exists no professionalism in the police. So long as there exists lack of professionalism in police, the detective ability of the police will be weakened and the politicization of the police will be strengthened. Just go through the syllabi or course contents of the induction training courses for policemen and officers of various ranks during the British raj. One might laugh at the contents as the contents contained nothing for intellectual improvement and the development of detective efficiency. What about the syllabi of police training after the independence and up to the recommendations by the Central Committee on Police Training appointed by Government of India in 1971? Professionalizing the police, policing the police service, converting a repressive police force to a people-friendly police service - all these were not the objectives of police training. Just study the qualifications of the members of the faculty in police training institutions and look at the credentials of the teaching faculty. Enough to say that the observations made by Prof. M.S. Gore in his report on the police training (Report of the Central Committee on Police Training) are a living testimony to prove how poor and deplorable was the state of the police training in India. How could the people expect a policed police service in such situations? In 1977, Government of India appointed the National Police Commission and their observations are painful for any police-loving citizen in the country. This is a time of information technology and the police training does not receive adequate attention and care. The objectives of the police training, of criminal justice, of victim justice, of professional police work, of politicization of the police, of police community relations, of policing the police, etc., have considerably changed over the last 50 years - over the last 10 years - over the last few years. The police till yesterday dealt with passions, instincts, anomalies, illegalities, maladjustments, etc., in many ways. But, today the people want professional approaches to all of them and precisely therefore the police training has to be professionalized. The senior law instructor who is an inspector of police might have been enough to teach the laws in the past, but today the police trainees want professionally qualified lawyers to engage classes for them. The Dy. S.P. (Indoor) who is a history graduate was more than enough to teach police subjects and police science in the past. But, today the police trainees want forensic experts and police scientists to teach forensic subjects to them. V.R. Krishna Iyer, a former Judge in the Supreme Court of India in his article on forensic justice in Pathological Crisis writes: "A radical agenda for change in the judicial system must be drawn up by a Judicial Planning Commission and a Five Year Plan formulated with creative imagination geared to better performance, independence, modern management, introduction of high technology and fundamental reform in the adversary process, laws of evidence and archaic, expensive, tantalising methodology, plus periodic monitoring, discipline and control over the judges and the judicial process. The new dimensions of justice delivery and the new visions of alternative justicing will have to be explored and executed if the First Promise of the Constitution were to be actualized". If this is what Justice V.R. Krishna Iyer tells about changing the judicial system in democratic India, then any person interested in policing the society will talk a lot about changing the police system in India. Dharma Veera and the members of his Commission made many suggestions and recommendations to improve the police system. Government of India recently appointed a committee to reform the police. Do they speak anything about policing the police? - or - do they speak only about policing the society? A society can be policed with a police force, but a police force cannot be policed without a police force. As such policing the police is more important today than policing the society. A police service is policed by the high standards it maintains. No police officer, be he ever so high in office or seniority, or even so powerful because of his unholy *nexus* to the Minister of Home, has any authority or power to misuse/abuse his authority/power. The police is an institution which is the repository of abundant public esteem and an unscrupulous police officer must not destroy the public confidence on the police by his non-policed policing.

Functions of Police Today and Policing

Some police commissions appointed in States and the National Police Commission say that the functions of the police have been enlarged after the independence in India.

Correspondingly, the strength of the police from the constables to the directors general too has been increased. There are States where the posts of senior level officers (including the posts of Additional Directors General of Police) are created just like that for political reasons or to accommodate certain favourite officers of the ruling politicians. In a particular State, the Chief Minister has pilot and escort vehicles whenever he is on the road. He is the Minister for Home as well. Whenever he goes from the State capital to anywhere in the State, the people see all police officers on the road. The purpose of these officers was found to give him a *smart salute* when he passes through their jurisdiction and they spend hours together for saluting the Chief Minister cum Home Minister. Later a situation comes into being that the Chief Minister feels unhappy and restless when he does not see police officers on the road. This is not policing, rather it is pleasing politicians. Studies conducted on the 'pleasing behaviour' of police officers show that they neglect their prime duties like investigation of crime just for pleasing politicians. How many policemen are seen on the roads in the name of offering security to V.I.Ps? It will be cheaper for the States that all these so-called V.I.Ps and V.V.I.Ps use helicopters and bullet-proof cars rather than misusing police manpower, resources, energy and money for their security which is not threatened on many occasions. Once I was travelling in a State Capital by an autoriksha. We were detained for over 40 minutes and on enquiry I understood that the Chief Minister of the State was moving in his car through that way. Thousands of vehicles were detained on the road and thousands of policemen with their resources were seen on the road. If the Chief Minister of the State wanted so many policemen for his security in the State Capital, then V.I.P. security itself would be the main police functions. Which democratic country in the world could afford to waste so much money and policeman-power for such interpreted insecurity of politicians? I have seen some films mocking at the police and politicians when they resorted to such V.I.P. security strategies. The dialogue in the films could reveal how the people appreciate the police strategies in V.I.P.

security duties. Security must be offered to V.I.Ps/V.V.I.Ps, but must be done not at the expense of other prime duties of the police towards the people.

What type of job do the police do? Police Commissions and research scholars have studies them. The questions are :

(1) Do we need the services of a trained police personnel in the investigation of crimes for V.I.P. security?

(2) Do we post trained police personnel in V.I.P. duty for the duties connected with the security of V.I.Ps?

(3) Policemen/officers in traffic units are posted to thana police work and are they competent to do the Thana police work?

(4) Policemen/officers who have little or no training in intelligence work are posted to collect intelligence. How?

There are one thousand questions and the answers to the questions will show the lack of policing in police work. This is a world of professionals and nothing can be a substitute for professionalism. The Code of Criminal Procedure may say that an investigating officer can interrogate a suspect, but an interrogation psychologist will argue that police interrogation is a highly professional job and an expert in interrogation psychology must do it. Police interrogation is not a muscle work, rather it is a work that involves a deeper understanding of the human psyche and its dynamics. The Indian Evidence Act enacted in 1872 may say many things which the experts scientists and psychologists may call "non-sense" today. Creating evidence, concocting evidence, producing touts and tutored witnesses, etc., are not police functions. But allegations are plenty that the police do so and naturally such works consume a lot of police time, energy, manpower and money. This is not policing! If the Indian Evidence Act-1872 is not a good piece of legislation during 2002, it must be substituted. Instead, producing evidence in a non-police way is not the method to tackle the situation.

In his article about *Glasnost and Perestroika for Judicial India*, V.R. Krishna Iyer, a retired judge from the Supreme

Court of India says: "The condition of the subordinate courts, where most litigants seek relief especially the poor and the weak, is deplorable. Rickety buildings which accommodate the courts are dismally inadequate, what with fish market jostling, and client crowds wrangling, broken furniture and absence of standing space for lawyers and members of the public, confusion, pollution and corruption - making proceedings insufferable and inaudible. A wasteful 'roll-call' praxis when noises, not voices, are heard and cases adjourned for the first fresh hours of the forenoon everyday, sometimes stretching till afternoon, and when regular hearings begin all concerned are tired and jaded judges and fatigued staff sigh relief when the next date is fixed, the client breaking down at the prospect, since bankruptcy not final disposal, is his lot .... These hearings, performed with peevish presiding officers and cantankerous advocates, compound the waste of time". He writes a lot, but to it I may add that the antique laws, folklore assumptions of human nature, museum piece Indian Evidence Act, non-police methods of collecting evidence, etc., make everything a sort of mockery of justice. To quote Justice Krishna Iyer once again: "One of the major factors aggravating the lawlessness in society is the destructive delay, unbearable expense, judicial irresponsibility and gambling appetite of the court process, apart from the procedural irrationality, mismanagement mess, medievalese and inhumanity of the system. These maladies are amenable to remedies but myopic tinkering can never do where surgical procedures are the desideratum".[3] The destructive delay in police work is pointed out as a major factor in policing the police. The allegation is centred around the delay in response time when situations threatening law and order are reported. What about the delay in inspecting the scene of crime? - in completing the investigation? Do the police manipulate records? - Do they concoct evidence? - Do they resort to human rights unfriendly approaches? If they do so, people will blame them as they lack proper policing. Despite the non-police approaches and cruelties that existed in the Indian police ever since its inception, crimes existed and continue to exist. If that is the truth, a policed police service and a police service without cruelties may guarantee better dividends in the police work and ensure better human relations with the people. If every criminal is killed, then crimes can be eradicated within no time. But can we do so? The police must exist with criminals and amidst crimes. They can control crimes and that can be done only through proper policing. Non-policing strategies or lack of policing while policing the police - both are crimes in every sense.

What are the police functions? In 1861, when the Police Act was enacted, the police were given those functions which are no more relevant or valid today. A computer, a photocopier and a few other modern gadgets do wonders now. Even today, the carbon copies of witness statements are given by the police and it is just impossible to read them by the accused or his defence counsel. The antiquated features aggravated by the bigoted refusal to update the police mechanics make police functions lengthy and unduly time consuming. Government of India (2002) now makes attempts to amend the Code of Criminal Procedure to administer speedier justice, but God alone knows whether or not the proposed changes in law will complicate the police functions. In 1973, a new Code of Criminal Procedure was enacted. But the police did not get any special advantage by the newly enacted Code of Criminal Procedure-1973. Policing the police by a new Code of Criminal Procedure is possible if the law-makers want the police to police the police and thereby to police the society. About the functions of the police under the Code of Criminal Procedure-1862 and the Police Act-1861, David Arnold, a British scholar writes: "The creation of the police by the State to serve its own needs and the lack of public accountability contributed to a further characteristic of India's emergent police raj - the coercive strength and disposition of the colonial police".[4] The same police continued to function when India became independent and the Acts under which the police performed their functions were the same. Instead of the colonial administration, various political parties made use of and misused the police for their advantage. David Arnold continues: "Since it was not made to feel responsible to the public and since its officers almost invariably enjoyed, thanks to the government, immunity from prosecution, the police were free to use violence, including the use of fire arms, to an extent that would have been unacceptable in a police system like that of England". The same situation continued for a long time even after India became independent. Now regional political parties come to power in many States and precisely therefore the police functioning during the previous rule is subjected to scrutiny. In some States, criminal cases are registered against the police functionaries so much so that the police become more accountable in these days than what they were earlier. There is a positive content in every police act and the police are to express the positive content in their functions, If they express negative contents in their functioning, they are made accountable for what they do. The Human Rights Commission, Lokayukta, Criminal courts, Sub-committees of the Legislature, Women's Commissions, the Press and the Media, Public Litigation Societies, Civic-minded people, Legislature, politicians of the ruling front and opposition, etc., evaluate the positive and negative contents of the police actions/functionings. Today, I read in the paper that the National Minority Commission have summoned the director general of police and the chief secretary of a South Indian State to appear before them to answer police responses to a law and order situation which affected adversely a minority community. The recent trend is to evaluate police functionings from many angles and they are not allowed to enjoy immunity from prosecution and victimological compensation to the affected parties. Lack of policing in the police is not tolerated. People want a policed police service and they cannot claim immunity for what they do in policing, in the name of policing or under the pretext of policing the society. People ask the police: "Oh, physician, cure thyself before you cure others". The illiterate, ignorant, over-enthusiastic, repressive, oppressive, people unfriendly police force policed the society earlier, but today they are made accountable for everything they do. People want transparency in the police work. Police violence is treated as violence by the policemen. A coercive police force is not accepted but rather a people friendly police service is acknowledged. People accept the functions of the civil police. They are not to execute any coercive functions. The armed and paramilitary police force may perform the coercive functions of the State. Yet, they are accountable. They have to manage a law and order situation as per the law and by the procedure established by the law. The brutal suppression or brute repression of demonstrations, disturbances and agitation may not be tolerated in a democracy. The colonial police could afford such brutalities, but a democracy's police cannot and should not.

Police Functions, Policing and Justice System

Victim Justice was an unknown concept for the colonial police. Hence, the police could abuse their power or misuse their authority without having any fear of anyone. Allegations are there to show that they have been doing so till recently, but today the police are made accountable. In a sensational espionage case involving top level scientists and foreign nationals, the National Human Rights Commission allowed an interim relief of Rs. 10 lakh for the suffering a single scientist underwent at the hands of the police. A situation has now emerged that any non-policing when the police police the society is now raised before courts, tribunals and commissions for getting victimological compensation. The need for policing without torture, inhuman and degrading treatment and punishment - becomes a Nation's cry today - an international demand and a millennium wish. There is one thing in everyone and that is his "humanity". The "man" and the "woman" in a person must be respected by every policeman when he executes the law. The police must be "human" and police functionings must be humane. "Humaneness" is now considered as the measure of success in policing a society. Hence people say that policing must have "humanity" as its *measure* and any police act which does not have "humanity" is no police act at all. A policed police service will have humaneness and humanity whereas a non-police police service will have animality and brutality. Victimologists argue for victim compensation for any police act/functioning which does not have humanity/humaneness in it. The eighteenth, nineteenth, twenteeth century use of police torture, methods of extracting confessions, strategies of humiliating crime-doers, violations of human rights become now issues for victimological compensation. The police are treated as a sub-system in an Equal Justice System and precisely therefore every system keeps a watch on the police doings and misdoings. Policing the police is a noble concept and the people want to see it when they police the society. Policing has a purpose and policing by torture or inhuman and degrading methods, means or strategies is not policing. Policing has a promise, but the promise is not to be contaminated with human rights unfriendly attitudes and approaches. The movement for humanizing and reforming the police - and for controlling the functionings of the police is not a recent phenomenon in India. About 40 years back, I remember to have seen an article expressing the strong desire to humanize and reform the police. Today, the demand has become stronger and more frequent. No liberal society - no democracy - can keep its citizens under a police raj - in fear and torture. The police function for the people and a policed policing is deemed to be the best in a democracy. The British who came to rob the country wanted a deterrent police force -soldiers and armymen-and they established a police raj for maintaining their self-interest. When they established such a police system in India, they had a different - people friendly - police system in England. The Indian Penal Code enacted by the British in 1860 provided *transportation* as a punishment in India while it was dropped in Britain. Why? Although they spoke a lot about the Magna Carta, they could not see human beings as similar everywhere. They felt happy when they saw the Indian policemen fighting against, injuring, suppressing, oppressing and repressing

Indians. In White Mutiny, disaffection and insubordination among the local European troops were found. Nevertheless, the Indians were found to be faithful to their British rulers. When India became independent, the political parties which came to power used, misused and abused the police power, strength and authority for political gains. The political parties in the opposition objected to some of the police strategies and thus the police in India have been in a transition period and they wanted to get out of police clutches. The National Police Commission: 1977-81 made some strong recommendations with that in mind. But, the governments which came to power from time to time did not accept the recommendations and the impact has been that the police functionings are controlled to a considerable extent by the politicians and political parties in power. Whatever that may be, the people make the police accountable for what they do and therefore some policemen/ officers want to get out of the political clutches now.

Police Functions, Democracy and Policing

The police are a part of the society, of the people and of the democracy. Hence, policing the people means policing the police as well. Well policed police means half well policed society. A non-politicized police means a just and impartial police. In sensational cases, the governments appoint special police officers who are upright in character and conscience. People accept them. Why? They find an impartial, non-politicized, just police investigation in such instances. This is called policing the democracy and the police get public confidence, people's participation and popular support and cooperation. During the British rule, the police was of the British government and now? It is and ought to be of the people of India. Does it become so? If not, it cannot be called a "policed police", rather it may be named a "politicized police". The transition from the colonial police, with its extreme loyalty to the British administration to a democratic rule which accepted equality, liberty, dignity, etc., was a transition from one form of police functioning to another form of police functioning. But, the police in India did not understand it in the newly formed democracy and therefore they continued to function as the colonial police with their muscle power and brutality. When police officers saw the caption "Modern India and Role of Police" in the syllabus prepared by the Central Committee on Police Training, they did not understand the relevance of the topics like democracy, fundamental rights, directive principles of State policy, political framework, economic frame work, people, political parties, etc. They asked: "Why should we teach all these topics to the new entrants to the police service?" Hence, even today, no qualified faculty has been appointed in many police training institutions to teach such vital topics. Some institutions invite guest faculty to teach Police and Democracy and even after 25 years, the same deplorable conditions prevail in some police training institutions. If that is the truth, how can we think of a policed police service in a democracy? The accounts and narrations of the police training during the nineteenth century in Phillaur (1892), in Saugor (1869) etc. still fascinate many and they fail to understand the changes in the concepts of police training in democratic countries today. Policc for them is and ought to be a muscle power and they do not and can not think about a police service in a democracy in a people friendly way. Community policing is an idea which cannot work for them, for, they think that police can police the society without the people's support and cooperation. It is true that the British held India and exercised their power through the use of police force and muscles. Every time the British had the difficulty to suppress the Indians, they increased the police strength. Some political parties too follow the same strategy. Whenever they come to power in a particular state, they want to recruit as many party men as possible to the police. They do so, if possible so, that they can have their men in the police. For them, the police is a force and not a service. It means that even the political parties are reluctantly accepting the fact that the police is a service or a public facility in a democracy. The political parties and politicians are found interfering even in petition inquiries and they want to see that the police settle the issues through threats and muscle force. This is not policing a democracy, rather it was a characteristic of the colonial police from which, experts think, the police in post-independent India have not got out so far - even after 50 years of freedom.

The National Police Commission: 1977-81 has surprisingly found out that 40 per cent of the time is spent by constables on mechanical duties such as sentry duty, escort duty, tapal duty, drill and parade, messenger duty and arms cleaning. My considered view is that there is no police duty or function which is purely mechanical. A sentry constable is the first point of contact in a police station and he does carve out a good or bad image of the Thana police. I have seen the sentry constables misbehaving with the members of the public and behave in an arrogant manner to the visitors to the police stations. The non-policing of the police can be evaluated from the way the sentry constables behave towards the people. In a public opinion survey conducted by me, some people honestly made the frank opinion that the police stations ought to be free from the unenviable behaviour of sentry constables. The Police Commission: 1977-81 could not see the dangers in the behaviour of the constables on sentry duty. According to the same Police Commission, the escort duty by a police constable was just a mechanical duty. The constables escorting ministers in the democracy sometimes make such a noise and behave in such an undesirable manner that the public feel disturbed at the police misbehaviour. Some utter epithets on the road-users, on the foot-path sellers, on vehicle drivers and so on. No doubt, the non-police behaviour of the escort constables/officers make the political leaders (ministers) unpopular among the people and how could the Police Commission see such abnormal behaviour to be just mechanical? I do not think that the drill and parade are just mechanical duties. The one who studies the working of the human psyche when one is engaged in drill and parade may subscribe to the view that they have a decisive role to play for the shaping of the police personality. The police

Commission could find that nearly half of a constable's time - 49 per cent was spent on mechanical duties and I totally disagree with the view of the Commission.

According to the National Police Commission: 1977-81, more than one third of the constables time - i.e., 37% - was spent on duties which involved a combination of mechanical duties with duties that required application of mind and exercise of judgement. The Commission enumerated night-patrol, surveillance, licence-check, conducting raid, attending court, imparting training, service of summons/execution of warrants, motor vehicle driving, wireless set operation, miscellaneous other duties under this category. I do not know the criteria by which the Police Commission could make such judgements on the police functionings. I think that the duties enumerated by the Commission under that category did not have any mechanical content. Night patrol, surveillance, conducting raid, etc., are considered to be very sensitive jobs and there requires a lot of human initiative, application of mind and exercise of judgement. The people evaluate the policing of the police by observing how the police conduct night patrol, surveillance, licence check, conducting raid, etc. If they see the policemen receiving a bribe during a licence check, showing no respect to the people and property during a raid, behaving in a disorderly or indifferent way during a night patrol, the people blame the police in many ways. Allegations are raised and complaints are sent. The police constable is more highly visible than the director general of police by the people. In a democracy, policing the police is seen and evaluated by the people just by observing how the lower level functionaries behave towards the man on the street during the patrol, during the license check, during the service of summons/execution of warrants, etc. Most unfortunately, the Police Commission could not see and appreciate the importance of the constable functionings in a democracy.

The National Police Commission: 1977-81 noted further that a little more than one seventh of a constable's time - i.e.,

14 per cent - was spent on duties which require initiative and the exercise of discretion and judgement and also interaction with the public calling for tact, courtesy, politeness and a proper attitude on his part. The observation of the Commission was not based on facts and realities. The Commission enumerated day patrol, traffic control and regulation, inquiry into complaints, collection of intelligence, assisting investigating officers, bandobust duties, V.I.P. visits, bandobust on other occasions like fairs, festivals, etc., and clerical work in police stations.

The superior ranks including the director general of police get the police functions performed by or through their subordinates. The success of the police functions depends heavily on how the constables at the bottom levels perform their duties and functions. If the constables are not policed well, it means the entire hierarchy lacks proper policing. The police is basically a man-oriented service and precisely therefore there is not a single function (in police) which does not have a social dimension - a human angle. Whether it is the escort duty, the checking of licence or collection of intelligence, all of them have human and social dimensions. Politeness, tact, courtesy, understanding, humaneness etc., are required in all police works. The Police Commissions' narrow look at the constables' functions in a way underestimates the importance of the policeman in policing the police.

Police Functions, Social Legislation and Policing

A policeman is only a policeman and so is the director general of police. They enjoy some powers and authority. Every power/authority has its limits and limitations. A policeman including the director general of police is limited in time and space. There is retirement and that is the surest thing in any service. The exercise of authority is understandable but the exercise of pseudo-authority and assumed authority by a policeman is an expression of lack of policing. I think that some policemen/officers suffer from an *identity crisis* and some others think too much about themselves. Some policemen have an inferiority feeling or complex and they want to compensate for their deficiency by exhibiting non-police behaviour. They do more harm than good to a people-oriented service. I notice that many policemen/officers repress their feelings and frustrations and they express them through their non-police behaviour to the public. Some policemen/officers have a mistaken notion that policing a society means the exercise of authority, pseudo-authority or the expression of animal instincts, aggressiveness and attacks. Such people lack an upright conscience and adequate superego formation. The police need policing, for they are recruited into a culture which lacks adequate policing and brought up in a culture which needs policing. The British could develop a police culture which was antagonistic to the Indian people and the new entrants to the police service logically became antagonistic to their Indian brethren in democratic India. An antagonistic attitude and approach ensured several advantages to the police and therefore they nurtured and nourished the culture to develop even after India became independent. The development of an antagonistic culture was the root-cause of developing a human rights unfriendly climate in police culture. A man was found different in his police uniform and the reason for this change in his outlook and attitude is traced to the development of an anti-human culture in the police during and after the British rule. A policeman started to think that he was a *big body* whenever he violated the law or behaved in an inhuman way towards the people. The failure to inculcate proper values in the policemen and their culture might be one of the reasons for seeing lack of policing in the police department.

From the beginning of police organisation in India, one could notice desperate and unfortunate men joining the police as constables. They had high risks, poor pay, no leisure, no status, no education and in that way they had nothing with them to feel proud of themselves. The little men had a lot of power with them and they could abuse/misuse them if they wanted. In the entire history of the Indian police, one could observe the policemen committing a lot of crimes, conniving with dacoits, accepting corruption money and becoming atrocious to their fellow brethren. The history is not an enviable one which cannot be changed overnight when India got freedom. The patterns of police behaviour continued to dominate the police culture even after India became a democracy, and necessarily such a situation would mean lack of policing within the police department.

The policemen are not social reformers. There is a number of social legislations which is to be enforced by means other than brutal police force. What is the meaning of policemen forcefully taking people for undergoing family planning operations? Special laws relating to family, divorce, adoption, inheritance, etc., are not to be enforced by the police. Nevertheless, news appears sometimes in the press that marriages take place in police stations. Whatever is done by the police to solemnize a marriage in police stations does not come under police functions. Hence, as far as possible, don't take up such non-police jobs. It is heard that, sometimes, the policemen threaten the couples to marry and many such marriages end in desertion or divorce in due course. The enforcement of dowry laws, the laws relating to vagrancy, begging, discrimination against women are not police jobs, nevertheless, I see the policemen taking undue interest and enthusiasm to enforce such laws by resorting even to non-police methods. The officers and authorities entrusted with rehabilitating beggars approach the police to make their job easier. They make use of and misuse the policemen to round up beggars to march them to rehabilitation centres or to any such institutions. By doing so, these officers get an ego inflation and therefore the police must, politely but firmly, say "no" to such requests. They are not police problems. If they create any law and order situation, then it may become a police problem. But, even in such instances, remarkable restraint must be shown by the police.

The National Police Commission: 1977-81 has extensively dealt with the police role in the enforcement of social legislations in a democracy. The police service is not a substitute for education and awareness creation. Social changes may come into being slowly and any hurry in effecting social changes will have only adverse or negative consequences. Allegations are sometimes heard that social legislations are not properly enforced in police departments. For example, what about the dowry which some policemen/officers demand and accept when they marry? A police constable in a South Indian State is worth several lakhs in the dowry market today and officers are worth many lakhs, flats, cars, gadgets, etc. People ask: "How can the police enforce legislations which they cannot enforce among themselves?".

The relationship between the police and students, between the police and the media/press, between the police and the weaker sections of the society is very sensitive. All of them are a powerful part of democracy and precisely therefore any ruthless handling of students, pressmen and weaker sections in society may invite problems which have a multi-dimensional impact which the police alone cannot tackle. In a democracy, riots erupt in many parts of the country and the source causes may be anything from personal vendetta to communal or political vengeance. Industrial disputes, agrarian unrest, migration, mobility, economic growth, industrialization, urbanization, youth unrest, women empowerment, women education, upliftment of the handicapped, etc., are part and parcel of a developing society - a growing democracy. The police have to take them as they are and to deal with them with utmost care and responsibility. A muscle approach may not yield any enviable results; rather a mature approach can ensure great success. "What is demanded by the people in a changing society is that the police should exercise their powers with due regard to the citizen's dignity and constitutional safeguards". The social approval of the police actions is the greatest reward that can be/must be desired for in a democracy. In such a set-up, blinding episodes, custodial rapes, torture, humiliation, unnecessary handcuffing, calling of epithets, illegal detention, informal arrests, incommunicado interrogation, manipulation of records, concoction of evidence, corruption, corrupt practices, bribery, corruption-money fixing, police-politician *nexus*, enforcement criminality, *nexus crimes*, unholy relationship with business men, participation in organized crimes, etc., have no place in policing the society. But, the problem today is more of policing the police rather than policing the society. "Justice without power is inefficient; power without justice is tyranny... Justice and power must, therefore, be brought together, so that whatever is just may be powerful, and whatever is power may be just". (Blaise Pascal)

References

1. Michel Foucault, *Discipline and Punish: The Birth of the Prison*, Penguin Books, London, 1977 (Trans. by Alan Sheridan).
2. Anandswarup Gupta, *The Police in British India*: 1861-1947, Concept Publishing Company, New Delhi, 1978.
3. V.R. Krishna Iyer, *Justice at Crossroads*, Deep & Deep Publications, New Delhi, 1992.
4. David Arnold, *Police Power and Colonial Rule - Madras: 1859-1947*, Oxford University Press, Delhi, 1986.
5. *Ibid.*
6. James Vadackumchery and John Kattakayam, *Human Behaviour and Law Enforcement*, Ashish Publishing House, New Delhi, 1995.

7

Police Praxis and Policing the Police

The British Indian Police, modelled on police muscles and ruthlessness, had a limited objective and many imperial values. The police praxes therefore were not to ensure social, economic and political justice to all the citizens in India. Article 39 A of the Constitution of India was not available to the British when they reorganized the police force in 1861. The colonial police culture, customs and practices never took into account the categorical imperatives of a social philosophy found in a liberal democracy. The repression and oppression of the Indian people were the police praxes and in such a strategy, human rights and the dignity of the individual had no place. The British administration did not want to rely on their military power for internal policing. They, at the same time, wanted a brutal force under civilian control. They wanted a police force armed and available for doing anything for retaining their power in India. The police for them was a coercive weapon. It being their objective, they militarized the police. They shaped the police personality on that of a soldier. Hard behaviour, ferocious looks, threatening eyes, frightening moustaches, strong muscles, etc., were the characteristics of the police in British India. A sober language, a human face, a humane attitude, sympathy, consideration, decency in behaviour, etc., were unknown to the police then and the British never wanted to inculcate the finer points in human behaviour into the British Indian policemen. A properly policed police service was not their objective; rather they wanted sorne illiterate and ignorant "animal men" to work as policemen. They created a partly militarized police force under a departmental structure which would maximize control and supervision by the white officers at the top. Thus they created a militarized police force with an attitude of "yes sir", "no sir" to their European masters. The police praxes were such that they said "yes sir, no sir" to everything - sense and nonsense - told to them. They were told that the Indians were to be repressed and oppressed and they most faithfully executed their superiors' orders.

In 1829, Sir Robert Peel established the London Metropolitan Police. The British administrators were fully aware of the excellent success of the London Metropolitan Police system, but they did not want to implement the system in India. Why? The police praxes which the police in the imperial metropolis in London developed were people friendly and therefore they felt that such praxes would not protect their vested interests in colonial India where they wanted a people unfriendly police system. They saw the Irish Constabulary and took it as a model for the Indian territory. The police of the colonial Ireland were a centralized - paramilitary - force and their chief was the Inspector General of Police. He was very authoritarian and paramilitary in his walk, talk and outlook. The semi-military character of the Irish Constabulary was transplanted into India. About the Irish Constabulary, David Arnold, a police historian writes: "... Unlike London's Police, there was the semi-military character of the Irish police. The senior officers were often men with military experience: the ranks, subject to virtually military discipline and training, were equipped with carbines and houses in barracks. Though primarily a gendarmerie and the first line of defence against insurrection, their responsibilities were wide-ranging. They kept Dublin Castle informed of the agrarian discontent and political agitation". Sir Hugh Rose, in 1861 (He was the Commander-in-chief of the Indian Army then) said categorically that "No system of police had ever worked better for the suppression of political agitation, or agrarian disorder, than the Irish constabulary". It means that the police praxes were developed in such a way as to suppress political agitations or agrarian disorders. Their praxes could not be to develop a healthy police - people relationship. They wanted the people to look at the police from a distance and never wanted any transparency. In 1860, out of 38 district superintendents appointed, thirty three were military officers and naturally they knew only the military ways of policing the society. The militarization of the police destroyed police-public relations and the British administration was happy at the deterioration in the police-people interactions. The "Deter and Rule" policy made the British safe in India and the police like wild animals caused fear and anxiety among the Indian population. Until recently, some policemen/officers were nicknamed as lions, tiger, vulture, etc., and they felt proud of such nicknames.

Madras Police Act - 1859 and Police Praxes

The Indian Penal Code was enacted in 1860 and the Code of Criminal Procedure in 1861. Crimes were classified into two categories -cognizable and non-cognizable. The police were given authority to register cognizable crimes and to investigate them. Naturally, a police force that was created in a para-military style with military training could not investigate crimes under the Penal Code-1860 and, as per the procedure established by the Code of Criminal Procedure-1861. The British were not serious about crimes. They were concerned only with law and order issues. The inspection of the scene of crime, the interviewing of witnesses, the interrogation of suspects, the collection of scientific evidence, etc., were Greek to the armed constabulary trained to fight against those who created law and order issues. In Madras, they wanted unarmed constables and in each district they created an armed reserve. The reserve constables were used for quelling local disturbances. With the advent of an armed reserve, the police in Madras became partly civil and partly military. The Madras Police Act 1859 was enacted thus and later the Madras system was appreciated by the police in other parts of the country. Today, we have a three tier system in the police and they are : (1) the police of the General Executive, (2) the police of the Armed Reserve, and (3) the police of the Armed Battalions.

The police of the General Executive perform all police works and those of the district Armed Reserve are considered as the second source of defence in law and order situations. Those in the Armed Battalions are the third source of defence. The police of the General Executive have contacts and interaction with the public. Those in the district Armed Reserve and in Battalions have nothing much to do with the members of the public. When the members of the public make complaints against the police or raise allegations against the police, they are often directed against the police of the General Executive. This does not however mean that allegations/accusations are not made against the police in the Armed Reserves or Armed Battalions. Once a constable from the district Armed Reserve picked up a quarrel with a member of the civilian public. To cut the story short, some constables left their barracks and did beat the members of the public. Why did they do so? An organization which was meant by the British to maintain law and order failed to perform their duties - not only that, but created law and order situations.

The police is an organized strength and sufficiently armed to meet any law and order situation. If they abuse their strength or misuse their authority and attack the people in a democracy, it means lack of policing within the police organization. From where did the police learn the strategy of attacking the public? Has the police praxis any historical explanation? Psychologists are of the view that the British primarily used the police in the Armed Reserve for suppressing civil disturbances and therefore whenever they had any interaction with the public, it was to show their muscle strength and to demonstrate their skill in the use of arms and ammunition. They were taught drill with arms, without arms, unarmed combat, musketry, mob-operation, lathy drill, parade, etc., and they were taken out to demonstrate their skill and efficiency to suppress/oppress the people. They did not have human dealing with people and did not have human faces. They knew well that they were a force - a coercive weapon -and well organized to repress the people who are disorganized. They were fully aware that they were not accountable to the Indian people, but rather were answerable only to the British administration.

Even today, I notice that the police give maximum priority to law and order situations. Whenever the law and order situation is disturbed, the ruling Government is disturbed. The investigation of crime is of secondary importance to the police in many States. Why? The investigation of crime, failure or success, delay, etc., normally do not affect the Government in power unless the crime is politically sensational in nature. In British India too, the investigation of crime by the police was not of great importance or had an importance very much less than law and order maintenance. There is ample evidence to prove that the police conducted perfunctory investigation of crimes and had been using torture and other third degree methods to prove the crimes. Necessarily, the police strategies were human rights violations.

About police investigation during 1950-60, my father-in-law once told me that torture was the oft-resorted method to get a confession from the suspects in a crime. In the history of the Indian police, before and after independence, one could notice any number of police atrocities during the investigation of crime. One of the main reasons for employing torture had been the ignorance of the investigating personnel about scientific investigation. The people in India did not react to the police torture in the past, for they thought that the police was primarily meant to torture people. The older generation did believe that the police were to torture people and some old policemen/

officers did subscribe to the view that it was their right to torture people or they were legally bound to do so for the interest of society. Owing to the development of human rights consciousness, people started reacting to the police torture, misbehaviour and atrocities. Today, the people do not tolerate any sort of police torture. Moreover, the Supreme Court of India in D.K. Basu Vs. State of West Bengal has given the directive that an arrestee has a right to be examined by a medical officer immediately after his arrest and in every 48 hours thereafter. The injuries of the arrested are recorded at the time of arrest and an inspection memo is prepared. All these laws were not in existence during the British rule and there was no one to control properly the aggressiveness exhibited by the police. W. Kaye Committee which inquired into the working of the police in 1890 (N.W.P. and Oudh) observed: "...one of the first points that struck us in conducting this enquiry was the intense dread which the police as a body inspired....". Why did the people exhibit extreme and excessive fear towards the police if they were convinced of the fact that the police were to protect their life and property? - if the police were policed sufficiently enough to protect the people? The Kaye Committee was candid enough to speak out that the police did not care much for the provisions contained in the Code of Criminal Procedure - 1861 (enacted 30 years ago) and were violating the law. The Committee accused the police of tyranny, oppression, corruption, fabrication and abuses of power and authority. The Committee further observed that the defects in the police was either due to the material of which the force was composed or the system which was totally defective. Lack of policing or defects in the police system was fully known to the British rulers; nevertheless they did not do anything much to remedy the defects and correct the system. One could not expect the English to ensure a just and decent police system - policed well enough to administer justice in India. Of course, they did it in London and that was a different story altogether. Their interest in India was collection of revenue and for that they wanted a police system. They made certain laws to give an appearance that they were honest in enacting good laws, but their hypocrisy was exposed when people saw that the law-makers were not keen enough to enforce the laws they enacted. What was more? The laws in the statutes were not the laws in practice. The police praxes - i.e., the conventions, habits or customs - which were established in the past became the unquestioned rules and practices when India became independent.

Law in Principle and Law in Practice

Earlier, mention has been made that the law in principle was not the law in practice. The people therefore did not/could not know exactly what the laws which were enforced by the police and how they ought to be enforced. For example, sections 330 and 331 of the Indian Penal Code-1860 dealt with voluntarily causing hurt or grievous hurt to extort confession or to compel restoration of property. According to section 331, I.P.C., whoever voluntarily causes grievous hurt for the purpose of extorting any confession or any information which may lead to the detection of an offence, or for the purpose of compelling or causing the restoration of any property shall be punished with imprisonment for a term which may extend to ten years and shall also be liable to a fine. No doubt, the law takes serious note of custodial violence and prescribes very severe punishment. What about the police praxis? Imagine for a moment that all police functionaries who employed violence in police custody to extort confession or to compel or cause the restoration of property were punished, then how many of the serving police personnel would have gone to jails? It proves that the law is not enforced by the functionaries who are to enforce them, rather they encourage the violation of the laws. Psychologists say that the mere repetition of an illegal act - undesirable act - will make it an acceptable act in due course and that is what has happened in police subculture. Custodial violence/torture is an illegal act. But, it was repeatedly resorted to by the police. In due course, it got an acceptance and approval. The police praxis thus becomes a custom, a tradition and an accepted strategy. A Malayalam poet once sang that the mistakes committed yesterday would become customs/traditions today and then would further become a science in due course. Perhaps, this was what happened in the police subculture in India.

A policed police service is a myth - a director general of police feels so and he has his own explanations for his view. He thinks that the Indian policemen/officers have not seen a policed police service in their lives and how can we expect that they must be policed then? The British perception of policing the police could be identified with the militarization of the police. Militarization is not policing. Police is "an organized civil force for maintaining order, preventing and detecting crimes and enforcing the laws". This meaning as given in the Random House College Dictionary is not accepted fully now as the civilized society is not prepared to treat the police as a civil force. The police today is a "service" and a "public facility" for the people. In such a perception of the police service today, militarization does not have any meaning or relevance. Throughout the history of the police in India, the British increased the strength of the police and they did it not for extending the police service to the people but to repress and suppress them. For making a repressive police force, they recruited illiterate/ignorant men. At one time (around 1889), it was found that "eighty nine percent of the rural police consisted of menial and quasi-criminal classes paid partly in cash and partly by the grants of land. Their net wages averaged between Rs.3 to Rs.4 p.m. in the N.W. Provinces and Rs.2 to Rs.3 p.m. in Oudh."[2] How could they be law abiding? How could the members of the quasi-criminal classes police the society? They were paid very low salaries and necessarily the policemen at the bottom level were men from poor community. Even today, the policemen come from poor economic background and some of them are from labour or coolie community. Lord Curson appointed a Police Commission in July 1902 to inquire into the working of the police system in

India. The report of the Police Commission has been a living monument of how deplorably the police system worked in India. The report contained a lot of descriptions about the police praxes which were illegal and intolerable. There would be no organized criminals in the entire British empire whose record of crime would be as big as those committed by the British Indian Police. They were a disgrace to the police community. To quote the Commission: "Everywhere they went the Commission heard the most bitter complaints of the corruption of the police...by non-officials...by officials of all classes including Magistrates and police officers, both European and Native". What more is required to speak about the integrity, honesty and policing of the police during the British rule in India? Could the National Police Commission: 1977-81 appointed by Government of democratic India find a better policing? Can the researcher in 2002 A.D. see a still better policing? Corruption, *nexus criminality, enforcement crimes*, syndicate partnership, Mafia involvement, unholy relationship with politicians, with bandits and underworld criminals appear more often in the press than what they were in the past. Researchers subscribe to the view that only a part of the police crimes - the iceberg phenomenon - is visible to the public. Police praxes assume very sinister dimensions now when the police organize seminars, workshops and symposia on policing the society. The gap between the police in law and the police in practice becomes very large as days go by and years pass by.

Human Rights and Policing the Police

The police in India was never brought up in a human rights friendly climate by the British. The Irish Constabulary was not a people friendly police organization and necessarily a police system which was developed on the model of the Irish Constabulary could never become people friendly. The Torture Commission Report really exposed how human rights friendly were the police in the erstwhile Madras Presidency ! The Indian Police Commission:1902-03 further elaborated the findings of the Torture Commission when they said that serious offences were "generally very fairly reported, though the corruption, oppression and inefficiency of the police already described, and the delays, expenses and vexations too often involved in the prosecution of cases have led to the suppression of crime to a greater or less degree everywhere". What do the National Human Rights Commission do now? The reports of the National Human Rights Commission show that human rights violations are not rare in police work and the Commission awards very heavy compensation to the victims of the abuse of power/misuse of authority by the police. The police practices appear to be human rights unfriendly even at a time when human rights are honoured by the international community.

Police administration at the intermediate ranks of the police is of importance in the protection of human rights. India has a Thana-based police administration and the Station House officers play an important role. The sub-inspector is the kingpin. Indianization started during the British period. Head constables were promoted and posted as station-house officers and they were to investigate crimes and keep surveillance. By 1890s, the Europeans understood that the Indians who held the office of the station house officers lacked education, integrity and investigative expertise. The investigation of crime is a professional job and lack of professionalism means perfunctory investigation, human rights violations and miscarriage of justice. In fact, the Indians were conditioned to suffer human rights violations by the police over centuries. The Police Commission: 1902-03 realized the defects and therefore they recommended to recruit directly sub-inspectors to be appointed as station house officers. Government of India in 1905 agreed with the recommendation of the Police Commission: 1902-03. Thus, people possessing matriculation certificate (S.S.L.C.) were appointed as sub-inspectors directly. The Indian Penal Code-1860, Code of Criminal Procedure-1861, Indian Evidence Act 1872 which were written in Queen's English were hard nuts to crack for the Indian sub-inspectors who possessed only S.S.L.C. qualification. About the newly appointed sub-inspectors, the European officers were not happy. To quote David Arnold: "The sub-inspectors who were directly recruited were said to be on the average inferior to the picked head constables and were reputedly less in touch with their men. An S.S.L.C was no guarantee of aptitude for police work, and their education and social position (to which the Police Commission had attached such significance) made them too big for their boots and disinclined to talk or associate with their men or with village officers". If this was the attitude the directly enlisted sub-inspectors showed to their fellow subordinates, naturally, it would be worse with the ordinary mortals on the street. The sub-inspectors were not prepared to respect the human dignity of their own subordinates and how could they be expected to show respect to the dignity of the suspects, arrestees and crime doers in police custody? Charity begins at home and if that quality is lacking at home, then who must be blamed for it? Human right is a concept which relates to the right to life, liberty, equality and dignity. If police functionaries do not show respect to the dignity of man and do not respect the human person in the individuals who work with them, then one can not expect them to show respect to human rights of others who are outside the police department. A policed police service will show respect to human rights.

About policing the police - and about the newly recruited sub-inspectors, David Arnold says again: "Allegations of police corruption and high-handedness, formerly directed at the constables and head constables, were now made against subinspectors and inspectors as well".[4] *Indian Patriot* wrote about the police officers: "Honest men cannot serve in the police". Did the situation become better after India got freedom? The National Police Commission: 1977-81 found that corruption has spread more extensively and widely. A situation has now emerged that people do not understand what exactly is meant by policing. They are inclined to think that corruption money fixing, corruption money splitting, corruption Mafia and corrupt practices, etc., become a part of policing and police subculture.

Amnesty International, a world organization endeavouring to protect human rights says that Indian police has institutionalized torture and Government of India accuses the Amnesty International alleging that it is an unnecessary interference in the internal affairs of India. Accepting the truth fairly, a researcher may subscribe to the view that the real truth must be in between the two positions taken by Amnesty International and Government of India. No doubt, there do take place human rights violations in police custody and certainly it is an indicator of lack of policing/proper policing in India even after 50 years of democratic rule and freedom.

People friendly police, human rights friendly investigation, scientific interrogation, etc., were not in the centuries old agenda of the British regime. They had the Indian money and English education. They had their parochial interests and idiomatic English language. They had their vested view and excellent ideas of justice. They enacted laws, innovated the police and made an atmosphere of terror and fear allowing the police to behave as ferociously as possible to deter the people. People hated the police and treated them as their enemies. The people shouted against the police and raised anti-police slogans. The police were called the *"goondas"* of the Government in power. Even today, some mike-announcements address the police as the *"goondas"* of the ruling government. Though the British made the Indians to shout at the police with anti-police and anti-government slogans, they could make a people friendly police in London. Herbert Spencer (1820-1903), the English Philosopher spoke loudly in England that "no one can be perfectly free till all are free; no one can be perfectly moral till all are moral; no one can be perfectly happy till all are happy". The British heard the philosopher's voice, but did not want to enforce the idea in Indian territory. They made the police to make the people to be not free - to be not happy and they claimed that they had the best sense of justice. They propagated the phrase - "the British Sense of Justice" - and the phrase meant that it was the best justice in the world. Indians understood the British plans and agenda and therefore Mahatma Gandhi said at Ahmedabad:

"Affection can not be manufactured or regulated by law. If one has no affection for a person or system, one should be free to give the fullest expression of his disaffection, so long as he does not contemplate, promote or incite to violence. But I hold it to be a virtue to be disaffected towards a Government which in its totality has done more harm to India than any previous system". The British left India half a century ago; yet the police system which they created for serving their self-interests continues to rule the country. What a tragedy indeed! Under the presently existing laws and police system, no one can make the police people and human rights friendly. The police will continue to be the people's enemy and the people will continue to shout anti-police slogans. Policing the police to police the society, as I said elsewhere in this book, has never been an objective of the British imperialism. The political parties which came into power from time to time to rule the States too never wanted to police the police to police the society. The police hierarchy who enjoyed power and authority in independent India too did not want to police the police to police the society. Certainly, the people wanted to police the police to police the society, but their voice was so feeble that the politicians and the powerful did not so far take the issue seriously. The politicians, the police, the powerful know fully well the international thinking on policing the police and on protecting human rights. The Manila Human Rights Proclamation said:

"Human rights today have become increasingly all-encompassing. Today as never before and especially in the developing countries of the world, there is a crying need for respect of all human rights, whether civil, political, social, economic or cultural, so as to ensure to all peoples of the world the enjoyment of a decent life in safety, justice and dignity".[5]

If the Police Act-1861 and the State Police Acts framed in agreement with the Central Police Act - 1861 do not allow the police to become human rights friendly, then the Act must be substituted by a new Police Act which ensures to all people the enjoyment of a decent life of safety, justice and dignity. There must be a political will for the same and until that political will comes into being, policing the police will be an unachievable task. If the public opinion is not in favour of the police, police behaviour and police administration, then it means that there is lawless law enforcement and loss of respect for law and justice. If law enforcement becomes a casualty now, it is certain that the administration of justice will be the next casualty.

Police Praxis and Political Influence

Once curfew was declared in the capital city of a State. A political party conducted a procession and the police kept mum. Other political parties became furious and called the police as violators of the law - as people not respecting curfew orders. Curfew means an order establishing a specific period during which certain restrictions apply, especially that no unauthorized persons may be outdoors or that places of public assembly must be closed. The police praxis of ignoring or overlooking curfew orders in favour of a political party may carve an image of the police that they are not policed enough to police the society.

Once a ruling political party asked the police to keep away from performing their police duties and the police faithfully obeyed the politicians' orders. The impact was that there was large scale arson in the city. Ultimately the Indian Army was called to establish peace and restore order in society. What does it mean? If the police become puppets in the hands of ruling politicians, they will have only puppets' value in law enforcement. No police will play the role of puppets as the police role in a democracy is not a puppet show.

When ruling political parties declare general *hartals/ bandhs* in India then the police become spectators to the atrocities committed by the *bandh* activists. Whenever political parties in opposition do the same, the police overenthusiastically initiate actions against the *bandh* activists. The double standards adopted in police praxes make the people suspicious of the police role in a democracy - suspicious of the extent of policing in police departments.

During the British rule, the police was the coercive force of the British Government in India. In a democracy, the police are public servants and are to enforce the laws as per the Constitution of India and the laws made thereunder.The policemen may approach courts of law for getting their rights established if and when they find the decision of the ruling Government is against their interests. During the colonial past, it was not possible for the police to go to courts against the decisions of the Government. There is a growing realization now that the undue influence exerted by the political parties in the ruling front put the police in difficulties. The power of transfers and postings which the Government enjoys make the political parties to make use of and misuse of police powers to their political advantage and others' disadvantage. Criticisms are sometimes levelled against political parties for their undue influence in police affairs. The unholy *nexus* and undesirable relations which some politicians establish with individual police officers/policemen or vice versa make police service unenviable - sometimes crime-prone or criminal. Whatever that may be, the political interference in police work has its positive and/or negative effects. Politicians can use and misuse the police power and uniform for their advantage just like individual policemen/officers use and misuse politicians for their advantage. Some policemen/officers, it is seen, surrender their power and authority before the politicians and how can they be called law enforcers who police the police to police the society?

Police Praxis After Independence

Police behaviour towards the public has been a major hurdle for the people to come closer to the police. What did the police do to bring the people closer? Before independence, the British never wanted the people to come to the police. They constructed walls and barriers between the people and the police. The European officers thought very big and they never mingled with the Indian public. Even Indian officers recruited to the middle level of police administration did not mingle with the common people. The middle level police functionaries in the police came from the upper castes and there were caste barriers too for them to mix and mingle with the people. They were better educated than the general public as they had S.S.L.C. as their qualification. How did the common man see the policemen and police officers? I have asked my father and father-in-law to tell me how they viewed the policemen? They lived in pre-independent and post-independent India. The word, police, itself produced a certain degree of pain in them. Seeing a policeman in pre-independent India was a torture for the people and therefore they withdrew from the very sight of the policemen. The police praxes were such that old women used to threaten their grand children by uttering the word "police" which for them was a human monster in uniform. The police just picked up the people and kept them in detention incommunicado. Everything the police did with the people in police custody was opaque to the public, to the kith and kin of the detained and to the detainees themselves. When India got freedom, the people still ran away from the police. Neither the Governments nor the police departments did anything meaningfully and honestly to bridge the gap between the people and their police in the newly formed democracy. The distance between the people and the police was maintained for a long time after independence. If some policemen/officers went to the people and established some good relationship, then it was considered to be a charity done to the general public. In police training centres, the importance of police - human relations was not told or taught. "People must come to the police" - attitude was entertained. To see a superintendent of police was a difficult task for a man on the street even during 1970s. An entry into the room of a superintendent of police was considered to be a rare privilege for the common man. The .303 rifles, the sentries, the rules, the regulations, the customs, etc., made things highly complicated and police public relationship has been an unattainable hope for many. Even in 1976, people could see the police officers only from a distance. Head constables were addressed as Esquires by the ordinary mortals. The higher-ups were "Their Lordships" for the common man. As a rule, the people had contacts with the constables/head constables and many did not go beyond them. The Central Committee Report on police training came out in 1973 and afterwards the higher-ups in the police started to feel that public cooperation and their willing participation were necessary for policing the police to police a democracy. They realized the fact that the people in a democracy did not want a militarized police force to police the society. They understood that the people had stronger power than the police and the police were only public servants to serve the people. What was more? They accepted the fact that the people were the police and the police were the people. But, the new perception of the police and their relationship with the public did not percolate down to the level of the constabulary.

Petty Ego, Ego Projections, Power, Pseudo-Authority and Policing

Although the police accepted the golden principle that the people were the police and the police were the people, they found it extremely difficult to put the principle into practice. It was not possible for them to have such a 'frog jump' from their pre-independence concepts of police and policing. I knew a police officer. He joined the police before India became independent. He was nicknamed as "Thalakanam" and the word meant "Headweight". "Headweight" in Malayalam culture has a special meaning and that is - a person who thinks too much about himself. In other words, he thinks that "I am the King and above Grammar". When "Thalakanam" was in police service, he exercised his police authority and pseudo-authority and certainly some people who had the bitter experience with him said: "Look, he is not a policed officer".

"Thalakanam" represents many in the police ; he is a legion and is found among directors general of police down to the constables. The higher one goes in rank, the more humble must he become - the more people friendly he must behave. But allegations are there that some do not. Why? Ego - false Ego - perverted Ego concepts create policing, false policing and perverted policing in a democracy. A change in one's Ego causes - must cause - corresponding change in one's perceptions. But such a change did not take place in the police functionaries when India became independent and the Europeans who occupied the higher posts in the police left the Country. Indians came to occupy their posts and they started to serve the people in Indian democracy with the *European police officers' ego*. They certainly did not have an ego to serve the people, rather their ego was to repress and suppress the people. Psychologists think that the failure to have a change in the police Ego when India became independent made the police to follow the same police praxes even when the power to rule was transferred to the people by the colonial administration.

The police in pre-independent India, historians think, to the surprise of sceptical colonial administration, remained very loyal to the European desires. They did not become people friendly, rather they remained remarkably resistant to the people's appeals to join in their endeavours to oust the British from India. The Congress made appeals, threats and entreaties, but in vain. Historians find that the colonial administration was very successful in getting police support to remain in power virtually to the last. David Arnold views: "The Congress never succeeded either in undermining the colonial police or in establishing a nationalist hegemony over them. When it took over the police in 1937 and again in 1946, it did so as the ministry in office, with an institutional and constitutional command of the police rather than an ideological ascendency. It was partly for this reason that the police were able to survive the return to direct British control at the end of 1939 and the shunt back to the returning Congress Ministry in 1946. The

Congress did not seriously try when in office to reorient the police by making them more accountable to the public, and even the attempts to make them answerable to the party were frustrated in 1937-38 and 1946-47. One of the most significant aspects of the colonial police - its public unaccountability - remained unchanged. The difference was that the police were now under the orders of an Indian government rather than a colonial administration".[6] The British historian frankly tells that the Congress did not seriously try to reorient the police by making them more accountable to the public. The governments which came to power from time to time made all attempts to make use of and misuse the police to their advantage. The *politicians in the police* made attempts to politicize the police to get more and more political advantages for them. The police functionaries established loyal relationship with the powerful politicians and made them more accountable to the politicians than to the public. The people in a democracy are the patrons of the police, but the politicians and the police did not think so, As a result, the public unaccountability of the police remained more or less unchanged until the passing of the Protection of Human Rights Act in 1993. Today, there is a greater awareness among the police functionaries that they are ultimately accountable to the people who are the tax-prayers. They realize the fact that hypersensitive self-importance is harmful to any profession, particularly to the police which is created and maintained for protecting the life and property of the people. They cannot and must not show annoyance and become intolerant to criticisms even when they are justified in their actions. Their performance will be counterproductive if their actions are not pregnant with integrity, morality, dignity and social sensitivity. They must be concerned with people and their welfare. If that is lacking in democracy's policing, it means that the police lacks proper policing. One reason for the police unaccountability to the public is traced to the excessive politicization of the police after independence. Allegations are there that the appointments to the post of the directors general of police in many States are politicized. Why think only of the appointments to the post of the directors general of the police? The appointments to every important post in the police are politicized! The tendency of misusing the government's power of appointment to various posts/positions in the police has been used for political purposes, advantages and benefits to the political parties in power and it is getting more and more strengthened in these days. If the tendency is not put down, policing the police becomes an unachievable pious wish. Police praxes are now tuned in such a way that the politicians and not the people are always happy and the trend is of bad taste. Any police officer who has occupied a particular post out of political patronage could not become accountable to the public. The decision and praxes of such police functionaries would be matters of considerable comments and speculations from the people, press and politicians themselves. Their actions and decisions would be more for the service of the political party which favoured them than for the people who paid them every month.

Indeed I hear complaints from many people against the head constables who manage matters at the police station level - against the superintendents of police who manage and manipulate matters at the district head quarters - against the directors general of police who do things to the advantage of the political parties which favour them to occupy the chair in police head quarters. They ask: "How do they police the society if they take decisions in favour of the political party which patronizes them? Are they not accountable to the public?" People expect the police in the civil service to be of the highest integrity and they want the law enforcement officers to be people of impartiality and independence in decision-making as per the law and procedure established by the law. They must not be people made of clay and can be moulded in any way. They must be men of principles and morality - men of legality and people friendliness - men of integrity, independence, impartiality and public accountability.

V.R. Krishna Iyer, a former Judge in the Supreme Court of India, in his article on *"A Jurist's Reflections on Indian Secularism"* writes about judicial functionaries as:

"To an extent, the judicial candidates disgrace the office by lobbying. Judges of the Supreme Court, selected from among the judges of the High Court or the Bar, must win the support of the Chief Executive who is the political leader of a party. His actions are often based on political mileage. So it is that aspirants lobby politically. It is a pity that many do canvas and ingratiate themselves into the favours even of local cadres. Some are seen shamelessly pacing anxiously the corridors of Shastri Bhavan; others go to the Law Minister, even the Attorney General". After reading so in his article, I posed for a moment and reflected on what was going on in the law enforcement fields? Yes, I can see police officers going with local level politicians - praying for favours from the service association leaders who have political patronage - waiting for the politicians in government guest houses - offering "pleasures" in the form of money and materials - prostrating before politicians when others are witnessing what they are doing. Why do they do so? The answer is obvious and the outcome is almost certain. How can they be accountable to the public? The Judge continues: "Indeed, weak Chief Justices, backing candidates, advise them to cultivate minister and attorney general, apart from the local party chiefs who have direct access to the Prime Minister. Nor is lobbying confined to political branch. Attempts are made to persuade the Chief Justice since he too has a voice and is human and has affections. All considerations, regional, communal, even gender based, old friendships and new relationships are passed into service both with the Chief Executive and the Chief Justice. Those who have no pull, however brilliant, may lose the race. Sometimes, a bargain is struck between the Chief Justice and the Chief Executive and unworthies make it. Many a manipulation, not printable, takes place ... since the whole operation is a kind of secret chamber negotiation unbecoming of a high public office". I stopped reading his article then and there as I could not imagine the underhand dealings in Indian democracy. Where are we going to?

My curiosity to read more observations of a learned Judge of the Supreme Court of India made me further to read the article. I read: "Names are in circulation but are suddenly jettisoned; new rumours jacking up the chances of hitherto unknown candidates surprise everyone. The entire wheeler-dealer business is unedifying and oftentimes, save where the political Government is very weak, the Chief Justice bends or bargains and the Chief Executive has his way". If this is what a Judge has to tell about the postings to the higher judiciary, the story is indeed painful and deplorable in the cases of appointment to the executive branches. Once an inspector general of police did not yield to the Home Minister's whim, then he found an asylum in a place more than 3000 kilometres from his home town. Another director general of police did object to the fanciful ideas of the Home Minister in policing the police, then he found his place in a newly created post for which no duties were assigned. One may enumerate any number of such real instances and any number of police officers who adore politicians and accept postings to do things in the way politicians want them to do. How can they police the police? Certainly, they will be able to politicize the police and their names may appear in the media as people of the ruling politicians. This has been a curse of Indian democracy and the situation is moving from bad to worse as years pass by. Are there any police praxes without political patronage? Researchers must study the problem in a deeper way; nevertheless, people complain that they require political patronage to get justice from the police even in simple petition inquiries to investigation of political murders. The laws do not have any relevance when politicians come to the field. The politicians are capable of getting cases registered, investigated, dropped or charge-sheeted. Even the specialized police agencies are not free from political interferences and as such the people lose their confidence in law, law enforcement and law enforcement machinery. The politicians of British India cried "Police Raj" when they saw the British Indian police repressing the people of India. Even today, the politicians of the opposition cry "Police Raj" when they see the politicized praxes of democracy's police. Once a political leader said: "I was beaten by the police as they were told by the ruling politicians to do so then. Now, we are in power and we can tell the police to beat our opponents". This is of bad taste. Governments come and go in a democracy, but the police remain for ever. Hence, politicians must not develop a feeling that they can manage and manipulate the police as they want when they are in power. No Government can rule the people in a democracy by terrorizing the people through the police. No government in a democracy can eliminate their political opponents through the power of the police. No democratic government can make the police a coercive power and the politicians must recognize the fact that no politician, however powerful he might be, ever could subdue the people by the strength of the police. The policemen/officers too must accept the fact that they have limits and limitations and a political power, however strong it may be, cannot and will not extend support to the police if they do things violating the law. The law can save the police and protect them - and only the laws will do so. Politicians can not do things which the law may do and therefore police praxes as per the law and procedure established by the law must win the confidence of the people.

Police Praxes during the Third Millennium

Everyone speaks about the *millennium police* and how they must be. No one wants to have a *police raj,* but at the same time, everyone favours community policing. But a police system that developed over a period between the Mutiny and independence had its praxes further developed over the last fifty years in a democratic set-up cannot jump into a new police system forgetting the past. The millennium police is therefore a continuation of the police system which was in existence in the country from 1850. During the 1890s, the military connection of the police was finally severed. Nevertheless, the police was given a military type training until the new syllabus proposed by Prof. M.S. Gore Committee (Central Committee on Police Training) was accepted by the States. The police in India as the coercive weapon of the colonial rule and as the oppressive force of the British imperialism could do marvellous jobs against Swadeshi movement and the Home Rule agitation,[1] Non-cooperation and the Khilafat, Civil Disobedience and Quit India, labour unrest, Kissan movements and rural insurrection, etc. The colonial police were anti-people and after India became independent, they continued to work as a repressive and oppressive force depending upon the desires of the governments and political parties in power. The police could never function as an independent agency for law enforcement. In order to make the governments stronger and stronger against their political opponents, each government which came to power from time to time strengthened and increased the police force. The police was not treated as a service by many political parties till recently. Millennium police means a police service which is people friendly. As a result, the police become accountable to the public. They become transparent and the millennium police cannot afford to become opaque in their transactions. Policing the police to police the society means accountability and transparency. The aloofness from and the unaccountability to the public will never be tolerated by the people in the third millennium. The role of the police in a democracy becomes more prominent now; but it must not become more controversial. The police is maintained by the people in a democracy and precisely therefore they are not to serve the political whims and fancies of the ruling politicians and political parties. The police are accountable to the people and not to the political parties in power. The police in the past enjoyed immunity from prosecution for many of their acts. The British wanted it to misuse the police strength to their advantage. But, in the millennium, the police may not be enjoying immunity from prosecution as they used to have in the past. The police will not be free to use violence, including the use of firearms. Everything will be scrutinized by several official and unofficial agencies including civil minded people, the press and the media. The police in the third millennium have to play a lot of positive roles - protective roles - promising roles. The frequency of police violence or State sponsored violence will come down and the third millennium police will develop better police - people relationship. The police praxes will be tuned accordingly. The police relations with nexus criminals, underworld and Mafia operators, politicians and the affluent will be watched and their alignment with them will be checked and controlled by the people and the press. The transfer of power on 15 August, 1947 did not effect any change to alter the intrinsic character of the police. The basic structure remained as it was in the past and even today in 2002 A.D., the basic structure of the police remains unaltered. The gap between the rank and file and the departmental superiors has not narrowed since 1947. But, the formation of police associations has strengthened the ranks and they are in a stronger position to look after their interests with the wholehearted support of the higher/highest echelons in the police. The millennium will see further strengthening of the activities of police associations. The authority of the superior ranks over their lower rank is getting more and more reduced. A human rights friendly approach within the police department becomes an urgent need of the hour in the third millennium. The fifty years since independence have done nothing much to enhance the overall prestige of the police. At the same time, the corruption and *nexus dealings* of the middle and top levels were exposed over and over again by the media. The prestige of the police thus has gone low in the recent past. The brutality, partiality and favouritism of the police become topics of discussion in the press, the media and the public. Acquittals of criminal cases go up and the professionalism of the police is suspected. To quote the British historian David Arnold again: "If anything, the reputation of the police is worse now than it was at the time of the 1902 Police Commission or during the Civil Disobedience Movement of the early 1930s. While becoming no more answerable to the public than in the past, the police have fallen increasingly under the politicians' sway. The politicians are the new masters, to whom the police show deference and obey".[7] What is there to speak about police praxis and policing the police to police the society during the third millennium?

References

1. David Arnold, *Police Power and Colonial Rule: Madras 1859, 1947*, Oxford University Press, Delhi, 1986.
2. Anandswarup Gupta, *The Police in British India: 1861-1947*, Concept Publishing Co., Delhi, 1979.
3. David Arnold, *op.cit.*
4. *Ibid.*
5. Manila Conference on the Law of the World, August 26, 1977.
6. David Arnold, *op.cit.*
7. *Ibid.*

8

Police Power, Philosophy and Policing the Police

People may enforce the law in any society more than what the police do or can do about it. I made a study on the increase/decrease of crimes in India from 1901 to 2002 A.D. I could learn that the crimes showed increased/decreased trend irrespective of the increase/decrease in police strength. The police history of India showed that crimes were on the increase when the strength of the police was increased. The explanation then was that the more the police, the more will be the detection of crimes. O.K., agreed; nevertheless, the crimes decreased considerable during the following year. Why? The explanation was that the more the police, the less will be the commission of crimes. Amidst these arguments pro and contra for the increase in police strength or in crime statistics, the fact remains that crimes do occur in spite of and amidst the police. People commit crimes, because people want to commit crimes. People do not commit crimes, because people do not want to commit crimes. Applying the same analogy to the police, we may say that the police become policed, because the police want to be policed. They become not policed, because they do not want to be policed. Police want the people to be policed and the people want the police to be policed. What are the crimes committed by the police? They commit all types of crimes which people commit in a society. Also, they commit special types of crimes which they can do with some immunity from prose-cution as they are policemen/officers. Examples are:

(1) custodial torture,
(2) concoction of evidence, and
(3) acceptance of corruption money.

The policemen/officers are a privileged community in so far as they are able to commit crimes and cover them up without being detected. If police situations have tongues to speak, then many police crimes would have come up. When the foundation of a police station was dug, people could see nine human skulls. This is an old story in a remote village in India, but the people still speak of the same. Certainly, each human skull would reveal some stories which could be crimes.

Police Power, Authority and Policing

A person who has the power and authority can use/misuse his power and authority. A policeman may arrest a person who commits a cognizable offence; he can as well ignore it. If questioned, he may say that he did not see the crime being committed. When I was seven years old, a person was stabbed to death on the day of a church festival in the church compound. Hundreds of people witnessed the incident. A murder in the church compound! No one reported the matter to the police for about two hours. At last, the vicar of the church informed the police and he said: "Let the police do their job; or what else are we paying them for?" The police have the power to investigate criminal cases and they have the authority to arrest, interrogate, raid,. search, detain, interview, etc. In the above case, the police did many things, but the case was acquitted by the court. Recently, when I went to the village, I saw the murderer in the church compound. He happily told me that he was not punished by the court and he added: "The police were inefficient to investigate crimes". Yes, he might be true.

Nevertheless, inefficiency in police work is not a crime. The penal laws do not define inefficiency as a crime. If a police officer becomes purposefully inefficient, still it is not a crime.

Once I found a college boy running away from a scene of law and order. I asked him: "Why do you run away?" He told me that the "police have just arrived". I asked him: "Still, why do you run away?" He told me: "They have power and authority. They can order for a lathy-charge or can fire at the mob". I thought then: "Let him run away as fast as he can".

There is a difference between an ordinary man and a policeman. If an ordinary man is injured in a lathy-charge, the police may register a criminal case against him and he may not get any financial help for treatment. On the contrary, if a policeman is injured on duty, he gets protection. He is covered by hospitalization at government expense. Usually no criminal case may be registered against him even if he becomes aggressively atrocious to the members of a mob. The people with power and authority are privileged in many ways and precisely therefore lack of policing or non-policing in them is not considered as serious defects.

An innocent person found at a scene of law and order management was beaten up - hospitalized - charge-sheeted for committing a criminal offence. What moral, legal or satisfactory explanations have the police to give to such atrocities on the people whose human rights are recognized. I asked this question to a police officer. He told me: "If no criminal case is registered against such people, even if they are innocent, then they will register criminal cases against policemen/officers who managed the law and order situation". There is a point in what the police say - and what the victims of police actions speak. A dilemma exists and no solutions! Can we say that the police is not properly policed in such situations?

The police officers of the General Executive Branch face greater dilemmas. Under the existing laws, they enjoy power and authority to use force at a scene of law and order management. Often, they have the policemen of the district Armed Reserves/Armed Battalions. The policemen/officers of the Armed Reserves/Battalions are caged men. Their interactions with the people are minimum. When they are given orders for a lathy charge, they do it, more often than not, in an aggressive way. First of all, these armed men are unaccountable as the accountability is generally fixed on the police officers of the General Executive/District Magistrate present at the spot. Lack of policed policemen in Battalions/Armed Reserves can cause serious headaches for the officers of the General Executive. If paramilitary police force is used, they may do more harm than what is required. They have no accountability and they enjoy immunity from prosecution for what they do under the orders of a competent authority. They possess 'docile human bodies' to execute superior orders with immunity from prosecution.

British Regime and Police Atrocities

There are no statistical accounts to show how many times the police of the colonial regime lathy-charged Indians, fired on them and tortured them. Torture was institutionalized by the British police in India. Torture by the police was not a news in imperialistic rule, for imperialism implied torture as well. According to some studies conducted by British researchers, India did have more than adequate strength in the police to suppress/repress the people who agitated against the British rule. After the independence too, the police in India have been widely employed to manage law and order situations. If the British did enact a law, then it was more for their advantage than for that of the Indians. The British policed the police not to serve the people of India, but to act as a coercive force to subdue the people to the British wishes. "Might is right" - the British believed and they became mightier every day by increasing the number of the police force. The number of the police force in India during 1913 was as under :

Police Forces in India, 1913

Province	Average population per policeman
Bombay	773
United Provinces	1,299
Central Provinces	1,155
Bihar and Orissa	2,537
Bengal	2,181
Madras (1014)	1,257

Source: G.O. 2561, Jdl, 23 Oct. 1915, INA

What was the need to appoint so many policemen in India? The intentions were obvious and they enjoyed seeing the Indian policemen fighting against their own brethren. They understood that the more aggressive and atrocious the Indian policemen were towards their brethren, the more successful they were in subduing the Indians to the British rule. They encouraged the policemen to be mercilessly ruthless towards the Indians. That was the policing of the police by the British.

Laws, Power and Policing

Once I saw a superintendent of police reading a novel - *God of Small Things* - after a cruel lathy-charge in the city. There was blood on the roads, broken lathies, chappals, stones, etc., were scattered everywhere. Injured human bodies were being treated in the nearby Government hospitals and the superintendent of police in a cool - very cool temper - was enjoying- reading a novel.

Yes, some people release their tension by that way too. The pressmen, politicians and the people were rushing to the spot - taking photographs - discussing - organizing *jadhas* and street corner meetings - press conferences and the superintendent of police reads a novel!

A strange phenomenon !

Seeing the behaviour of the superintendent of police, his batch mate - another superintendent of police asked him: "What are you doing, man?"

The superintendent of police just smiled and said: "An imperialistic Government has enacted laws which empowered the police to use force to disperse unlawful assemblies and to repress the people. Why do you worry then?"

Yes, there is a point in what he says!

Hence the middle level police functionaries will see to it that the *'papers'* are made legally perfect so that the police can justify their actions. The police in British India enjoyed vast powers to employ force on the people and the 1973 Code of Criminal Procedure reproduced the sections which contained in the earlier Code. Police in free India cannot and should not become cruel to the people as the British police could afford to do. The police in India are accountable and the people want them to be more policed than the police of colonial India. The British police officer might give orders to lathy-charge/fire from a remote place, but the Indian police officer has to be on the spot to give orders. Today, one may see senior/very senior police officers on the trouble spots and they see to it that the police actions are justified - are so policed that the police are not criticized. Yet, the reading of the novel is too much! People ask: "what type of man is he when the people bleed on the road and in hospitals?".

The superintendent of police was transferred immediately afterwards. He was not a well policed policeman. A lathy-charge is not a pleasant spectacle. It is a spectacle that the people do not want to see. In every lathy-charge, there remains a trace of 'torture' and the police who torture the people are criticized and condemned by many in society. Fifty or sixty years ago, the people in India received blows from the policemen and suffered them. Today, they go to lawyers and to the press to consult them for initiating legal action and for giving wide publicity on police atrocities or interpreted atrocities on the people. In a democracy, no police action dies as it comes up often for attacking the ruling political parties. Opinion surveys on policing the police show that people are unhappy about police brutality, prejudices and cynicism in performing their job in many situations and especially in a law and order situation where they often show excessive enthusiasm to use excessive force. It is said that a trained policeman in lathy-drill and in mob-operations and caged in a police battalion or barrack feels excessively jubilant when he is offered an opportunity to express his skill and talents. In a law and order situation, the policeman who uses the lathy does not often have any accountability as the accountability is fixed on the higher levels of administration.

I have observed many policemen/officers at the scenes of law and order management. I have noted well policed police officers who were calm and collected. I have also seen police officers/policemen who were very much disturbed and who showed symptoms of excessive anxiety to deal with the situation. The laws are the same - the police powers are the same, but the way a situation is managed differs from individuals to individuals. I find that the personality of the policeman/officer is an important factor in determining how he performs his role as a policed policeman/officer. Police officers who possess a personality pregnant with suspicion shall never be sent to a law and order situation to take decisions. For, they suspect everything and everybody. They give orders accordingly. The police officers who have special affinity to political parties must not be entrusted with duties to deal with situations having political significance. They may interpret the gestures, language or behaviour to be either in favour of or against their political likings/linkages. They may use/misuse/abuse their power and authority to tackle the situation.

Police officers are taught laws - particularly the provisions in the Indian Penal Code, Code of Criminal Procedure, Indian Evidence Act. They are also taught the provisions of law in Special and Local Acts. They are taught what is required for them to perform their duties as policemen/officers. Officers of the General Executive Branch are taught more laws than those in the Armed Reserves/Armed Battalions. A little knowledge is always dangerous and as such they do not get a total vision of the laws, rule of law, rule of justice when they undergo training in a police academy/training centre.

Police officers are taught more about laws that they can use against the people. If they are taught by the police officers, then they are kept ignorant of how the laws can be used against them. Moreover, many policemen/officers get a wrong impression that they will always be on the side of the prosecution. A total vision of the laws, their applicability in a democracy, police accountability in their actions, etc., may not be made available to a raw recruit in a police training institution and whose academic background may be anything other than law and law enforcement. I think that many policemen/officers are transformed into authoritarian personalities by virtue of their ignorance about their role in a democracy and due to the lack of knowledge in law, social sciences and public relations. Coupled with their authoritarian/pseudo-authoritarian personality, they have a special love for power and toughness. I have noted the manner of "walking" or "strutting" in some policemen/officers, especially those in the higher echelons and it signifies to me that they simply love power, authority and toughness. The British made the policemen as tough as possible and they gave a militarized training. For they wanted ferocious policemen/officers in India. After India became independent, no conscious and honest attempts were made for a considerably long period to sober down the ferocious nature of the policemen/officers. As a result, they continued to love power and toughness. They wanted to frighten, threaten and deter the public. As a counterthrust to the police toughness, atrocities and actions, the people started attacking the police back and thus the number of policemen injured or attacked gets increased every year. Even during the rigid British rule, the policemen were attacked and killed by the people. Lack of policing in the police may invite public reaction against the police. In many parts of the country, policemen are attacked and the reasons for it must be identified; remedial measures must be initiated.

I for one think that there is something wrong somewhere in the police training. For, I find that unnecessary authoritarianism and pseudo-authoritarianism is increased while the police training is in progress and after the police training. Some trainees go out of the training centres and quarrel with the civilian public. On inquiry, it may be clear that many such quarrels have a beginning or start in the show of authoritarianism or pseudo-authoritarianism among the police trainees. What I have observed is that the authoritarianism which starts during the induction training period gets further aggravated within one year after the institutional training. I notice that some trainees who sir their teachers when they are in the training institution call them by name - without showing any respect to them - within one year after their induction training. Officers of the higher echelons are found to be worse in their show of authoritarianism/pseudo-authoritarianism. With police vehicles, policemen around, lathies and rifles, handcuffs and canes, wireless sets and telephones, law books and authority, some police officers become blind and do not see many realities in front and around them. They become authoritarian and attack the people with this attitude. They forget the fact that they are only police officers with limits and limitations in their authority.

I take note of the fact that some police officers do not know the difference and distinction between authority and authoritarianism. Authority means the power or command over others. It includes misuse of authority and abuse of power. When an authority is misused/abused, then it is called authoritarianism. Rational authority means the power or command over others based on genuine ability, competence, justness and fairness. How many police officers can claim that they possess such qualities. If they do not have such qualities, then they are not policed police officers. If the police exercise their authority properly, legally, morally and with an upright conscience, then the attitude of the people will be submissive, tolerant, adjusting, responding, docile, listening, obeying, proactive, recognizing and accepting. But do we find such public attitudes to the police? If we do not find such public attitudes to the police, it means that the police are showing authoritarianism instead of authority. Public attitude to authoritarianism will be violent, intolerant, reactionary, contemptible, disobeying, resisting, non-accepting and criticising. Why do the people criticize the police? My studies convince me to subscribe to the view that the police are authoritarian in their behaviour. Even after fifty years of freedom under a democratic rule, the police in India have yet to understand the vanity of authoritarianism.

I observe that the more time a person spends in the police garb, the more authoritarian he becomes unless he learns the vanity and meaninglessness of authoritarianism. The increased authoritarianism is likely to damage police image and reputation. Some police officers think that their occupation/profession/job is such that they have to be authoritarian in their approaches to the people. But, they fail to understand that the police officers who do not show any authoritarian attitude/approach perform their job better than those who exhibit authoritarian attitude/approaches not only in India but also in many foreign countries where policemen think that theirs is a profession/job created by the people not to show authoritarianism, but to exercise just authority and power over the people who live under their responsible care and protection.

Demands of the Immediate Situation during Law and Order Management

Some policemen/officers say that they do not possess the qualities of 'irisis' (sages or seers) when they manage law and order situations. Of course, the police have a lot of discretion when they take decisions, but human weaknesses and frailties may play their role. They do not and cannot see everything in its totality so much so that mistakes do occur. It is not non-policing or lack of policing, but rather these are human frailties in police actions. The policeman at a scene of law and order management relies on the characteristics and special features of the immediate situation in making decisions.

In order to assess the law and order situation and to make advance planning, the police have a good set-up. The intelligence wings under the superintendent of police and under the State Police Branch are meant to collect information on law and order situations. Their failure to collect intelligence or a *'don't care'* attitude to the information furnished by them make the police to have a poor show at a law and order situation. Are the intelligence units properly trained to offer professional service to the police in the operational/field level? This is a point to be discussed at length. Experts on police management of law and order situations are skeptical about the professionalism in the collection of intelligence and its dissemination for effective enforcement of law. The intelligence wings may be able to make a fair assessment of the perceived risk in an anticipated law and order situation. The police officers in the field can make an objective assessment of the actual risk at the real scene of law and order management. Often complaints are heard that the police managed the law and order situation in a non-professional way because of the lack of adequate police strength. The intelligence wing failed to provide a factual report and other details. Immediately, the intelligence wing may be shuffled and new people are appointed. Are they sufficiently trained to offer professional service? How are the new ones better than the old ones?

Adhocism is another curse in police management of law and order. Lack of proper training and the impact of improper training are other factors of non-policing/lack of policing during a law and order situation. Total surrender to the political wishes and politicians' demands are other factors. The police may be active/very active if that is the desire of the political party in power. Besides and beyond the political interests, the police have the Constitution in front of them and the laws made thereunder. Political patronage for the law and order management is not professionalism in the police. Maintaining law and order is one thing and investigating crimes is quite another. The professionalism required for maintaining law and order is not the professionalism required for the investigation of crimes. The British gave little or no importance to the investigation of crimes. Their interest was on the maintenance of law and order. They did not want professionalism in law and order management, rather they wanted, as said elsewhere, a brutal police force to repress the people in India. They were not accountable to anyone. Like a military force, they could do anything. But in a democracy, police brutality is disfavoured. Professionalism in crime investigation is often questioned in courts of law. Sometimes, the Government interfere and the investigation of crime is transferred from the local police to the crime investigation branch. The question is: "Are the investigators in the crime investigation branch professionals in their work?" Any police officer can be posted in any unit of the police department and one's posting in the crime investigation branch does not mean that he is necessarily a professional in the investigation of crimes. Crimes are of many kinds and professionalism means professionalism with respect to the special nature of the crimes under investigation. A specialist in the investigation of crime needs not necessarily be a specialist in the investigation of traffic offences. Today, we read in the paper that a share-broker in Mumbai is arrested and it means that it needs special and professional investigation which is different from the investigation of petty thefts and burglary. So long as the police do not become professional they cannot get public trust and confidence.

Use of Violence to Coerce Respect

During the British rule, the people in India were illiterate or moderately literate; but they had power and authority which they could use or abuse at their discretion. Instances are plenty to show that the policemen of pre-independent India misused their power to coerce respect for them. In an island of blind men, a one-eyed man is a respected person. Likewise, in a colony of illiterate people, the moderately educated policemen with some power and authority ought to be respectable. But history shows that the policemen then were not a respectable lot. In order to coerce respect from the people, they used to become aggressive, arrogant and abusive towards the people. The people showed an outward respect to the policemen, but in their heart of hearts, they had contempt for the police uniform. When India became independent, the people started expressing their contempt for the police uniform. The people started expressing their contempt in many ways in the newly created liberal democracy. The people became more and more educated. Technocrats, lawyers, management experts, chartered accountants, computer engineers, scientists, criminologists, marketing specialists and so on came out from universities in large numbers. The literacy rate in the country went up. Policemen/officers deal with people who are more educated and qualified. Before the technocrats, experts and specialists, police officers with one year's training in the academy/police colleges cannot and do not command respect. As a result, they demand respect. This is otherwise called coercing respect. If they do not get it, then they become angry and antagonistic to the people. They express non-police behaviour. They become violent and human rights unfriendly in their interaction with the people. The police must get the respect of the people through their expertise in law and order management, crime investigation or other types of police activities. What is to be achieved by education, intellectual training and acquisition of knowledge cannot be obtained by threats or use of violence. Knowledge is power and the policemen are to accept the truth that their muscles, bayonets, lathies, shells, bullets, epithets, cells, handcuffs, torture, etc., have no meaning or relevance in the years to come. At the same time, professional police work and policed police service will pay rich dividends. Galliher and McCartney write: "...policemen use the resource of violence to persuade their audience (the public) to respect their occupational status. In terms of the policeman's definition of the situation, the individual who lacks respect for the police, the 'wise guy' who talks back, or any individual who acts or talks - in a disrespectful way, deserves brutality".[1] How can the police demand respect where their behaviour does not command respect? How can a police officer who is inferior in education claim superiority in education before people who are highly educated? Non-sense is not respected by people who accept sense. A forensic expert who works as a scientific assistant may be honoured higher than an additional director general of police who heads the crime investigation branch if he does not possess good knowledge in forensic and police sciences. One thousand police interrogators will be sent out by a single professionally qualified police interrogator. About 10-15 years ago, there were *'veteran'* police interrogators who were famous/notorious for their interrogation techniques including third degree methods. Now, they are rejected and condemned by their own one-time admirers who appreciate professionally qualified interrogators who are human rights friendly in their approaches.

Sanctions Against Non-Police Strategies

Over several decades before and after independence, policemen/officers have been criticized for their non-police, cruel and brutal methods of policing by many people and agencies including courts of law. Yet, enviable result is not seen. Why? Is it due to the refusal of the police to accept the truth or is it due to the helplessness of the department that the deplorable state of affairs remains even in the third millennium? To quote, Galliher and McCartney once again: "...policemen cannot and do not employ sanctions against their colleagues for using violence, and individual men who personally condemn the use of violence and avoid it whenever possible refuse openly to condemn acts of violence by other men on the force".[2]

In the history of the police in India, many Commissions of Inquiry were ordered to probe into the police use of violence, custodial deaths, custodial violence, custodial rape, etc., and many Commissions of Inquiry did say that the police did them in a non-police manner - or there was lack of policing in police departments. But how many police officers would come forward to speak out openly the truth even when they were fully aware that the police were wrong? The National Police Commission: 1977-81 was candid enough to admit that even departmental inquiries conducted against police officers brought out conclusions which were suspicious in nature. Does it mean that there exists a sort of group support from the police for the prevailing situation which is deplorable. The police are not policed to police the society and they misuse/abuse their power/authority to do injustice in society.

Skolnick writes that a policeman becomes more dependent on another policeman because he feels isolated from the public. While I agree with Skolnick, I think that there is something called a *uniform affinity* in policemen. Each policeman represents the police department and many a time policemen work in groups. Hence people think that policing/lack of policing is a group phenomenon in the police. The policemen do their parade, drill, mob-operation, lathy-charge, house search, raids, etc., together and the togetherness make the police a single source of power and force. Some policemen/officers think that they together form a service while others view that they are a force. Whether or not the police in a democracy is a service or a force is an issue which is not settled so far. If they accept that the police in a democracy is a service, then policing the police becomes easy. But, some policemen/officers think that all police functions cannot be put under service functions. The enforcement of law and maintenance of order are not police services. That is a perception, yet there are policemen/officers who have different perceptions on the police and police functions. Comparing the police in the British past to the police in the third millennium, I think that the police today are less violent. Today's policemen/officers consider police jobs as more services than as police coercion. Hence, non-policing/lack of policing has no scope in democracy's police work.

Non-Police Ways: The Best Way to Solve Issues and Problems

For immediate result, non-police ways are found to be good. Once an army officer took his L.M.G. and fired at the people. Many died and he uttered: "This is the only language you understand". Can we do so in a democracy? Can the police do so against their own brethren? Torture may yield a confession even from an innocent person. Once I told some police officers the need for applying scientific methods for the investigation of crimes and interrogation of suspects. One of them reacted saying that these scientific ways and psychological methods were not good always and they did not yield immediate results. He advocated for the use of crude methods and I found him to be "argument proof". Then I said: "O.K., you apply your crude methods and suffer the consequences".

There may be many easy methods and short-cuts. They may yield good results, but are they legally acceptable? The police did many such atrocities in the past, but they were then not accountable. Today, the police are accountable to many and the people want policing the police first before they police the society.

Recently a deputy superintendent of police told me that the politicians of the ruling party in Government would not allow the police to perform their duties in an honest way. He was working in a place where there were frequent conflicts between two political parties. People were killed quite suddenly and the police were not allowed to arrest the real culprits. The politicians would interfere in the police work and they would assure that they could produce the culprits. They would bring some party workers as culprits and the police would be forced to arrest them knowing fully well that they were innocent people. If the police did not do so, then they would be harassed, transferred and persecuted. What kind of policing could be ensured then to the people particularly when the police themselves were found to be unable to police them? Surely, they would be the non-police methods, but could be the only methods in the changed socio-political climate. If the Indian police are prone to use some illegal and non-police tactics and methods, it means that the Indian society offers them the means and the climate to do so. The question then is: "how to remedy the situation?" A further question is: "How long can we tolerate the system?" People say that whenever there is a conflict of interest between the politicians and the police, many police functionaries protect the interest of the politicians and regulate the behaviour of the people so that they can protect their own self interest. This is not policing and it can never be. The police power is a people's trust and the police authority has a fiduciary component. The oath of office clearly implies the responsibility of the police to police themselves and the society. The Constitution of India guarantees justice to every citizen. The police ought to do so and the people have that trust on the police. To betray that trust is a sin against humanity; it is to bankrupt the institution of the police itself.

Police Methods and Non-Police Methods

I asked in a class consisting of college teachers: "What do you understand by police methods?" They said many methods and they included torture, harassment, connection, manipulation, victimization and thus the litany of the items was very long. I said that they had wrong notions about police methods. I added that police methods would be any method which would be fair, decent, just, human rights friendly, honest, etc. But, they did not seem to accept my view. According to them, what I told them were non-police methods. They said that experience was the best teacher for them and their experience with the police did not make them to subscribe to my views on police and non-police methods. Humanizing the police to police the police - that was what the college teachers told me. O.K., I asked the same question: "what do you understand by police methods?" to a batch of police officers.

They too answered my question exactly the way the college teachers said. I found congruence in their answers and thereafter I used to say to many that police methods meant decent, people-friendly, fair and just methods. But, one day I was shocked to listen to a superintendent of police who angrily uttered: "Don't compel me to employ police methods" and I understood that he meant the use of torture and violence. Police methods somehow or other got a foul meaning - i.e., torture, degrading and inhuman treatment to people. People saw the methods from the British past to the democratic present. It is therefore a herculean task to wipe out the public impressions about police methods.

Take for instance the arrest patterns in India. The majority of those arrested by the police are people who are not influential or otherwise powerful. Why? Allegations are heard that the police offer discriminatory treatment to those under arrest depending upon their status, position, influence, affluence, etc. Verbal and physical harassment may be offered to political orphans or to the economically handicapped. Joseph Lohman, a police officer once said: "The police function is to support and enforce the interests of the dominant political, social and economic interests of the town, and only incidentally to enforce the law".[3] If this is a true observation, the Constitution does not have any value. The power vested with the police must be utilized for the best interest of the people. But, history shows that the British misused it for their political and economic interests. The political parties after the independence of India abused it for their political advantage. The nexus between the politicians and the police became a burden for the people. As a result, corruption, enforcement criminality, Mafia operations, political exploitation and politicians' abuse of police power, etc. came into being. Different political parties have different aims to be achieved by the police and the police often applied the *principle of equilibrium* - i.e., they wanted to protect their interests by serving all the political parties as far as they could and avoiding criticism from the politicians. However, the *principle of equilibrium* is not easy to be achieved as each political party has its own special interests. Every political party that comes to power thinks that the police is a part of the political party and the politicians expect the police to play its part for the advantage of the party. The top level politicians expect the police to honour their small scale politicians so that their political party grows up from the grass root level. Some policemen/officers faithfully obey the politicians and they do so more for their personal advantage than for any political advantage. Nevertheless, there are policemen/officers who are proud to say that they belong to a particular political party and their mission is to see that the party makes political mileage through their service in uniform. Don't they have the accountability which they should have towards the people? What is meant by the social audit of police performance? The society does not and can not audit police performance from political angles. If the police force becomes political or becomes politicized, then inevitably credibility collapse will be the outcome. Some police officers may not register criminal cases against politicians. A crime is a crime, no matter whether it is committed by politicians of the highest level or by the poor men of the lowest level. The people see the difference in police approaches to the politicians and also to the slum-dwellers and they make social auditing. They pronounce judgements and according to some researchers, during the last fifty years of democratic rule, some police officers have not registered a single criminal case against certain politicians even when they were fully aware of their involvement in the commission of crimes; or even if they did register criminal cases, the cases were not seriously and objectively investigated. I quote the Bible: "If the salt has lost its savour, wherewith shall it be salted?".

What is lacking in the police? - morality? - legal sense?- Constitutional responsibility? Proper policing of the police? A performance audit by the public may show that a politicized police is a curse in any democracy. About the judges, V.R. Krishna Iyer said: "Some cowardly judges and opportunist brethren oblingingly bend their judgements when political heavy-weights and tycoons with clout happen to be parties".[4] If this is what is written by a former judge of the Supreme Court of India about his brethren in the judiciary, let the senior police officials speak about their brethren in the police service. But I am sure that there may not be many to speak as they lack the moral courage to say loudly about their felt feelings and impressions on the police-politicians *nexus*. To quote Justice V.R. Krishna Iyer once again: "Of course, politicians in or out of power and bureaucrats in or out of office sometimes commit shocking crimes"[5] and how can the people call it to be policing? *Nexus crimes,* police - politicians' *nexus, enforcement criminality* etc. are widely and frequently discussed in the media, the press and research papers. Police power, philosophy and policing the police receive a lot of importance in these days so much so that the social auditing of police performance is now accepted everywhere.

Police Powers and Limitations

No policeman/officer can please a politician for a long period. No policeman/officer can please all politicians alike at all times. A close contact with a politician means a rupture of relationship with him at a later time or with other politicians at the same time. If they are truths, then why do policemen/officers go closer to the politicians? The question was answered by a police officer who said: "The magnetic power of the politicians is such that only the policemen/officers who have an upright conscience and an unspoiled ego can or will escape the magnetic attraction". How many policemen/officers possess such resisting capacity? Many yield and become the political adherents of the politicians of the ruling Government. Many a time, it may be for temporary or pecuniary advantages and the politicians shower them lavishly so that they can misuse police powers for their political advantages.

The law may confer many powers on the police, but the politicians put limitations to the use of police powers for their political advantage. Study the contents of the telephone calls reaching the police stations, district and State police headquarters from the politicians. Count the number of "Don'ts" to the police and the researcher will be surprised to note the limitations exerted by the politicians on police functioning. Count the number of *"Dos"* to the police from the politicians and it will show the intensity of their demands to violate the laws for political advantages. The police officers sometimes say that the limitations put by the law on police powers are understandable and necessary; but the limitations imposed by the politicians on the police are un-understandable and illegal. What to do then? Either get out of the magnetic field of the politicians or yield to their whims and decisions. In any case, the politicians will be able to get things done in the way they want. The judiciary may be able to control the police and save the police from any political interference. The judiciary too has limitations to do so. Then, the question is: "How to police the police in the existing political climate?". One policeman told me: "...the purpose of policing today is to make friends with politicians and see that they like you. If a policeman reacts rough to them, naturally they will prosecute or victimize the poor policeman". As many policemen/officers at the bottom level come from the lower economic class background, it is easier for the politicians to bring them to their magnetic fields. Since a good number of the police officers at the middle and higher levels like to have power and authority for actualizing their vested interests, they too can be brought to the magnetic field of the politicians. The social audit of police performance for the last 50 years of democracy shows that the law enforcement has not been primarily for the protection of the general welfare of the society, but was for the protection of the interests of those holding power, money, respectability and authority. The National Police Commission too expressed a similar view, but were helpless to see that their recommendations were accepted by the governments which subsequently came to power.

Police Power and Money Power

Police power or money power: which is the more powerful to police the police? The emergence of *nexus criminality* - i.e., the police-politician-businessman relationship-opens new areas for deliberations in academic and administrative circles. The police functionaries have been found often supplementing their regular salaries by accepting monthly pay-offs from the affluent Mafia criminals and underworld operators in exchange for their official support to what activities they do. The poor policemen thus became rich and the rich ones became richer and richer all on a sudden and surprisingly for many did so. The policemen know the methods of selling their power and authority for pecuniary advantages and the affluent - the Nexus Operator - know the methods of cashing on the police powers for their advantages. The unholy relationship and *nexus* dealings gave birth to *goondaism*, corruption, political murders, *enforcement criminality* and many other types of crimes. Policemen were thus called criminals in uniform by the press and the media. The criminalization of the police captured research attention and many articles on the subject appeared in print. Some researchers said that the police could essentially serve only the private interests of big businessmen at the expense of the general public and also serve their own vested interests. Amidst these exaggerated versions and interpretations of police-businessmen nexus, some policemen/ officers were detected to have involved themselves in nefarious activities and *nexus* transactions. Whenever the police become weak, *rowdies* parade the street and tax-payers become alarmed of the safety and security of their lives. Some unofficial estimates show that there are as many as 700-900 *rowdy-gangs* in medium size cities having a population of 7-9 lakhs.

India has a history of police which was military in character and the British regime made use of their police force to suppress and repress the riotous disorders. When the country became democratic, the military or paramilitary nature of the police became thinner and thinner. Not only that, they started establishing unholy relations with the unscrupulous politicians and bandits of the underworld. As a result, riots became so frequent that the police could not suppress them by employing military forces in an effective way. Every riot in a democracy has its political patronage and the politicians who patronize the riots, chaos, crimes and banditry are the people who patronize the police as well. Police laws, police powers and police authority thus become ineffective for sustained law enforcement. The lack of policemen/officers with values and principles might be one reason for the development of non-policing of police departments.

Police and Prevention of Crimes

The police in a democracy are to prevent the commission of crimes. The glory of an army uniform for the Indian police helped them to perform their job in a meaningful way. The army uniform, the lathies, the pistols, the rifles, etc., which the police have, do help them to maintain public order - to prevent crimes. But recently reports are seen in the press that the police have become inactive - immobile when political tensions take place - when politicians involve themselves in the commission of crimes. Why? Researchers attest to the view that the police and the legal system serve thc interest of the powerful politicians more than the interest of the people in a democracy. To the people in the slums, the police show roughness and they do so for ensuring that they respect the policemen and also to maintain law and order. But the same roughness is not shown to the powerful and the affluent. The police adopt a double standard in their approaches to the powerful and the weak. Lack of power for the people might prompt the police to employ roughness and to ignore the "due process" in law enforcement. "How many policemen/officers will make a pledge that they will simply refuse to comply with the requests of the powerful, of the affluent, of the politically influential for favours for themselves and their friends?" - I asked this question to a batch of policemen/officers and none of them replied to the question. Most them asked me a dozen counter-questions and I was made to answer their questions. Some explained their difficulties to answer my questions while others quoted a number of examples which amply proved that those who refused the requests from the powerful, the affluent and the influential had to pay for their refusal and to suffer the consequences. Sometimes the police are below the men who are above the law. In such instances, the police are forced to protect the gambling dens, bootlegging business and Mafia operations. The prevention of crime is an impossible task and policing the police or policing the society in such cases becomes a mockery in its real sense. The mimicry artists mock at the police and the police laugh at the mimicry of their own functioning. In films and other cultural programmes, the policeman is mocked at and their meaningless attempts to prevent crimes are exposed to the public who laugh at the police. Just recently, a political leader was convicted for corruption/ corrupt practices and he was jailed. After a few days, he was released on bail from the jail. Thousands of partymen came in hundreds of vehicles to receive the "political leader" and they shouted anti-police slogans and fooling the police signifying the meaning: "Do what you want and we have our leader to lead us". The policemen felt humiliated and some of them shouted slogans in their mind supporting the political leader who became a "hero" just because a crime against him was investigated and he was convicted. The political leader challenged the police and the legal system and said that he would take the case to the "People's Court" for their final judgement. He is contesting for the election and an opinion poll-survey in his constituency shows that he is sure to win the election. Once again he becomes a M.L.A. and leader. The police who investigated the case and got him convicted might be victimized if he were to exercise his power unjustly after the election. Researchers have to find out solutions to such issues which the police in a democracy face today. Another political leader was arrested by the police and got the leader convicted. There are appeals against the convictions and it is now learnt that the political party is likely to return to power. If that takes place, then what will happen to the policemen/officers who investigated the crimes? There is uncertainty and there exists a possibility of victimization of the policemen/officers.

Researchers have to find out solutions to such dilemmas faced by the police functionaries. When one political party comes to power, the politicians including the ministers involve themselves in several corrupt practices and *nexus* transactions. When another political party comes to power, they order for the investigation of the many transactions/dealings by the politicians in the previous government. Sometimes special investigation teams are constituted to conduct the investigation. Lakhs and lakhs of public money are spent by the investigating team and sometimes they may leave the investigation half way and at other times, they may complete the investigation. In the meantime, a lot of things happen in politics and the politicians become one with other politicians to fight against the policemen. There is no permanent friend or enemy in politics. But the police investigation has a harassment value and the police investigators become targets of political vengeance and vindictiveness. There are any number of cases in which the politicians of the ruling government misuse police authority to harass the politicians of the opposition. The damage done to the reputation of the police department by these unscrupulous politicians is very severe and the police investigators victimized to the maximum. How can the police be policed if the politicians are people of dubious integrity? Some cases against certain politicians are investigated for many years or even several decades and the result is a big "zero". Of course, the politicians get political mileage by such police investigations.

I know the case of a senior police officer. As soon as a new government came into power, a number of vigilance probes were ordered against him. The officers in the vigilance and anti-corruption department honestly felt that the intention of the vigilance probes was just harassment and victimization. How far can the police powers be misused/abused by the people having no principles, values and philosophy is an area that needs further research and reflection. Looking at the injustices practised and perpetuated in the law enforcement department, one safely comes to the conclusion that policing the police is just a dream or a pious wish. If crimes are violations of the State laws, then the officers of the State become the greatest violators. They enforce the laws against those without power and authority. The law enforced is the law of those in power. Selective enforcement of the law is what is seen in Indian society and certainly the selective enforcement is not policing, rather it is misuse or abuse of police power and authority.

Police Work: A Dirty Work?

Is police work a dirty work? No, police work can never be a dirty work. Nevertheless, it can be sullied by dirty policemen/officers. How many lakhs of innocent people were taken to police custody and how many of them have come out sound of mind and body? We don't have an accurate account of the tortured people in police custody, but many people say that they suffered humiliation, starvation, fatigue and physical abuse at the hands of the police. Everett C Hughes narrates a case of torture and it reads: "Prisoners were ordered to climb trees; guards whipped them to make them climb faster. Once they were out of reach, other prisoners, also urged by the whip, were put to shaking the trees. When the victims fell, they were kicked to see whether they could rise to their feet. Those too badly injured to get up were shot to death, as useless for work. A not inconsiderable number of prisoners were drowned in pits full of human excrement".[6] They were horrible acts, but they did not take place in India. During the British past, the police atrocities were so cruel that even human imagination could not conceive of them. What about democratic India? The atrocities committed by the police during, before and after the Internal Emergency in 1975-76 were sometimes worse than what the British Indian police did during pre-independence period. If they are known, people may say that police job is a dirty job. Nevertheless, on the other side of the coin, the police have a lot of achievement stories and when they are listened to, any person will say that the police job is a noble and divine job. A policed police service is always loved by the people and a non-policed police service is always hated and condemned by the people in any culture.

The police have a notoriety that they have been aggressively atrocious to the people and they have earned it over a long period of time. It is not easy to wipe out the notoriety one day too soon. A smuggler has a "status" a Mafia criminal has a "status", a professional criminal has a "status", and they are accepted in society by the people because they enjoy a "status". A bootlegger enjoys a "status" and people give him some "respect" which poor people do not have. The notoriety itself is a "status" for many. The people know that the police employ torture, use epithets, behave in a people unfriendly manner, informally arrest people and detain them incommunicado. The policemen too know that the people know their behavioural pattern and in that way they have a notoriety. But, for some, the "notoriety" itself is a "status" and they openly admit that they do such things in their work. Once a policeman said: "They do not know the police and they have not tasted the police" and he took pride in saying so. Psychologists believe that the police ought to feel ashamed of their notoriety if they want to police them. Taking pride in the notoriety and having the feeling of a sort of "status" in having such a notoriety are not conducive for policing the police in any country. In an enthusiasm to police the society, one must not forget to police the police. When the policeman points with his index finger to a person violating the law, he may remember that his three fingers - the middle, the small, etc., point at him. When he says: "you are wrong", he should not hear back: "you are wrong; you are doubly wrong".

"Do not judge, and you will not be judged; because the judgements you give are the judgements you will get, and the amount you measure out is the amount you will be given. Why do you observe the splinter in your brother's eye and never notice the plank in your own? How dare you say to your brother, "Let me take the splinter out of your eye" when all the time there is a plank in your own? Hypocrite! Take the plank out of your own eye first, and then you will see clearly enough to take the splinter out of your brother's eye".[7] This is a management thought and every policeman must remember it when he enforces law - when he investigates crime - when he prevents and controls criminal activities. Otherwise, he will be called a hypocrite and hypocrisy is a sin against his uniform and humanity. Some policemen blame their superiors and say that they are wrong in their methods of policing the society. Hence, they don't take them as their methods of policing the society. Hence, they don't take them as their role models. Some policemen have told me: "We are ashamed of our officers whenever we think about them. They are brutal and cruel, but we often keep our mouths shut and do as we are told". What type of policing they do? The police have power, but they must have a philosophy which must guide their behaviour. This is lacking and that is the problem in policing the police and policing the society. If 'P' in Police stands for power, then that power must be exhibited, expressed and enforced in a powerful way with a philosophy which is praiseworthy.

References

1. John F Galliher and James L McCartney, *Criminology: Power, Crime and Criminal Law,* The Dorsey Press, Homewood, Illinois, 1977.
2. *Ibid*. Also see, William A Westley, *Violence and the Police*, American Journal of Sociology, 59 (July), 1953.
3. Arthur Niederhoffer, *Behind the Shield: The Police in Urban Society,* Doubleday and Co., Garden City, N.Y, 1967.
4. V R Krishna Iyer, *Judicial Accountability, from Justice* At Crossroads, Deep & Deep Publications, Delhi, 1992.
5. V R Krishna Iyer, *op.cit.*
6. Everett C Hughes, *Good People and Dirty Work*, from Social Problems, Vol.10, No.1 (Summer, 1962).
7. St.Mathew, Chap.7, verses 1-5, Holy Bible.

9

Leadership and Policing the Police

Who will?—who can?—who must?—police the police? The questions are not asked by many as they think that the police do not require any further policing? Policing has two dimensions and they are: (1) individual policing and (2) group policing. A director general of police does not make a police department. Yet, he can do a lot of things to police the department. Likewise, a superintendent of police may be able to police the police in a district; a sub-inspector can do the same in his jurisdiction. But, all of them must have a *charisma* to do so. By *charisma*, I mean the special quality that gives an individual influence or authority over large numbers of people. This Random House Dictionary meaning of *charisma* was not seen in many police functionaries in the pre-independent or post independent period. "The special virtue of an office, position etc.", the dictionary gives further elaboration of the word *charisma,* "that confers or is thought to confer on the person holding it an unusual ability for leadership, worthiness of veneration or the like". How may police functionaries can claim such *charisma* or charism? Many cannot and many do not, for many occupy a post not out of their merit but out of the grace of some politicians who vouch for them. Their presence will be mutually beneficial for the individual police officer and for the political leaders/party. In such a situation, an officer's *charisma* or charism does not have any meaning. How can an inspector general of police who made attempts to cheat and thereby obtain two university degrees simultaneously have the charism to police the police? How can a circle inspector of police who accepted Rs.20000 to refer a criminal case claim charisma to police the police? Officers and men who have character, integrity and uprightness in behaviour certainly will have the charisma not only to police his subordinates but also to police his superiors. Whatever may be the position one holds or the post he occupies, the character and integrity count more than his official power and muscle capability to police the police - to lead the police to the right destination.

Solomon E Asche said: "...The decisive psychological fact about society is the capacity of individuals to comprehend and to respond to each other's experiences and actions. This fact, which permits individuals to become mutually related, becomes the ground of every social process and of the most crucial changes occurring in persons. It brings within the sphere of the individual the thoughts, emotions, and purposes of others, extending his world vastly beyond what his unaided efforts could achieve. It brings him also into a far-flung relation of mutual dependence, which is the condition of his development into a person and, if the social process becomes maladaptive, the source of his greatest anguish. It alters the psychological scene of each, since to live in society is to bring into a sensible relationship private and public experience. It is also an irreversible step; once in society we enter into a circle of mutuality that cannot be undone".[1] In police, how many men/officers comprehend and respond to each other's experiences and actions? There is excessive secrecy in many areas of police work and this opaqueness makes people suspicious of one another. Though the policemen/officers come together on a parade ground, one doubts seriously whether or not there exists any mutual relationship. They do not extend beyond them and do not make attempts to know the thoughts, and emotions of others. As such rightly found, there must be a sensible relationship and a circle of mutuality in social life. I find that the police lack such a relationship and mutuality which may be the cause for the lack of policing in police service. Neither the hierarchy nor the rank and file want to establish and strengthen such a relationship. The white police officers imported from England during the British regime kept the Indian policemen at a distance and the Indian hierarchy after independence did not make any honest or positive attempts to bring the rank and file close to them.

Earlier, I said that there are individual and group behaviour in the police. Every person, be he the director general of police or the police constable, is an individual. The individuals in the police are not separate phenomena, but are people who work together. They have a relationship with one another and the relationship can be developed in a positive and right way only if they are given facilities to respond to their emotional environments created by significant individuals who occupy senior positions in the service. Is the hierarchy capable of producing such environments in the police? The junior-most officer of the Indian police service may address the senior-most deputy superintendent of police by his first name. The junior-most sub-inspector of police may call the senior-most head constable by his surname. Once I asked a sub-inspector to tell me why he did so? His answer was: "Sir, earlier, the head constables had only numbers and no names. Now, at least we call them by names". Yes, that is true! A number has been changed into a name and according to some police officers, the change from a number to a name deteriorates the discipline in the police department ! I am yet to understand what he meant by discipline in the police department. Without an emotional exchange in human transactions, can we think of discipline? Hearing the number or name, the head constable reacted: "I am as old as your father and yet you address me by my surname?" They become psychologically at a distance and never come closer in life. The kind of head constables the police have today is to a large extent a product of the interactions they had experienced with other people in the police hierarchy. The British police officers looked at the Indian constables as illiterate and ignorant muscle men and they looked down upon them. After India became independent, did the hierarchy look at the constables and head constables as individuals with dignity? If they did not, it would tell upon the policing of the police in a democracy. The former orderlies and the present security staff of the police hierarchy have to tell a lot of stories about their interactions with their superiors.

Formative Periods and Shaping of Police Personality

A policeman's formative period starts with his entry into the police service. The interactions which they experienced during their childhood, of course, have made them what they are when they enter the police service. After entering the police service, they develop their personality and in that process, their current relations with other fellow policemen/officers matter a lot. Their home experiences with their parents, siblings, family members, friends, school mates, etc., are to a great extent and degree reflected in their basic attitudes, feelings and values as new entrants into the police service. After entering the service, a new 'formative period' begins. During that period, the police personality is shaped and developed. The "self-concept" is formed and developed. The British coloured police officers during the British rule shaped their ego concept as privileged people imported to India to rule the illiterate and ignorant Indian policemen. The disparity in the salary of the British police officer and the Indian policeman was so large that the British extracted free police labour from the Indians. When India became independent, the Indian police officers too started thinking that they were British police officers with Indian skin. The Indian policemen were unskilled labourers and even after 50 years of freedom, the controversy as to the nature of the police job - i.e., skilled or unskilled labour - is not yet settled. Necessarily, the "self-concept" formed in the policemen will be different from that formed in the officers who occupy higher posts in the police. The formation of the two types of "self-concepts" is not conducive for policing the police in a democracy. A head constable told me: "I was an orderly for seven years to a senior police officer. I did everything he, his wife and children asked me to do. One day, I did a mistake and my officer placed me under suspension. I knew "I am I" only then and thereafter I could not respect him or all officers who occupy higher positions in police". I do not know whether or not it was a strange incidence? - it was a common incidence? In any case, the "self-concept" of the officer who suspended his orderly and the "self-concept" of the victim of suspension will be different. Other people in the police are important to any police officer just like he is important for others in the department. The mistaken notions about the *self-other* relationship is perhaps another cause of lack of policing in police service.

The Self and Others in Policing the Police

The human needs 'esteem' - this is seen both in the policeman and in the director general of police. When the director general of police is saluted, he gets a feeling of esteem and this feeling of esteem can be given only by others. Each one in the police wants to have such feelings of esteem and the director general of police must be prepared to offer such feelings of esteem to his subordinate men/officers if he wants to police the police. Who will respect a director general of police if he does not respect his subordinates? Respect is reciprocal and a give-and-take policy is better rewarding than the demanding respect policy which is now seen.

The police is a group of people and everyone has to associate with others. Associate with others means prepare to suffer a loss of a great deal of autonomy. An autocratic way of administering the police was possible, perhaps, in the British imperialism and not in Indian democracy. It took a lot of time for the Indian police higher-ups to understand it and as a result the police hierarchy during 1950s, 1960s and 1970s took an attitude which was against policing the police in a democracy. In many States, there broke out police strikes as a consequence. The principle is that one must give up some of one's identity as an autonomous individual in exchange for the identity one receives from the group. Were the higher-ups in the police prepared to do so? Were the rank and file prepared to do so? A superintendent of police from the State cadre got into the Indian police service. Naturally, he received a great deal of group acceptance and esteem. He thought to be "big" and went to call on the inspector general of police. The inspector general of police asked him to wait and later when he called on him, he was not offered a seat for two/three minutes. He felt slighted in front of the policeman who was in the room of the inspector general of police. Such experiences are quite unsettling to anybody. First of all, the superintendent of police had a different "self concept" when he took the decision to call on the inspector general of police. After meeting the inspector general of police, he could understand that the inspector general of police had a different perception of the officers who were promoted to the IPS cadre from the State service. He understood that his identity and self-concept depended upon others. In the police, every higher rank shows an attitude that the lower rank is to obey the higher rank without questioning. I think that the higher rank officers are yet to understand that their identity becomes important only if it is recognized and respected by the lower ranks as well as by the higher ranks. I do not have a rank in the police hierarchy. I have been a criminologist of the police department. One day, I went to meet an inspector general of police with whom I had no earlier contacts. Immediately after meeting him, I said that "I am a civilian member on the faculty of the police training college". He told me: "Yes, what can I do for you?" I think that he never considered me as an outsider - a member of an "out-group". I felt happy that I was recognized and respected by him. Afterwards, we had many occasions to associate closely and we developed mutual respect. But, do the policemen get it? If they do not get it, then it becomes extremely difficult to police the police. There must be mutual respect, recognition and rapport between the lower and higher ranks to have an effective policing of the police.

Group Affiliations, Self Concept and Policing the Police

I have asked many young assistant superintendents of police who have come to the police training college from the Police Academy, Hyderabad, to tell me who they were. I got the reply almost like this from many—

"I am *so and so*. I am an engineer (MBA, MCA, B.Com (Hons), M.A.). I belong to...State" and I have noted always that they enumerated the group with which they were affiliated. I have asked the same question to the newly enlisted sub-inspectors and the newly recruited police constables. I could specially take note of the fact that the constables had ego concepts which were different from those of the officers of the Indian police service who, as a rule, spoke very highly of their "self-concepts". The constables spoke very lowly of their "self-concepts". The officers of the Indian police service were talking about inspectors general of police, about deputy inspectors general, about officers of the Indian administrative service, secretaries to government, etc., and their associations with them and the constables were talking about the people of their status and levels and their associations with them. Can the top level and the rank and file come closer? If not, policing the police will be an unachievable task. Realizing this, vertical interaction courses are organised all over the country, but there too, one sees a three tyre vertical interaction - the top level, the middle level and the lower level. Will it bring the different levels closer?

I have not so far got an opportunity to stay in constables' barracks. At the same time, I have got ample opportunities to listen to the talks among them. I have heard that some of them talked always ill of their superior ranks. They abuse, curse, call names and speak about them with hostile expressions and words. I had opportunities to listen to the talks that took place among senior levels and they never or usually talked seriously anything bad about constables. I conclude now that the policeman must be brought closer to the higher ranks if the police want that they must not develop hostility against their superior or higher ranks. By association and contacts with the higher-ups in the police, the constables must develop better "ego-concepts", feelings of status and importance. So long as the lower levels have the ego concepts which they have at present, policing the police becomes a difficult affair. If they do not get due status within the department, they will go out to get it from others. They will establish their contacts with corrupt politicians, underworld criminals, Mafia operators, unscrupulous businessmen and so on. The impact will be detrimental to the proper policing of any police by the hierarchy.

Presently, I find that the policemen have an in-group feeling. The middle level and top level officers too have such in-group feelings. When a sub-inspector was placed under suspension for a custodial death, the middle level police officers contributed enough money and funded him to win the case. The constabulary and top level police officers did not do anything. When an officer of the Indian police service faced a similar problem, the officers of the Indian police service raised adequate funds for helping their brother in the service. So long as the in-group feelings exist in the police, it is difficult to have a feeling of oneness in the police service. If the feeling of "oneness" is lacking, necessarily policing the police becomes difficult. The associations with the people of similar status and rank provide to them to develop a feeling of identity - an identity that is very powerful enough to counteract any feeling of mutual attraction and appreciation. Whenever dinner parties are arranged for top level officers in hotels, the constables are asked to wait outside to provide security for the officers. This too helps to develop a feeling of identity which may not be helpful to have a feeling of oneness in the police service. The higher ranks expect submissiveness and passivity among the lower ranks while they want to show dominance, strength, leadership, etc. Every person, irrespective of the rank he has in the hierarchy, has the same needs - to maintain himself as a human being, to grow and develop and to maintain social relationship with other fellow individuals, etc. But how to achieve one's needs? The police have a culture. The police are a group. The police hierarchy permits each subgroup in the police to behave in a particular way and that makes the members of the subgroup to become unhappy. A policeman, if he comes to his office every day by his own car, the middle level or top level officers do not generally tolerate it. When a constable uses a mobile phone, he is looked upon with suspicion. Why? As a member of the constabulary, he is not expected to use such luxuries which are meant only for the higher-ups in the service. A bicycle for a constable is all right, a bike for a sub-inspector is O.K. and a car for the new assistant superintendent of police is understandable. Identity with a particular subgroup in the police means a lot. A member in a particular subgroup wants to go higher and higher. He wants to go to the next higher group. But, he may not get promotions. Yet, he can climb up to the next higher rank by identifying with the luxuries which are used by those in the next higher rank. Those who have a bicycle thus purchase a bike. Those who have a bike thus purchase a car. Those who have a second hand car want to have a brand new car. Those who have a new car want to change to a better model with more human comforts. By legitimate means one cannot go up. And therefore, many vices such as corruption, bribery, *nexus transactions, enforcement crimes,* etc., have connection with the identity feelings of policemen/officers. So long as identity feelings exist, policing the police or making the police free from illegal/corrupt practices becomes a practical impossibility. The more the feeling of identity, the better it is for policing the police. Today, I see constables owning computers, cars, internet connections, credit cards, mobile phones, club membership, etc., which were once upon a time the privileges of the higher-ups in the police. I do not know how they make money to maintain them. That is a secret which neither the constables nor the top ranks like to divulge.

Status Feelings and Policing

A constable has a status and a director general of police also has a status. I think that there is a confusion in the police as to what is the "status". May be due to the historical factors the status in the police is decided by "who you are" rather than "what you have done". If you are the director general of police, you enjoy a higher status than what a constable may get. But recently, I find a change in the outlook. Policemen and officers evaluate the person, his personality, achievements, etc., before they decide upon the status. "Earned success" is given more weight than any other thing. Suppose an officer of the Indian police service is appointed as the director general of police. The moment one is appointed, the policemen/officers assess his capacity, eligibility, suitability, personality to decide upon his "status" in the department. If he does not have "earned success", he is not considered as a leader and his efficiency in policing the police may not be much. Think about a constable and as a constable, the status he enjoys may not be very enviable. But, he may earn success and enjoy better status than many officers in the department. Therefore ascribing status by the post one holds was an older strategy. When the backgrounds and the socio-economic positions of the lower, middle and top level personnel in the police are taken into account. I find that there are more points of similarity than differences. Therefore, it is difficult to find out the differences in their behaviour owing to the class they belong to. There was a time when the officers thought of the lower level functionaries as stupid, dirty, uncultured, unreliable, boorish, etc., but now they don't think so. The white police officer thought so because the policemen were illiterate and ignorant. But today, there are highly qualified policemen, sometimes more qualified than the officers themselves. Hence, the officers cannot afford to think of the policemen as inferior to them. They may be inferior to them only in rank when they wear the uniform; otherwise they may be superior in many respects. The facts are facts and they have to be accepted in fairness. In the changed socio-economic and political climate, individual dignity and the status of a human person must be recognized and honoured. If that is not done, policing the police becomes a herculean task. Terrorize and lead, threaten and rule, frighten and subdue, etc., are strategies which are rejected and as such a democratic style of leadership is proved to be better and more effective than the older autocratic methods of leadership. I have authored a book titled: Police Leadership: The Inside Story and it deals with police leadership in the present day policing.

A Kerala Study

Policemen have less pay and therefore less social status. Policemen have less income and therefore less social status. The policemen have less education, hence less social status. The policemen have less power and authority and therefore less social status. Conversely enough, the director general of police has more pay, more education, more power and authority, etc., and therefore more social status. How do the people evaluate them when they speak of the status of the constables and that of the director general of police. I asked this question to 972 people selected on a random basis and I could learn that a considerably large number of people subscribed to the view that the status for police work was given by them not from the point of view of the income, power, authority, etc. Instead, people give status looking into the behaviour patterns. For example, a constable behaves well in his uniform, his status is raised higher than that of the director general of police who behaves indecently. I could learn that the income, power, authority, government car, telephone, mobile phone, wireless set, orderlies, etc., which the higher echelons in the police have are not the sole criteria that decide upon the status of the person. As far as police duties are concerned, the behaviour patterns and character decide upon the status. C.D. John, a constable worked with me. He left me long ago. Once I found his photograph in the news paper and the photograph was published for the good work he did. A few days ago, I met him and he told me that his status has gone up after that incident.

Teachers in schools, social workers, priests, nuns and so on have lower income than the deputy inspectors general, inspectors general of police. But, certainly they enjoy good social status. Hence, income, car, rifle, salutes, power, etc., are less important than good behaviour. My conclusion from the study was that a police officer who possesses good behaviour pattern, character, manners, etc., enjoys good status. A person with good status has got good command/power. He commands respect. He is a stronger person to police the police than a person having no character and personal qualities. A drunkard cannot be a good model if at all he occupies the highest post in the police. He is looked down upon by the superiors, subordinates and the rank and file alike.

The status is decided by other criteria as well. The nature of the work one does, the regular income one gets, the illegal income he makes, the muscle power he exercises, the way he deals with the people, the reputation he has, etc., decide upon his status and charisma in the department. Everyone observes all in the department. Every one takes note of the cigarettes one smokes, the type of clothes one wears, the magazines and periodicals one reads, the hotels and restaurants one visits, the vehicles one uses, the company one enjoys, the liquor one consumes, the school to which one sends his children and a variety of other factors. The lowest rank in the police and the highest rank in the service are not very much different in many of the above areas and therefore deciding the status of the constables basing on the scales enjoyed by the British may not be correct now; it may be harmful to police the police.

Communication, Leadership and Policing

The British police officers during the colonial rule spoke in a language normally not understood by the illiterate and ignorant constables or by the moderately educated (with S.S.L.C.) Indian police officers. Speaking English/writing in English was considered as a symbol of status and even today, it is so. Owing to the enlistment of better qualified personnel at all levels in the police service, a situation has emerged that everyone understands the language spoken by others. Communication is the very life blood of police life and there must be communication among all in police service.

Every policeman/officer communicates to himself and others. Whenever a superintendent of police comes late to his office, he communicates to others that he is not concerned with punctuality. He cannot then insist on punctuality from his associates/subordinates. Whenever a deputy inspector general of police misuses his official vehicle, he communicates to others that misuse of vehicle is not a serious misconduct. Whenever an inspector general of police abuses his power, he communicates to others that abuse of power is not seriously taken into account. Whenever a police constable accepts bribery, he communicates to others that there exists an environment in which corruption and bribe-taking are tolerated or encouraged as the case may be. Any good thing that one does communicates to others that good things take place. Hence, communication has a decisive role - sometimes a destructive role - in policing the police. Communication as it is generally understood in police circles, is the transmission of orders/information to the members by oral or written methods. Such communication may be necessary for policing the society and to police the police in a formal way. But policing the police takes place more by informal methods of communication.

Every policeman - constables upwards - is a member of a group and as such there exists a communicative relationship among the members. Once a deputy superintendent of police told me: "*so and so* talks like an IPS officer" and he meant that he did not talk "*like* a police officer". The tune of voice, the manner of talking, the body language, the signals he emitted, etc., gave an impression - communicated - that he belonged to a category different from the ordinary police. I understood that his talk did not have any impact upon the deputy superintendent of police. Once a director general of police himself prepared a complaint against one of his subordinates.

Afterwards, he called him to his room, asked him to sit down, offered him a cup of tea and showed him the complaint he has with him. He then said: "No, I am not taking any action against you" and thereby he communicated to him that he has sufficient material with him to put him in trouble. Hence "be careful and be with me". He thought that he could police his subordinates by such threatening methods. Later, it was learnt that his subordinates disliked his methods of policing the police.

A superintendent of police assumed the charges of the head of the district. He told his subordinates/policemen that he would look after their welfare and safety if they administered fair justice. Once a politician came to a police station and asked the sub-inspector to do something which he could not do. To cut short, he was transferred to the police control room from the police station on that very evening. The sub-inspector met the superintendent of police and reminded him of his promise to the subordinates. The superintendent of police then said: "Don't teach me. You obey the order". The behaviour of the superintendent of police had great communication-effect to police the police. Thereafter, his subordinates did not trust him. Certainly he could not police the police if he behaved the way he did.

A deputy superintendent of police told his driver to go to a particular place and do a personal work for him. On his way back, he met with an accident causing the death of a college student. The deputy superintendent of police just disowned him and thereafter the news was flashed among his colleagues/ subordinates that he was an untrustworthy person.

Personality clashes, interpersonal rivalries, hostility, vengeance, vindictiveness between two officers/men communicate themselves and damage the smooth policing of the police. They create tension and every person has an optimal level to tolerate tension. If the tension goes beyond the climax - the optimum point, then he becomes less effective, less comfortable, more aggressive, more maladaptive, etc. Some may resort to drinks/drugs, others may withdraw from the situation. Some may show swollen faces while others may spread rumours. In any case, all these communicate a lot and the result is less of policing in the police.

One day an additional director general participated in a seminar and the participants found him smoking foreign cigarettes. The participants then said to themselves: "How can he smoke such a costly cigarette with the income he has?" Another participant added: "Ask his associates, subordinates and friends. They will tell you how he makes money". The discussion continued for some time and they drew the portrait of the police officer. If outsiders have so much information about a police officer, then one can fairly guess the information the insiders have about him! Doubtlessly, his policing the police will be of a suspicious nature.

During the British rule, the hierarchy - the white police officers - could afford to do many things in a clandestine way. Transparency was minimum and communication was practically nil. Today, the situation has changed a lot. Judicial activism is seen, the press has become vibrant, the people and policemen have become conscious of their rights and privileges, human rights awareness has come into being, the secrecy is lost. Many things are leaked out and the police hierarchy becomes a target of attack. Some of the high ranking police functionaries are detected and arrested for their nefarious activities. Their charisma is lost and they fail to exert any influence on the rank and file. Their leadership is questioned and they are criticized.

Group Processes and Policing the Police

A policeman/officer has a feeling that he belongs to a group - he is a part of a force which has power, authority, weapons and muscle power. Whenever he behaves, he thinks that he can mobilize the strength of his force if he wants to do so. As such, when he behaves in an aggressive way, he knows that he can afford to be so because he has a force behind him. When a policeman tortures a person, he expects that he must suffer it. He does not expect him to react to his torture. Contrary to his expectation, if he sees that the tortured person attacks him back, he sees to it that his associates/subordinates come forward to torture him. He is lifted to a place where he is tortured by many in his group. His membership in the police force makes him courageous enough to resort to such strategy with some sort of immunity. Immediately, a case will be registered against him and he makes his position safe and the entire group helps him to do so. This is not policing, rather it is misuse of authority/abuse of power. If the person tortured dies in police custody, the group support may be withdrawn and he may be made the accused in a crime case. It is not unusual to see that the people (in the group) who support him become even hostile to the accused. The group members then will be responding to different internal and external stimuli and the accused may be isolated in the group.

The policemen during a jeep patrolling - when a suspect is questioned by all of them in a crude way - when a lathy charge is ordered - when firing takes place-behave in a different way - behave in a way different from the way one would behave if he is conducting the patrol alone or interrogating the suspect in isolation. As a policed policeman, one must accept the fact that his individual behaviour will be different from his behaviour as a member in the group. There is something called group behaviour which is different from individual behaviour. A leader in the police tries to create a feeling of "groupness" in the service. They are told to do things together and think as a group. When he does so, he sees to it that the feeling of "groupness" is created to do the lawful things in a lawful way- that the "doing things together" is to do fair things in a fair way- that the "thinking as a group" is to perform police functions in a human rights friendly way. This is essential to police the police in a democracy. During the British past, they developed the feeling of "groupness", "thinking together", "doing as a group", etc., to suppress and repress the people in India. Somehow or other, this perverted approach continued to dominate the Indian police even when India became independent. The result has been that the "groupness" in the police sometimes helped them to commit atrocities on the people and thus the policing became a target of attack from many quarters. The British police did not allow the Indian policeman to think that he was a member of the Indian community. They made him feel that he belonged to the British government in India. They promoted to develop in him that he was hostile to the Indians and thus he became a member of a group which was alien to the Indians. After India became independent, no honest attempts were made to change the attitude of the policemen to the Indians. As a result, the policemen continued to behave as a group hostile to the civilian community in India. They did not think that the police were the public and the public were the police. The "groupness" thus seen or developed made the policemen to keep away from the civilian population. The people too kept the policemen at a distance. They developed an avoiding attitude and sometimes hostile to the police. Even the good works the police performed for the public were interpreted as acts of hostility. The police became a group and the civilians became another group hostile to each other. The public did not participate with the police to police the society. The police too did not want to involve the public in their policing functions. The police administration understood the defects in keeping a distance between the police and the public. Hence they initiated some programmes to make the police and the people to come closer and closer. But, they were more ritualistic than realistic. Hence, there was no perceptible impact by such gimmicks on the police - citizen relationship. I remember an incident that took place in 1980. While coming to the Police Training College, I found a police jeep on the road. The driver and the officer had difficulty to start the jeep. They understood that the battery of the jeep was weak. They asked the people to help them to push the jeep. The officer sat in the jeep and the jeep was pushed. After a short distance, it gained enough speed for the engine going forward. The officer asked the driver to accelerate and they drove the vehicle from the people. They did not say a "Thank you" to those who pushed the jeep and the people said: "These policemen are always like this". In 1991, I found a similar situation. I found the driver shouting

"Thank you" to those who pushed the jeep and the people shouted back as O.K. and went their separate ways. In 1999, I again witnessed a similar scene. The officer in the jeep politely thanked those who pushed the jeep and shook hands with some of them. The people responded the good gesture and said: "Nice officer. The police must be like this". I found the differences and I used to narrate my experience to police officers in my class on improving police-public relationship. This is a time of community policing and the police and the people think together that they belong to the same group. The "groupness" is to work together and when such a feeling is developed both in the police and in the public, then policing the society becomes easy. When such a feeling comes to a reality, then policing the police becomes better and more perfect. Every group has a purpose and whenever the police and the people behave as they are the members of one and the same group, then the purpose of policing becomes meaningful. The purpose of the police is the same for the policemen and the general public. It cannot be two.

Policing the Police with People's Participation

Policing the society with people's participation is a widely discussed area. I take note of the fact that some policemen/officers are for it and some others are against it. The latter group is of the view that policing the society is not the people's affair. I think that they need more information about policing itself and they must think that they form a part of the society. There is no difference between the police and the people except that the police are paid for what they do or what the people are to do. I go a step further and may argue that the police must get the people's participation not only for policing the society., but also for policing the police. Some problems are created by the lack of policing and the people can tell them where the police go wrong. Some human rights activists, journalists and so on keep a constant watch and vigil on police activities which make the police to behave in a controlled way. During a law and order situation, the people, pressmen, politicians and so on exert control on police behaviour. Now the acts of the police at a scene of law and order are videographed and a situation has come into being that the police cannot behave in an unruly way. Before videos were brought to the scene of law and order management, policemen could afford to lathy-charge people in any way they wanted. The British taught them jabs and cuts and if the police are going to attack people with jabs and cuts, then they will be branded as human rights unfriendly. In many ways, the people do police the police. About two decades ago, the films in the press photographers' camera were forcefully taken by the police and exposed to light. Today, they do not do so, for the press photographers take the photographs of a scene of law and order management from great distances using telelense and zoom-lenses. The police are helpless before the pressmen and people. This feeling alone helps to police the police. In the case of illegal arrests, the people approach the court and get search warrants issued. The publication of the names of those arrested by the police in police control rooms aids the police to police the police. The directives of the Supreme Court of India about the formalities to be observed by the police are exhibited before police stations by non-governmental organizations or citizens' fora. Public litigation societies file suits against the police. The press and the media give a wider publicity of what the police do. They write editorials against the police. Some politicians and political parties organize *dharnas, jadhas* and street corner meetings against the police. The Legislature Sub-committees, Women's Commissions, Human Rights Commissions make the police accountable to what they do. The cultural media expose police behaviour and thus exerts influence to police the police. The role of the people in policing the police is as important as the role of the hierarchy in policing the police. Hence, policing the police through people's participation assumes more importance in the days to come.

How many complaints are received against the police? The volume of complaints will be an indicator of the effectiveness of the public's role in controlling the police. When the people are not satisfied with the investigation of a crime by the local police or when they smell rat in the investigation of a crime by the local police, they demand the transfer of the case to special units including the Central Bureau of Investigation.

Group Morale and Policing the Police

Whenever the people see the police not policed well, they react and raise their voice. In democracy, the voice of every person counts. Sometimes, the people's reaction to police behaviour/misbehaviour compels the Government to initiate action against the police. Immediately, some policemen/officers say that the Government action affects adversely the *morale* of the police. I think that some of them have misconceived notions about '*morale*'. When we say that the police have a high *morale* we mean that they accept the goals of the group and are very optimistic about the chances for attaining those goals. For that purpose, each policeman/officer is prepared to invest something of his own and is willing to collaborate with the other members in their attempt to achieve the goal. Then what is the goal of the police? Non-policed police behaviour is not the goal of the police organization. When a raid in a village was conducted, some policemen misbehaved with the womenfolk. There was a public agitation and the Government initiated action against some policemen/officers. Immediately, the policemen/officers said that the Government action would affect adversely the *morale* of the police. They said so because they had perverted ideas about the morale itself. Misbehaving with the womenfolk in the village during a raid is not a police goal in a democracy. The view was expressed by individuals who were pessimistic, cynical, apathetic, resentful or simply unable to take the goal of the police in a meaningful way. People having a low morale would behave in a non-policed way - sabotaging the efforts of the police organization to attain its sublime goals. The people may overlook some wrong acts which the police do in society- but never will they forgive any serious wrong acts. Shouting at people with epithets in public may be overlooked by some, but not at all torturing of women in public.

It may be remembered that morale alone cannot make any organization, including police efficiency. If senior officers issue an illegal order or an order which is against the goal of the organization, it will certainly lower the morale of the policemen. During the internal emergency in India (1975-76), some police officers issued orders to arrest certain people and the police were misused by them. Later the Shah Commission of Inquiry was appointed to probe into the police excesses. My studies after the period of emergency revealed that some of the orders issued by senior police officers and executed by the subordinates could help to lower the morale of the police service. Such orders and exercise of pseudo-authority would produce displeasure, resentment, anger and apathy among the subordinates. Certainly, they would defeat the goals of the organization.

India is a democracy and the politicians of the opposition are as powerful as the politicians of the ruling front. The press in India and the people in India are very vibrant. They openly criticize the police and the Government when they are inconvenienced or when their comforts are adversely affected by the police activities or by the exercise of pseudo-authority by the over-enthusiastic police functionaries.

I wanted to know whether or not the morale of the police is adversely affected by the working conditions of the police. I could find that the working conditions have some effects upon the morale of the police. Inadequate facilities in the working environment, lack of human comforts, difficulties in transportation, inadequate facilities to sit, to write, to take rest, to drink water, to eat food, etc., have some impact on the morale of the police. The lower level police functionaries compare their working environments with those of the higher-ups who have good furniture, a room, a vehicle, air-conditioners, T.V. sets, etc., and they feel unhappy and rejected in their service. Some officers therefore see to it that the lower levels are made as happy as the seniors in their working environment. When the policemen are posted in sensitive areas where human comforts are not provided, they become annoyed and angry at it. Some senior officers see to it that they are provided with adequate facilities there and they too accommodate with them to give a feeling that they are one among them. Naturally, it has a higher impact on improving the morale of the policemen and officers at the lower levels. If senior levels do not become one among them, it creates murmuring and resentment.

I have noted that the lower levels would tolerate or accommodate with the inadequacies in their working environment provided the hierarchy looked after their opportunities for promotion and ensured psychological rewards for the good works they did. The promotion prospects of the lower level functionaries are poor when they find the same, for the middle level are brighter and for the top level are the brightest. A person joining as a constable may retire as a constable/headconstable while a person enlisted as an assistant superintendent of police retires as the director general of police. This necessarily affects adversely the morale of the police at present. No policing the police worth its name will be possible if the same situation continues longer. The lower levels lose their confidence in the leadership of the higher levels when they realize the fact that they are not interested in their promotions and welfare. Peanut rewards now given to a few selected members (the selection process is questioned often) of the lower levels cannot make their morale high. If the morale of the lower level is not high, then they will transfer their aggression on to others who will be the general public. They may behave in a non-policed way then. On the job, frustrations seem among the lower level police functionaries to affect adversely the policing of the police today. The British successfully did it for their vested interests. They wanted frustrated policemen to oppress and suppress the people in India. But we do not want frustrated policemen and therefore their morale must be raised at any cost.

Group Cohesiveness and Policing the Police

The police have very many cadres from constables upwards to the director general of police. For the effective functioning of police duties, there must be group cohesiveness which is nothing but the mutual attraction that the members of a group have for one another. The police activities are many and precisely therefore there must be mutual attraction that the group and its activities have for its members. Cohesiveness is also called *morale* by some. The success of the director general of police lies in getting maximum cohesiveness in the department. Do the various ranks in the police have the mutual attraction for one another? No studies were conducted in this direction. How can they be attracted? The constables and the superintendents of police are miles apart and the director general of police are poles apart. Rigidity in the rank structure does not allow them to come closer. The white police officers of the British period were invisible to the policemen at the bottom of the hierarchy. But, in the democratic set-up, the director general of police is quite visible; nevertheless he does not come down to establish an attractive relationship with the constables. Of late, the superintendent of police on some occasions become one among the policemen to manage law and order situations, to conduct raids, to perform search operations, to investigate crimes, etc. This sort of cooperation with the subordinate staff is appreciated not only by the police personnel, but also by the press, politicians and the people. They forget about their rank consciousness and work in unison as members of the same service for a common objective. In connection with a hooch tragedy in a South Indian State, the director general of police came down from the police headquarters to the policemen in conducting raids and searches. The press published the photograph of the director general of police and appreciated the good gesture to create group cohesiveness. Some senior police officers who were still under the Old-British-School of thought commented that the behaviour of the director general of police was unwarranted. At the same time, his behaviour was appreciated by many and they said that his behaviour was good enough to create mutual attraction among the various ranks in the police. In connection with the law and order management during a communal riot, the inspectors general of police, the director general of police and so on went with the patrolling team consisting of policemen and subordinate police officers. Again, in a clash between two political parties in a sensational area, the director general of police participated actively to settle the issue. This sort of behaviour was unseen or unheard of during the British rule or during the period following independence. A retired police officer once told me that the head of the police department- i.e., the inspector general of police as the post then was known - used to come to the police headquarters only once a month and that day was a great day in police headquarters which would be decorated with flowers and plants, etc. What is more? In a police conference, some police officers from some bigger States told me that the director general of police did not/could not know many of the sub-divisional/circle officers in their States. The relationship between them was practically nil and, in such a state of affairs, it was just impossible for the constabulary to know the head of the police closely. As a result, group cohesion was not possible. If group cohesion is not visibly seen, then *morale* is lost and policing the police becomes difficult. The mutual attraction among the members will be zero or even negative.

The *morale* of the police force is not the *morale* of the director general of the police at the top or of the constable at the bottom. The *morale* of the police depends on the *morale* of its members. One may speak of the *morale* of the director general of police and if he has a good *morale,* it will exert influence upon the *morale* of the entire police functionaries to a limited extent. The *morale* of the director general of police is not and cannot be the *morale* of the police department. The *morale* and cohesiveness of the police as a group are closely related. If the department has a high *morale*, it increases the cohesiveness which in turn multiplies the attractiveness which again guarantees efficiency in the police work and good policing of the society and the police. If the *morale* is high, then the members get pleasure and find satisfaction in working together on common objectives. The policemen, sometimes, catch hold of notorious criminals. The press gives publicity to the creditable work the policemen have done. But, in such news flashes, the names of the policemen are not seen. The entire credit is taken by the superior ranks and the policemen often make complaints about this sort of robbing the credit by senior levels. It affects adversely the morale of the policemen. Some senior police officers are not prepared to give to Caesar what is due to him and to God what is due to Him. They assume the entire credit and laugh at the policemen who do the real work. This is treachery and is bad from the point of view of policing the police. Researches show that cohesiveness is always an aid to effectiveness.

Can threat increase cohesiveness or *morale*? I mentioned earlier that cohesiveness is the mutual attraction and it cannot be ensured by threats. "If you do not do as I tell you, then I will see that your annual confidential report is damaged" - said a superintendent of police to a sub-inspector thinking that his threat would increase cohesiveness. The same superintendent of police threatened many of his subordinates with the same strategy. I wanted to study the after-effects and I could learn that his threat could not increase cohesiveness. The subordinates who worked under him under a condition of threat developed behaviour which was no *'cohesiveness-prone'*. Instead, some of them took the attitude: "come what may". Some made attempts to strengthen the bonds among those who were placed under similar conditions of threat. They made attempts to see that the superintendent of police got a transfer from the jurisdiction. Some yielded to the threats without developing any cohesiveness. So, the approach was not found to be conducive for the development of cohesiveness and *morale*. Consequently, the superintendent of police failed in his attempts to achieve the goals of the department in an enviable way.

Group Climate and Policing the Police

Psychologists describe certain emotional aspects of group life by using the terms *'morale'* and 'cohesiveness' particularly in terms of the attitudes and behaviour of group members. For policing the police, *'morale'* and *'cohesiveness'* are essential. In the police, there are three wings which are : (1) police of the general executive, (2) police of the armed reserves, (3) police of the armed battalions. Even in one and the same group, there are subgroups. For example, in the police of the general executive, there are the (i) Thana police, (ii) crime investigation branch, (iii) special branch, etc. In every branch, there are (a) policemen, (b) head-constables, (c) assistant sub-inspectors, (d) sub-inspectors, (e) inspectors and so on. The constabulary, the subordinate service, superior service, etc., have further sub-groups. The officers of the Indian police service form a separate group. Thus, it may be observed that the police consist of sub-sub-groups, sub-groups and groups. I have noted that the emotional factors operating within a sub-group, sub-sub-group are unique and therefore the emotional factors operating in the police of the general executive are not the emotional factors which operate in the armed reserves or in the armed police battalions. The emotional factors which operate in the constabulary are different from those that operate in the sub-group consisting of the officers in the Indian police service. Group climate means the atmosphere of a group which is its general psychological or emotional state as of a given point. In that way, it is difficult to find a group climate in the police as a whole. Each sub-group (sub-sub-group also) has its own group climate. For example, the members of the constabulary may think of themselves as policemen who enjoy a low social status, receive a low pay, etc., whereas the officers of the Indian police service may feel themselves as highly paid officials who can enjoy a lot of perks, privileges, comforts, etc. Since one notices a special kind of atmosphere which prevails in a particular sub-group (sub-sub-group also), he can refer it to be the special climate of that sub-group (sub-sub-group). It is but natural that the members of a particular sub-group (sub-sub-group) may be inclined to behave in terms of their perception of the prevailing atmosphere/climate in their sub-group (sub-sub-group). What about the group climate in the subordinate service? A sub-inspector may be the leader of a certain number of constables. If he is an autocratic leader, then he may produce two kinds of climate in the group - i.e. (1) aggressive and (2) apathetic. The aggressive climate, psychologists find, is characterized by rebellious behaviour from the members of the group. The apathetic climate is characterized by extreme dependence on the leader. The members exhibiting such a dependence will show low capacity for initiating any group actions. Psychologists are of the opinion that an autocratic leadership may not be conducive to police the police in a democratic set-up. The British officers showed an autocratic leadership and made the members of the police either aggressive or apathetic. Those who showed aggressive behaviour were ruthlessly punished or dismissed from service. In the history of the police in pre-independent India, such punishments/dismissals were plenty. After India became independent, the group climate in the police was more or less autocratic. As India became more and more democratic, the autocratic leadership inherited from the British past was challenged by the members of the police - particularly, the constabulary. We see police strikes in many States as a consequence or due to many other reasons. When the British found the members of the police becoming aggressive, they did not change their style of leadership. Instead, they became more and more autocratic. Lack of education and ignorance of better leadership styles might be the reason for the British to adopt such an objectionable style to police the civil police in India. The British who wanted an oppressive and repressive police force in India accepted the same approach to police the civil police who showed aggressiveness to the police leadership. The police hierarchy which administered the police after independence were not management experts and therefore they followed the same autocratic style until it was challenged or questioned. The Gore Committee included management subjects in the training syllabus to the various ranks and recommended to appoint a permanent faculty in police academies/colleges to impart the principles of management to the officers of various categories. Nevertheless, a sudden shift from the autocratic styles to other forms of leadership was not easy in the police.

Management experts are of the view that a democratic style pays rich dividends to police the civil police in a democratic set-up. The democratic leadership is characterized by a high level of friendliness among the group members and toward the leader. Today, one may observe some police officers adopting a democratic style of leadership and I notice that the democratic style improves the group climate better than the autocratic leadership. In the autocratic leadership, the members do their work satisfactorily only in the presence of the leader. In the democratic leadership, the group members continue to work with sincerety, dedication and honesty. In the democratic leadership, the *'morale'* and 'cohesiveness' of the members of the group are very high. The members become more aware and concerned with the goals of the organization. The *laissez-faire* leadership style produces more discontent, more hostility and less friendliness. Police the police means ensure maximum cooperation, friendliness, dedication, etc., in the work. For it, there must be a group climate which can be guaranteed only by a democratic style of leadership.

Task Orientation and Policing the Police

The policemen/officers have to perform a lot of tasks and they must be task-oriented. Researches show that a task-oriented policeman/officer will be resourceful, not dogmatic, self-sufficient, self-controlled, showing endurance, etc. Are the policemen resourceful? The allegation is that the police are resourceful, but not up to the mark or expectation of the public. They may have vehicles, weapons, man-power, funds, etc. But are they resourceful intellectually? The intellectual resourcefulness may not be adequate. One reason is that the police are not trained well and as such they lack sufficient knowledge to handle the situation in an effective way. The inefficiency to handle the situation in an effective way may be expressed in their inability to show self-control in live situations.

They become aggressive and some are hot tempered. They don't become sociable, sober, calm and mature in their interactions. If they become so or show such characteristics, then they are not policed people. Task-oriented people must be self-controlled and must exhibit due endurance in behaviour.

Leadership and Policing the Police

The police are a group and their work is task-oriented. Precisely therefore they need leaders. And who is a leader? I have asked many constables a question: "Do you consider the director general of police as your leader?" The answer was: "no, we do not". The policemen consider the director general as the "Head" of the police department. They do not think that they have easy accessibility to the director general of police. They can see him only through the proper channel and, therefore, more than a leader, he is only the visible/partly visible/invisible "Head" of the department. The policemen see him as a bureaucrat vested with a lot of powers. What about the other ranks in the police? Do the sub-inspectors see the director general as a leader? No. They do not. What about the superintendent of police at the district headquarters? He too is not a leader for the constables. Even the sub-inspector in charge of a police station is not respected as a leader. All of them are bureaucrats in the hierarchy.

A person becomes a sub-inspector or an assistant superintendent of police by virtue of his recruitment and not by virtue of his leadership qualities. The sub-inspector/superintendent of police/director general of police/anybody, in that way, occupying a strategic position in the police will be invested with a lot of power and authority to control his subordinates/administer the department. My studies show that they do not/cannot become leaders. They do not want to become leaders, rather they want to administer the department. No one becomes a director general of police as a result of a series of situations and circumstances that are bound to produce a strong leader for the police. A person occupies a strategic position by virtue of his appointment which is managed or manipulated.

I asked many policemen/officers: "Who is your leader in the department?" And all of them said that they had no leaders in the department; they rather had only superiors in the service. Studies conducted on leadership show that the leaders must have a strong sense of identity with the group they lead and the members of the group tend to identify, in turn, with them. How many directors general of police have such a strong sense of identity with the group? - ask the policemen. Often, the superiors initiate disciplinary actions against their subordinates and, sometimes, they are motivated by vengeance, hostility, vindictiveness and personality clashes. Conversely enough, how many policemen identify with their superiors? No, not many - not even a few. There is no sense of mutual identity and precisely therefore the superiors are not treated as leaders by the subordinates or the subordinates are not treated as followers in the police bureaucracy/hierarchy which is very rigid in the police.

A leader must communicate to the followers and the followers must communicate to the leaders. The leader and the followers understand each other only through communication. The police are said to be an autocratic or authoritarian organization. As such, the communication flows readily from the superior to the inferior and not from the leader to the followers. In the police, the provision for feedback is minimum. In the police, what I find is that there is a great flow of information from above and they come in the form of orders, instructions, dos and don'ts, oughts and ought-nots etc. As the police are an autocratic bureaucracy, what the superior says is very important because *he is important* and what the subordinates say or have to say is not important because *they are not important*. "Wisdom goes with the rank one holds" - is the principle with which the police autocratic bureaucracy works and in such a set-up, mutual communication is difficult, if not impossible. The British wanted a militarized police system in India and they did not want to have a free flow of communication. For them, the white superior was important-all important and every time important. How can such an attitude followed by the militarized police be applied to a 50-60 year old democracy?

Democratic relationship between the superior and subordinate or vice versa only will work in a democracy. The policeman is as important as the sub-inspector/superintendent of police/director general of police in certain situations. Each member in the police must get opportunities to initiate, receive and share communication. Instead, the attitude of "attention" followed by "double mark time" or other words of command suited to a militarized police force will not yield good result either in policing the police or in policing the society in a democratic set-up. A *pyramidal* type of group as the police has, provides for the flow of communication from the top to bottom and for the least sharing of communication. I have studied the autocratic - the bureaucratic - the pyramidal type of communication in the police and I have found out that it would result in the lowest morale, but best production under a fear causing climate. I think that the police hierarchy is yet to understand that the morale, cohesiveness, production, climate, etc., are very much related to the flow of communication from the top to bottom and from the bottom to the top. The autocratic superior in the police does not like his subordinates to propose new ideas to him. He thinks that it is a threat to his authority and superiority. He is threatened and shaken by the new ideas of his subordinates. Here, he tries to attack and suppress all those subordinates who outshine him. How can he improve the system? How can he police the police then? For policing the police in a democracy, the superior has to share his leadership, power and authority and encourage the subordinates to come up with their new ideas. The subordinates must play their leadership roles.

Once in a police conference, a selection grade superintendent of police started telling: "Excuse me, Sirs, if I am wrong. I may be pardoned if I am not correct" and I found him to be very apologetic and taking an *"anticipatory bail"* for making suggestions in front of the deputy inspectors general/

inspectors general/additional directors/director general of police. In the police autocratic (bureaucratic) group, the members are likely to look at the superior for solutions to their problems. Why should the selection grade superintendent of police make a suggestion apologetically? The policeman too takes the same attitude to the sub-inspector. The deputy superintendent of police does the same to his superintendent of police. I do not think that such an attitude is good or conducive to free communication, production of free ideas and policing the police in a democratic set-up.

A military pattern of police structure was probably the best for the British interest as they did not want the Indian constables to show any initiative and enthusiasm. They did not want the Indians to pass their responsibility to their white *"Lords"*. They wanted the Indians to be docile, submissive and literally obedient to their white masters - to be repressive and oppressive as they were instructed by the Britishers. *"Yours most obediently"* attitude taken by the Indians was the best to police the police then - but not so today.

The autocratic police superiors - with their bureaucratic power and authority - think that they are very efficient and effective. Once a deputy inspector general of police said: "I will cut your tail so close to the body that you cannot further wag it". Listening to the threat by the deputy inspector general of police, the circle inspector said in a cool and calm tune to his friends and associates that the deputy inspector general was yet to know that Hitler was dead long back. He was later called Kamsan, a character in Indian mythology and who was notoriously known for his evils. The psychological maturity of the superior is important.

The police in the British past accepted the authoritarian and autocratic leadership (superior status) of their white hierarchy. During the nineteen hundred and seventees (1970s), the police reluctantly accepted the autocratic and authoritarian leadership. Today, some policemen/officers positively show their unwillingness to accept the leadership of superior officers.

"What am I to the director general/superintendent of police or what is he to me"? - attitude is seen. The authoritarian and autocratic administration is questioned. This attitude is seen more among the young and the newly recruited policemen/officers than among the older generation which has a different cultural background. They want a clearly defined culture with the autocratic/authoritarian leadership. A senior inspector of police once told me that he was anxious and uncomfortable to see the newly recruited policemen's/officers' attitude to authority, authoritarian administration and autocratic leadership. He could not think of sharing leadership, authority and responsibility with the various members organized along democratic lines. Politicians may like to have democracy introduced in the police, but old and senior policemen/officers do not tolerate the movement. According to them such procedures will make the department weak and inefficient.

Today's newly recruited policemen/officers are born and brought up in a democratic set-up and they do not know what is autocracy or authoritarian administration. Hence, democratic approaches are likely to work better with them than autocratic approaches. I have seen that, whenever young and newly enlisted policemen/officers were put under autocratic superiors, they did disagree with their superiors in many situations causing hostility, interpersonal rivalry, non-cooperation, personality clashes and disciplinary inquiries. The group suffered from low morale and cohesiveness. When I joined the police as a civilian lecturer in 1976, I could find more of an autocratic administration than what it is at present. Once, I heard a "Cat-call" in the class and as a newly appointed member of the faculty, I did not know what to do then. I approached senior police officers who unanimously decided to award a "punishment parade" to all of them. On the next day, when I went to the class, I could see unpleasant and swollen faces in the class. I could see the hostility generated by the autocratic decision for several years among the trainees in that batch. I understood that the trainees who came for police training in 1976 were born and brought up after India became democratic and with them the old autocratic method might not work well. Thereafter, I never resorted to any autocratic approaches to the police trainees.

Director General of Police and Policing the Police

Can the director general of police who heads the police department in a 50-60 year old democracy become one among the group? Can he merge his personality with that of the group and become one among them? Or, should he remain isolated at the police headquarters administering the department by taking authoritarian/autocratic decisions? This is a problem that is not easily resolved in a hitherto hierarchy-based police structure. I have not done any specific researches in this special area of policing the police/police administration. Nevertheless, I have made some valid observations. A director general of police who does not come down from the police headquarters proves to be less efficient than the one who merges his personality with that of the group working under him. For, he must know everyone who jointly works with him for the success of the organization. "The one who enters through the gate is the shepherd of the flock; the gatekeeper lets him in, the sheep hear his voice, one by one he calls his own sheep and leads them out. When he has brought out his flock, he goes ahead of them, and the sheep follow because they know his voice. They never follow a stranger but run away from him; they do not recognize the voice of strangers".[2] The Biblical passage is important. For, some directors general of police are strangers to the subordinate ranks and policemen. The questions are: (1) Do the directors general want group solidarity or (2) do they want to maintain their inflated ego and autocratic authority? The answer to these questions will tell us how to police the police. I asked 75 policemen who had 5-7 years of service to give me the answer to the question: "Have you ever talked to the director general of police directly-face to face?" No, not even one among the 75 policemen had a face-to-face talk with the director general of police during 5-7 years of service. What about the talk with the superintendent of police? What about with the sub-inspector of police? This is an area of research and certainly the situation is really very deplorable.

Senior and very senior police officers come to police training colleges/academies to give lectures. The objective is, inter alia, to show their faces to the newly enlisted officers. The objective is good if they see the faces of the officers as well! A mutual acceptance/recognition is what is desired now to police the police. As I indicated earlier, the senior police officers police their subordinate officers and the subordinate officers too police their senior officers. The policemen police both subordinate and senior levels in the police hierarchy.

It has been seen that the more cohesive a group is, the more satisfying it is to its members? What do the police do to make the group more cohesive? Do the members come closer and closer emotionally? The rigidity with which each rank deals with the higher and lower rank does not allow them to come closer and closer. Each rank keeps the lower rank at an arm's length and there is no extra-departmental activities in which everyone participates without the rank-consciousness. If at all there is any, still the rank is a factor which keeps the individual members away or close to one another. The sub-inspectors cluster together, the officers of the Indian police service cluster together and the policemen cluster together and the different ranks rarely become close to one another. How can there be cohesiveness then? I may call this to be the "rank casteism" in the Indian police and it permits a sort of emotional untouchability among the various ranks. The psychological distance each rank maintains from the lower/higher rank is a factor that does not help to police the police. I think that each rank in the police is an *exclusive group*, a group whose satisfaction in the group activities is heightened by excluding the members in other ranks - higher or lower - or by making it difficult for the members of a particular rank to come closer and closer with the members belonging to other ranks. When police associations were formed in India during the British rule, they were formed on the basis of ranks. The officers of the Indian police had their association. The lower level functionaries have their own associations. When police associations were allowed recently, again three associations were permitted and they were: (1) an association for the officers of the Indian police service, (2) another association for the State service officers and (3) a third association for the constables and head constables, and so on. Each association functions as an *exclusive group*. They do not allow to expand the activities of one group by including the members of the other groups. Hence, we may call each association to be an *"inclusive group"*. In inclusive groups, individual equality and freedom are more accepted whereas in *exclusive groups*, they are not. In a democratic set-up, I think that each rank in the police must become more of an *inclusive group*, a group whose satisfaction is heightened by enlisting members from other ranks. This can help to police the police better. It can create more cohesiveness and raise the morale high. The police become a group - a whole group and everyone in the group share their feelings, emotions and norms. They feel that they are members of the same service and as the proverb goes, birds of the same feather flock together. Today, the members of the same rank flock together and as such they do not become or feel similar to others. I think that the members of each rank must come closer and have more cohesiveness to police the police better. The hicrarchy can do it and the top level officers/middle level officers who are to lead the lower ranks must recognize this fact to police the police during the third millennium in the democratic set-up.

References

1. Solomon E Asch, *Social Psychology,* Prentice-Hall, Engle wood Cliffs, 1952.
2. Holy Bible, St. John 10: 1-5.

10

Policing the Police for theThird Millennium

Policing the police with people's participation is a new concept of recent origin in India. So far, the police have tried to police the society and they thought that they could do so by their authority, power, muscle strength, etc.; nevertheless they faced a lot of problems. Police-people relations became far away from being satisfactory. No serious or honest attempts were made to bring the police closer to the people or the people closer to the police. The people developed an avoiding and sometimes hostile attitude to the police. As a result, the police association with the people did not offer happiness to the police. The people's association with the police too did not make the police happy. The police did offer a lot of services to the people, but they did not ensure any psychological reward to the police functionaries. For examples, when the people were sleeping, the police provided protection to them by foot patrol. During a law and order situation, the angry mob stoned at the police. The policemen were attacked by criminals and in spite of such difficulties, the police engaged in protecting the life and property of the people. The rewards which the police received from the people were criticisms for many things the police did for the people. Why? They did not get the people's affection, admiration and acceptance even for the risks which the police took on themselves for the people. Why? The people could see that the policemen were repressive and oppressive even after 50 years of freedom and democracy. No longer can the police be repressive and oppressive in the third millennium. They have to be people friendly.

Positive and Negative Attitudes of People to Police or Vice Versa

The positive or negative attitude which the people have towards the police plays a crucial role in the people-police interaction. Likewise, the positive or negative attitude which the police have towards the people play a crucial role in the police-people interaction. I have done some empirical studies to find out the public attitude towards the police during the early 1980s and the findings were published in the book *Police and the Society*. The public attitude then was avoiding, hostile and, so to say, far away from being satisfactory. In 2002, I find that the attitude is not considerably changed. Still the people keep away from the police! Should they not come closer? Yes, they must. This is necessary not only to police the society, but also to police the police in the years to come. What are the determinants of liking and disliking between the police and the people? I think that they must be identified at the earliest. We have no time to waste. The people and the police must come into some kind of contact with each other. This is essential to establish a positive relationship between the two forces in the society. The contact will certainly help to have a positive attitude in the people for the police and in police for the people. The Police Act-1861 did not envisage such a healthy contact between the police and the people. I think that the antiquated-rusted-Police Act-1861 must be substituted by a new Act which will ensure positive attitudes in the police towards the people. In order to police the police, the first thing to be done is to enact a new Police Act with objectives to create a people-friendly police service.

Behavioural scientists speak of *propinquity* when they talk about contacts. According to them, there are two kinds of proponquity which are : (1) physical and (2) functional. Physically, policemen are present in many places; nevertheless the allegation is that they have little or no contacts with the people around. Why? Some people think that a policeman in uniform feels *'too much'* about himself. He may not speak decent language or he behaves in an irritating way. People approach him with fear and isolate him from social intercourse. What about the functional propinquity? People complain that there is too much of secretiveness in police functioning. Transparency is not seen and as such functional propinquity is very weak. I have asked many people who stay near police lines/police quarters a question: "How is your relationship with the policemen?" They have answered me: "very minimum". I have asked many policemen: "Why don't you have close relationship with the people who stay around your quarters/ residence?" They have told me: "the more contacts the people have with the policemen, the more difficult it will be to perform police duties. They will come with recommendations to policemen". What about the relationship of the higher levels in the police with the people around their quarters/residence? It is seen that the relationship is very little or nil. The higher levels have security guards at home and the people look at them from a distance. "If you are a policeman/officer, you be so. We have our work" - this is the attitude people have towards the police neighbours. "I am a policeman/officer. So please don't disturb me" - this is the attitude the policeman/officer has towards his neighbours. Even the children do not mingle and play together.

Police officers come and go. They are transferred every now and then. As such, they do not stay in one place long enough for propinquity to have any effect. The newcomers take time to establish relationship with the people. The wives of many police officers complain that they feel neighbourhood isolation and clannishness in the newly transferred places.

People in Indian culture are afraid of the police. "If you are close to the police, you will be made witnesses in criminal cases" - this is a feeling in some. They think that the police create witnesses in criminal cases and some do not want to be the touts of the police. I think that some people have a wrong impression about the police and they continue to behave with such wrong impressions. Instances were reported that earlier the police used to make people as witnesses without their knowledge and they came to know about it only when they received summons from the courts. This practice which the police did in the past might have influenced the people to keep away from the police. Propinquity theories do not work well here.

A good majority of the people can live in society without establishing any relationship with the police. How many people go to a police station? How many people need direct police help? They are not many. Hence, they think that they can live in society without being friendly with individual policemen/ officers. India is a country of unemployment. Anyone employed in Government service feels superior to others who are not employed. The employed people develop a special "ego" and therefore many ordinary people who are unemployed wish to keep away from such a privileged group. If the employed have some power and authority, they exhibit an authoritarian ego before others and this is seen in Panchayat peons as well as in special secretaries to Government. How many countries are there in the world where one finds so many vehicles exhibiting "designation boards" on the roads? The designation boards of the vice-chancellors of the universities, members of the Public Service Commission, judges of the Courts, Public prosecutors, managing directors of banks, presidents of Panchayats, revenue divisional officers, show their "ego" on the roads and the people/road users give way to them. Policemen/officers have power and authority and they want to express them, exhibit them wherever they go. People do not like it and therefore they keep themselves away from the police. For example, people love a traffic constable on the road. They watch him doing the job in a desirable way. Nevertheless, if and when they observe the traffic constable misusing or abusing his authority or speak abusive language to vehicle drivers/road users, they dislike him. They go away from such a law enforcement officer. It being so, the physical propinquity, though good in establishing enviable interpersonal relation, is not always helpful to strengthen police-public relationship. My studies show that the propinquity between the police and the people helps to establish good interpersonal relations only if the people are convinced that the police do perform their functions in a legal and fair way. The third millennium police have to bear in mind that their presence amidst the people helps them to come closer to the people only if they consciously make attempts to perform their functions in a neat and people-friendly manner.

Propinquity Factors in Face-to-Face Relationship between Police and People

The police constantly come into contact with many people in their jurisdiction. They have practically face-to-face contact with the same people everyday. There are way-side sellers, footpath sellers, small shop-keepers and so on. In a city, the police may take action against them. In some cities, it is learnt that the police and the small scale sellers have unholy *nexus* by the help of which the police get a regular income for permitting them to carry on their business. A book seller in a bus station once said that he used to pay Rs. 80 everyday to the police who permit him to sell pornographic literature. Likewise, a footpath seller had to pay Rs. 20 everyday. The amount thus collected is shared among the police personnel. Hence, once there is a contact situation, people see the nature of the contact and then decide whether or not they must keep good interpersonal relationships. Functional propinquity in face-to-face relationship does not mean that the relationship will be desirable or good.

The police get in touch with politicians, lawyers, businessmen, journalists, social workers, the affluent people and so on. Does their functional propinquity affect the nature of relationship? Studies show that those who get in touch with the police on a regular basis have vested interests. More than the friendship with the police, they want to make use/misuse the police for their advantage. Reciprocally, the police too get some advantages. Hence the friendship with such vested interests is not friendship, but is a sort of relationship for mutual advantages. The public are not happy over it. They blame the police and vested interests for their unholy relationship. The policemen/officers are invited for marriages, birthdays, other celebrations in their jurisdiction. But, how many poor people invite the policemen/officers for such functions? They don't invite them and it shows the acceptance of the policemen/officers among the general public. It shows that the general public does not accept the policemen/officers as a part of the community to which they belong. On the other hand, the higher-ups, the affluent, the influential people see to it that the police functionaries are invited and give an impression to the general public that the policemen/officers are their own people. The susceptibility of the police functionaries to the high tea/dinner of the affluent keeps the common man away from the police. The third millennium police ought to see that they are for everyone, but belong to none specially or specifically.

The police have face-to-face contacts with witnesses, complainants, petitioners and so on. They are also seen by the general public in bus-stations, railway platforms, festivals, scenes of V.I.P. security, street corner meetings, during patrolling, etc. They have face-to-face contacts with many in society. People do not see an individual policeman then. They see the policeman in uniform and identify him with all other policemen in the service. If one policeman behaves properly, then do they see all other policemen behaving properly? No, they do not think so. On the contrary, if they see one policeman misbehaving, they see all other policemen misbehaving. Yes, it is so. Because, they have formed some impressions, rightly or wrongly, about the police and their behaviour. The impression is not in favour of the police and therefore they evaluate police behaviour in the background of their earlier formed impressions on the police. The third millennium police will have to wipe out the bad impression which the people have formed against them if they want to come closer to the police and thus improve police-public interactions.

The police so far did not see the social dimensions of their behaviour. From 1860, they wanted to suppress and oppress the people to make the British rule over the country. After India became independent, the police could not become the people's police in a democracy. In their over-enthusiasm to establish law and order in society, they forgot the social dimensions of policing and police behaviour. They worked amidst the people, but away from them. The psychological distance between the people and the police was a barrier to establish a good relationship between the two. In spite of the propinquity, the interpersonal relationship could not become stronger than what it was during the British raj.

Enforced Propinquity with People

Police departments could sense that the police, in spite of their propinquity, amidst the people could not bring the people closer to them even after serving the people for many years in a democracy. Hence, in order to bring the police closer to the people, the police department introduced several strategies such as celebration of crime prevention weeks, boys clubs, participating in sports and games, etc. But, they could not yield the desired results. Of course, the people considered such activities as an enforced propinquity of the police with the people. The public found a different policeman in the play grounds, in the boys clubs, etc., and they were different when they performed the routine police work. Without a change in the police attitude towards the people and without a change in the outlook of the people towards the police, no enforced propinquity could help to ensure better police-citizen interaction. A lot of prejudices against the police existed in the people and likewise a lot of prejudices against the people existed in the police. The people considered the police as anti-people and the police considered the people who approached them as crime-prone or people possessing undesirable personality traits. My studies prove that the prejudices are likely to be diminished only if the people are encouraged to participate with police activities in a more positive way. In England, the police take the people with them when they go for patrolling and they allow more transparency in police work. The third millennium police service requires the people to participate with the police in a more positive way and towards this end, probably, community policing can be of immense utility. It is only through people's participation in the police work that we can think of policing the police in the years to come. The more the contacts with the people, the better will the police be able to correct the distortions in the people's perception of the police. This does not however mean that all police contacts with the people will lead to a satisfactory relationship. As such, the police must be very cautious in bringing the people closer to them. For example, the people's presence during an interrogation of a suspect may be instrumental to cause an unsatisfactory relationship and, in such situations, it is advisable to follow the directives of the Supreme Court of India during the police interrogation of a suspect. The Supreme Court allows the presence of a lawyer - and not the members of the public - and that too, not all throughout the interrogation. However, there is nothing wrong in participating the people for traffic control or control of the people during a festival or V.I.P. security duties.

Sun Glasses and Police-Citizen Interaction

I have observed many police officers/policemen wearing sun glasses when they are in public. Police officers in junctions and policemen during traffic control wear sun glasses. The police version is that the sun glasses protect their eyes from the sun and dust when they are performing their duties in public. I have asked many people to tell me their felt impressions and attitude towards policemen/officers wearing sun glasses in public. The data I have collected revealed to me that policemen/officers wearing sun glasses were judged to be more suspicious of people - were more interested to observe people without their taking notice of the police watching them - were exhibiting their ego in a projected way than those who did not have sun glasses. People do not like the policemen/officers wearing sun glasses when they are on duty in public. They want to see the eye-contacts of the policeman/officer when they have interaction with the people. Likewise, the people want to have more interaction with the policemen/officers who have no lathies with them. They have no difficulty if the policemen/officers have pistols with them. In any case, they do not want the policemen to have a .303 rifle with them. People in general do not want to interact with a policeman/officer having a police moustache (i.e., moustache with a threatening appearance) and a cruel face. People do not want to interact with a policeman/officer who uses abusive language. People do not want to interact with a policeman/officer in uniform with a cruel face and a weapon when they go to police stations. People do not want to interact with a policeman/officer in uniform when they are interviewed as witnesses. People want to have a receptionist in plain cloth in police stations than a policeman in uniform. It appears to me that people respond to such cues as sun glasses, lathies, .303 rifles, police moustaches, cruel faces, police uniforms, etc., on the basis of certain prejudices they have already formed against the police in the past. Hence, in order to police the police and to enhance police public interaction, there is the urgent need to remove all the cues which work as barriers for a smooth police-citizen interaction. The British police is dead in India and the British-Indian police during the democracy till now is on the death bed. Hence, the new police must be people friendly.

Prejudices and Attraction

Sometimes, news appears in the press about police torture, custodial rape, death in police custody, corruption, police misbehaviour in public, adverse observations by courts on police work, politicians' comments on police activities, etc. They appear in the media repeatedly and certainly they help to strengthen the already formed prejudices against the police. Anything the police do in an enviable way appears in the media rarely or sparingly so much so that the people are not informed and attracted much to the good acts of the police. The good activities of the police have no news value as the journalists say that the police are meant to do only good activities.

People have already formed some impressions and prejudices against the police and they are not altogether baseless. It is not easy to remove the prejudices and preconceived theories or notions against the police. The police are viewed as people who are not well policed although they claim that they are to police the people in society. Such prejudices and prejudgements about the police inevitably affect the way in which people look at them - behave with them. For example, six people were brutally murdered in a south Indian town. The police said that the murders were committed by a single person. The press and the people believed that the murders were not committed by a single person. In the meantime, some people moved the High Court and obtained an order for transferring the case from the local police to the crime investigation branch. Side by side, a number of stories from corruption to high level political interference could be propagated against the police. The people are already prejudiced against the police and the stories of this sort will further worsen police-citizen contacts, interaction, trust and what not? To convince the people that the police are policed becomes difficult now.

The adverse news against the police in the media evokes only negative feelings among the people. People do not say "Hello" to the policeman once they read a news about custodial death or corruption in the police. Instead they avoid the police. Even little children develop irreconcilable hatred towards the police. How to remedy the situation? To serve the people and to survive amidst the people during this century, the police will have to change their strategies. Any strategy that evokes negative feelings towards the police will create reactions in the public and they may range from the conscious (or unconscious) ignoring of a policeman/officer to public demonstrations, general *hartals, bandhs* and war against the police administration.

Once, I was talking to some young men/women (age group was 18-30) and I asked them: "How many of you will like to have a policeman/officer as your personal friend?" I asked them to raise their hands up if they wanted to have a policeman/officer as their personal friend. To my surprise I found none out of 39 participants in the seminar wanted to have a policeman/officer as their *personal friend*. I asked them further to tell me: "how many of you will like to have a policeman/officer as your 'friend'?" To that question, I found 16 out of 39 expressing their desire to have police 'friends'. I asked them: "Why?" They said that they could make use of their friendship with the police for their personal advantages. They were not found to have some attraction for the police; on the contrary, they wanted to cash on the police to their advantage. They loved to have friendship with artists, social workers, teachers, religious people and so on and it showed the interest which young people had with them. In the meantime, I overheard two people whispering to each other: "Any friendship with a policeman or with an officer will be a liability and not an asset". Was it just a prejudice or a feeling unfounded on reality? Most of the young men/women had no personal contacts with a policeman/officer till that time, yet they did not like to have personal friendship with policemen/officers. It was quite probable that the lack of any contact with policemen/officers was at least partly responsible for the existence of prejudiced attitudes. Hence it is the responsibility of the policemen/officers to open more and more roads for the people to come to the police and mix with them. Already, some prejudices against the police exist in the people and the existence of a negative attitude itself prevents many from interacting with the police. There must be ample opportunities for the people to come and see what is going on in the police department and they must be convinced that there is nothing undesirable happening in the service - inside the service against the people.

Who is the greatest enemy of the police? I find that another policeman/officer is the greatest enemy of the police department. He who misbehaves (towards people) in police uniform is not a policeman. He is a traitor and must be isolated. He who applies torture (to an innocent person) in police uniform is an infamy to the police service. He who abuses others, utters epithets in public, misuses authority, concocts evidence, etc., is not worthy to be called a policeman/officer. Just ask the men on the street about the observable or observed characteristics of the policeman/officer. Ask them more about their attitude toward the policeman/officer Evaluate their responses and they will give a picture of the policeman/officer in the present society. Is it enough to have the same picture in the years to come? In order to project out the best picture of the police, there is no option but to effect changes in the police. If the picture is bad, it means that the picture is bad and it is the picture of the original which is bad.

Desire and Motivation

There is no meaning in saying that the police-citizen interaction is bad. The question is: "Do the police want to improve it?" If they do not want so, it is futile to do anything for improving the relationship. Again, another question: "Do the police want to police the police to improve police-citizen interaction?" Let the police be honest and say whether or not they really want to establish and maintain good relationship with the people? - whether or not they really want to cooperate with people - whether or not they really want to please people in order to get their appreciation and love. If the police genuinely want to be closer to the people, they have no option but to show good will, to be people friendly, to be sociable, to be trusting and good natured. The police expect a lot from the people when they police the society. The people expect a lot from the police when they are policed by the police.

I have asked some policemen/officers to honestly tell me whether or not they genuinely wanted to improve police-people relationship. I have learnt that many of them did not want to improve the relationship. According to them :

(1) The people must be kept at a distance.
(2) The people must feel the presence of the police but they must not see the police.
(3) The people must be afraid of the police but must not become friendly with the police.

If the people must become so, the police must not be very policed and polished in behaviour. According to them, in certain areas of police work, police public relations may be harmful. 'Public' does not mean a faceless mass. It means the individuals of the public. If so, friendship, frequent contacts and free mingling with the people are likely to bring about unnecessary influences and pressures in the police work. If the police do not yield to their desires, the result will be a broken relationship which will be damaging to the public interest and the smooth enforcement of the law. The police-politician relationship, it is alleged, creates very many problems at present and the problems will be multiplied if the police become closer to the people. However, the argument seems to be not acceptable to the people who believe in democracy and democratic principles in governmental administration. They ask: "how can the police in a democracy function without having public contacts?".

Police and People Complementary to Each Other

What are the needs of the police? To short-list the needs, one may say that they are for the control and prevention of crime and thereby establishing peace and harmony in society. What are the needs of the people? The people too want to prevent and control crimes and thereby establish peace and harmony.

If the needs are the same or similar, why not the police and the people become complementary to each other? In order to function as complementaries to each other, they need interaction. Police-public relation becomes inevitable and necessary. Third millennium society and the people require such a complementary role and for it, policing the police and policing the society become necessary.

I asked some policemen/officers and many people in the public to tell me what they need from a police service. I obtained their responses and the responses showed that the police and the people have the same needs which are :

(1) Peace and harmony in society
(2) Prevention and control of crimes
(3) Detection of crime and criminals
(4) Fair enforcement of law without undue influence and corruption
(5) Administration of justice in a just way-as per law and procedure established by law
(6) Proper maintenance of law and order without political linkages and personal preferences.

My study shows that the needs are the same or similar. Then, why can't the police and the people work together to achieve the goals? Psychologists say that similarity/sameness leads to attraction. There is a proposition in science that "opposites attract" and in my research, I find that interests or needs that are opposite to each other do not attract, rather the likes attract each other. The needs of the people and the police are the same (likes attract each other) and precisely therefore they must be complementary to each other in the years to come.

The British did not understand or rather they refused to understand the importance of such an approach. They made the police to think that their need was to retain the British rule in India and everything the police did was a means to achieve the goal. In a democratic set-up, the needs are the goals and the police and the people have the same needs/goals. During the British rule, the police had a different goal from the one the people had. The people wanted to evict the British while the police wanted to retain them. Hence, the people and the police could not work as complementary to each other. In a democratic set-up, the outlook is changed and correspondingly the police and the people become complementary to each other. The British bullet had a target and the target was always an Indian on the other side. But, in democratic India, the rubber bullets used by the police are fired to the air more often than they are fired at human targets. If at all they hit a human target, the police want to cause the least harm and damage to the people on the other side. There is a lot of difference between the two approaches.

Attitudes and Democratic Values

What was the police attitude to the people during the British regime? What was the people's attitude to the police during the English rule? An attitude is defined as "a relatively enduring, acquired predisposition to behave in a particular way (usually either positively or negatively) with respect to certain objects, persons and situations" (Henry Clay Lindgren et al). If a review of the last 50 years of studies on the attitude of the people to the police or vice versa is made, it will show that the attitude of the police to the people and of the people to the police was far away from being satisfactory - are negative, hostile, avoiding and antagonistic. But, Indian democracy cannot afford to entertain such attitudes any longer. I am fully aware that the attitudes were associated with a set of beliefs, opinions and values which tend to justify them. Beliefs and opinions depend upon those judgements that individuals in the police and the public make and they lie at some point between established facts and felt impressions. A person may believe that in the police department, there is torture of suspects or he may hold the opinion that the police in many parts of the country are corrupt to the core. The values of an individual are those objects and activities which are most highly considered to be desirable or acceptable. For an individual, justice done to a person in police custody may be valued more highly desirable than the same administered to the society as a whole. Evaluating the same from the police point of view, a policeman/officer may believe that the people in general are crime-prone or may hold the opinion that every one in society wants to corrupt the policeman/officer. He may value that a criminal can be tortured to administer justice to the people in society. Both, the people and the police form such views, values, opinions, beliefs and attitudes from what they learn from their experience. The attitudes are not the desirable ones in a democracy wherein the people and police must cooperate and participate in policing the society and in policing the police. A change in the attitudes is possible if honest attempts are made. But I find that neither the police nor the people make sincere attempts to effect changes in their mutual attitudes. The police talk a lot about improving police public relation, but how far are they earnest in their attempts to really better the situation? People want to improve people - police interaction, but how far are they sincere in their attempts to better the situation?

I have asked some policemen/officers to tell me honestly about their attitude to the people. I have verified the same with the views which they have about the police attitude to the people. I could observe no significant difference between the two views. Similarly, I asked many people to speak about their attitude towards the police and the police attitude towards the people. There too, I did not find any perceptible difference between the two views. It means that both - the people and the police - know each other well. The realization of this fact is certainly a positive step for improving the police public relation or vice versa. For it, there must be a will and I find that the lack of a will and determination is the major barrier in bettering the police-public relation or public-police relation. The identification of the areas in which the people and the police can cooperate is important and I observe that the police and the people are fully conscious of the areas of cooperation.

Nevertheless, nothing takes place and the reasons for this inertia must be located to find out the remedial measures.

Passive Contacts with Police and Police-Citizen Relation

Practically everyday, the same people see the same policeman/officer on the roads, traffic points, in front of police stations, etc. They may be passive contacts. Psychologists may argue that many passive contacts can lead to a nodding acquaintance which may further develop into conversational interactions out of which friendship can grow. The psychologists' view is not subjected to any serious studies to know the validity of the view in public police relations or vice versa. I have seen the same policemen at 9.30 a.m. in a traffic junction in a city. I have also noted the same people waiting to get into buses in the same junction. For days together, I have watched the passive contacts between the policemen at the traffic junction and the people waiting to get into buses. I could not however observe that the passive contacts between the policemen and the people developing into a nodding acquaintance which develops further into conversational interaction. I could learn that neither the members of the public nor the policemen on duty wanted to develop a friendship from their passive contacts. While I was travelling in a car in New York city, I observed a policeman greeting me and I too greeted him back. On the next day, I found the same policemen doing the same thing and I greeted him back. Thus I did several days and there came a situation that I wanted to greet the policeman before he greeted me. Consciously or unconsciously, his passive contacts with me could help me to develop a positive affinity towards that policeman and to the New York police. Can the policemen in India do similar methods to improve the police-public interaction? Once an engineer working in ISRO told me: "Near to my house, a deputy inspector general of police has his residence. He comes in his official car which has tinted glass panes and nobody can see him when he goes out of his house or comes to his house. As a result, we have little or no contacts". If he was true in his version, it meant that some police officers do not want even passive contacts to develop between them and the people. If so, how can the police better their police-public relation? About an inspector general of police, a priest once told me: "So and so comes to the church. He participates in the holy mass. He never enters the church. He remains outside with a mobile phone. As soon as the mass is over, he gets out of the church compound as quickly as possible. Neither I nor any member of the congregation is allowed to meet and talk to him". If his story was true, it showed that he was not interested to interact with people. How could he improve the police-public relationship? Once a pet dog of a professor entered into the house of a senior police officer. It irritated the police officer. He took his telephone and dialled to the next door neighbour to see that the dog was taken away. All these may point to a fact that physical propinquity, neighbourhood, passive contacts, congregational membership, etc., do not enhance police public relation. What to do and how to go about in such situations? Perhaps, a change in the police culture of behaviour and attitude may solve the problem. The British bureaucratic culture may be continuing and dominating the individuals in Government administration.

Still in Indian democracy, the elders (especially, parents, grand-parents and so on) threaten their children saying that they will call the police if they do not obey them - do not eat food - do not listen to them. The media too projects the policemen as atrocious people who torture or misbehave with the people. The newspapers too carry the cruelties of the police and the little children from their infancy develop a fearful attitude to the police. Hence, from early childhood, our children tend to fear and avoid policemen/officers and they fear a lot the policemen in uniform. Once a boy studying in standard-IV asked his father who was a superintendent of police to give him a police lathy to beat his class-mate who mocked at him. He said that the police lathy was a licence to beat the people if the situation demanded so. In simple terms, the cue of a police uniform, a police vehicle, a lathy, a .303 rifle, etc., is associated with threat and threatening. When policemen come in a police vehicle to arrest someone from his residence, as stated elsewhere, the entire people - children especially - make a loud cry as if some catastrophy has taken place. Why? It is time now to work hard to give an impression to the people that the police are not to threaten people, rather to serve them. It can be achieved only if conscious attempts are made to police the police and to behave in a people-friendly way. The prejudices which the people still entertain against the police must be washed out if the police want them to come closer and the prejudices are many. Though some changes have taken place in the police, they have not gone into the people. Once a film director came to me and said that he would like to produce a movie showing crime investigation. I understood that he had a lot of prejudices against the police. I wanted to clarify his doubts, but in vain. I found him taking a lot of interest in strengthening the prejudices which people have against the police - even in the changed socio-political environment. According to him, his film would be appreciated only if the police were shown in a bad shape as atrocious and anti-people.

People have some expectancy from the police. Expectancy determines attitude. When crimes are reported, people want the police to detect the crimes and arrest the individuals. When the police are unable to do so, some people say that the result was expected. "These policemen will not be able to detect the crimes and arrest the criminals" - they say so and that becomes the expectancy of the people. Correspondingly, they strengthen their attitude against the police and demand an investigation by the Central Bureau of Investigation (C.B.I.). How long can the police entertain such public demands? The third millennium police requires professionalism and thereby they must wipe off the negative attitudes which the people have towards the police. Highly prejudiced members of the public will not like raw policemen to investigate crimes which are pretty in nature. They may attribute many motives behind every step involved in the crime investigation.

I interviewed four young men. One was interviewed while the police investigated a murder case in which his brother was killed. The second was interviewed while the trial of a murder case in which his father was killed. The third was interviewed when a murder case (his father was killed) was convicted and the fourth was interviewed when a murder case (his father was killed) was acquitted by the court of law. The first one said that he had no hope that the case would be convicted; the second one told that he did not expect a severe punishment; the third one said that God was great and the police succeeded in getting a conviction and the fourth one told that everything happened as expected. I do not claim that the study was valid enough to make any generalizations. The sample was not representative. Nevertheless, one could see the expectancy among the people at various stages of the investigation, trial, after conviction or after acquittal. To a young man who had nothing to do with a crime, with police, with court, I gave a note and it contained:

"You have witnessed a person stabbing another and killing him. To your surprise, you see a police officer coming to your residence to interview you as a witness to the murder".

Afterwards, I asked him to tell me the most probable consequence of his interaction with the police officer. He said that he would not like to become a witness. I asked him: "Why?" He said that :

(1) He did not want to be harassed by the policemen;
(2) He did not want to get the displeasure from the murderers;
(3) He did not want to spend money from his pocket;
(4) He did not want to go to the court every now and then;
(5) He did not think that the police would treat him as a person valuable for prosecution;
(6) After all, he did not expect that the case would end in a conviction.

I felt so desperate to listen to his evaluation of police performance, proficiency and professionalism. No doubt, he was a highly prejudiced person who had no expectancy in police expertise in the investigation of crimes. Incidentally, the conviction rate in India has been steadily declining from 1971 and presently is deplorably low. Can the third millennium police allow such a deplorable condition to continue? If they want to get the trust and appreciation of the public, they must prove their worth. The cruel methods and crude behaviour of the police were tolerated by the people during the British regime; nevertheless they do not and cannot ensure success in the years to come.

A Millennium Countermove

British Indian police developed a peculiar behavioural pattern for achieving their imperialistic goals. They were successful in putting down the people in India. They had their muscles, bayonets, lathies, bullets and hard core attitudes to suppress and oppress the Indians. The atrocious police behaviour reached a climax not at the time the British left India, but at a point somewhere between Indian Independence in 1947 and the dawn of the millennium in 2000. A countermove started from that point and it got accelerated in 1993 when the Protection of Human Rights Act was passed in India. With the enactment of the Protection of Human Rights Act-1993, the acceptance of transparency in the police work, attaching of accountability for everything the police do, the countermove started to have more and more acceleration. By 2000, the acceleration received further momentum and the countermove is speeding up now. The police have been functioning in a particular fashion till the countermove started. As soon as the countermove started, the occurrence of various events within the police system began to upset the thereto existed normality or normal state in the police system. It irritated many in the police service and they started telling that the countermove would damage the entire policing in the country. The countermove activated certain mechanisms, processes, organizations and individuals to a synthesis of the move and countermove. By the countermove, the symmetry of the British police system was twilted. As a result, discrepancy in the system came into being. Consequently, the police system becomes asymmetrical and the system now moves towards a new symmetry which is yet to come. When the police do something to police the society, the people evaluate what the police do and raise their objections if they find them necessary. Some objections may be ill-motivated, yet objections are viewed seriously by the press and the people. They can and do police the police.

The people love the police if they do their job fairly and honestly. They start disliking the police when they see or suspect the police manipulating matters. The police is a public facility in a democracy and people's attraction, love, liking and association with the police varies with the frequency of being attended by them with justness and fairness. Just go to the premises of a police station and interview the people who come out of the police station. Some will be happy because they think that they find fairness and justness in police station. Some will be unhappy, for they do not see fairness and justness in the police decisions. People's love towards police increases in proportion to the fairness and justness in the police decisions and activities. The people love individual policemen/officers who are fair and just, and hate those who are not. Psychologists attest to the theory that dislike towards an individual or organization increases with the amount of negative reinforcement which he or the organization gives to the people. The police from the British past have given enough negative reinforcement to the people and now the people want the police to offer to them positive reinforcement. When the police and the people interact, they must feel that they are rewarded and not punished. They must have experiences which are reinforcing rather than extinguishing. The people have expectations and the police have obligations. The people want to have pleasant experiences with the police and their attraction to the police varies to the extent of having pleasant or unpleasant experiences. If the policeman speaks abusive language, then the listener has an unpleasant experience. If the policeman listens patiently to the complaints of a person, then the complainant has pleasant experiences. If a policeman receives corruption money, then he offers unpleasant experiences. On the contrary, if he refuses corruption money, then he expresses pleasant behaviour. How many policemen/officers have taken their job as a job to extend service to the people? How many policemen/officers have taken their job as a job to generate illegal income? The people in the third millennium want service-minded policemen/officers.

The history of Indian police from the British past showed that they did not consider their job as a service to the people. They did not take their job for generating only legal income as well. They functioned as a State apparatus to retain power. Some misused police power to their advantage. The people did not object to it earlier although one could take note of anti-police riots in Indian police history. But today? The people do object to the police behaviour which is unpleasant. The people want transparency and the police are made accountable to what they do. Even if there is no accountability for many things the police do while they do things under the pretext of administering justice, their behaviour, acts and activities have legal, social and political relevance. Any shameful abuse of power/misuse of authority is not tolerated. The illegalities and atrocities which the police committed during the British Raj are remembered as they occurred yesterday and the police are not given pardon by generations to come during the third millennium.

If Behaviour is O K, Everything is O K

If behaviour is O.K., then there is no need to police the police. When behaviour becomes misbehaviour, then the police interfere to police the society. When the police misbehave, the people criticize them. The imperial autocracy made the police to misbehave with the people. They became oppressive and repressive. Universal adult suffrage in 1952 in India made the people to elect their rulers. The State's apparatus thus formed made use of or misused police power for their political advantage. The police became the primary agency to protect the interest of the ruling government. The centrally administered armed police force and the State controlled civil police (including the armed reserve and armed battalions) continued to function just like the police of the colonial times. 1947 marked no difference either in the imperial police structure or in the behaviour patterns. "The very absence of the army from India's political scene since 1947 has been evidence of the continuing strength and political utility of the police. In this heavy reliance upon the police, the rulers of India since independence have been no more than faithful to their colonial inheritance".[1] The police worked often, as the allegation goes, for the ruling Government and sometimes misbehaved with the people who elected the Government to power. The colonial inheritance continued for several decades and during the internal emergency (1975-76) in India, the police became cruel and atrocious. Police misbehaviour, custodial violence, death in police custody, custodial rape, registration of false cases, concoction of evidence, calling of epithets, use of abusive language, *nexus* transactions, corruption and corrupt practices, misuse of power, abuse of authority, etc., appeared in the media time and again. The police administration could not take note of the deterioration in police culture seriously even after several decades of democratic rule. Policing the police did not receive any administrative attention. The administration wanted to modernize the police by investing a lot of money in acquiring technologies and scientific gadgets, vehicles and weapons, computers and handcuffs, rubber bullets and what not. At the same time, the behavioural aspects of the police were not attended to. The police behaviour became a target of attack on many fora, but the criticisms were unheard by many decision-making levels. The Central Committee on police training made recommendations for including some topics in the behavioural sciences in the training curriculum of policemen/officers. But the recommendations were indifferently implemented and the imperial behavioural patterns continued to dominate the police subculture. Those who spoke against the culture of police behaviour were branded as anti-police and yet the administration could not realize the fact that behind their so-called anti-police approaches, there was a lot of pro-people attitude and philosophy. They failed to accept the reality that an approval of police misbehaviour raised difficult problems of conscience for legally upright people. People have a right to demand the police that they ought not to take part in evil actions whatever may be the advantages by such acts. The willingness to carry out evil actions will not only cause scandal for the department, but also will weaken the credibility of the police in the eye of the public. The third millennium police, it appears, have accepted the truth more realistically than what they did in the past. This is a positive sign of development and will lead the police to become people friendly. The ruling Government often determines the character of police behaviour. The police behaviour may be sanctioned by the State authority, but the State does not decide the manner in which a service is to be ensured, extended, denied or delayed. Individuals have a lot of discretion and it is there that the police must give utmost attention. "The State shall strive to promote the welfare of the people by securing and protecting as effectively as it may a social order in which justice, social, economic and political, shall inform all the institutions of the national life"[2] - says the Constitution of India. The police have to strive to promote productive justice and distributive justice under an Equal Justice System by policing the police in letter and spirit.

References

1. David Arnold, *Police Power and Colonial Rule: Madras 1859-1947*, Oxford University Press, Delhi, 1986.
2. Article 38, Constitution of India.

Bibliography

Adams, Thomas, F (ed), *Criminal Justice Readings,* Goodyear Publishing Company, California, 1972.

Allen, Francis A, *The Crimes of Politics*, Harvard University Press, Cambridge, Mass, 1974.

Arnold, David, *Police Power and Colonial Rule: Madras 1859-1947*, Oxford University Press, Bombay, 1986.

Arthur, T C, *Reminiscences of an Indian Police Official,* Sampson Low Marston and Co., London, 1984.

Bahuguna, H N, *Perspectives in Police Administration,* Socialist India, 23 March, 1973.

Banton, M, *Policing a Divided Society,* Police Journal, Oct-Dec., 1974.

Bawa, P S, *Policing for People*, Rupa & Co, Calcutta, 1989.

Bayley, David H, *Police and Political Development in India,* Princeton University Press, New Jersey, 1969.

Berkley, George E, *The Democratic Policeman,* Beacon Press, Boston, 1969.

Bittner, Egon, *The Functions of Police in Modern Society,* National Institute of Mental Health, Rockville, 1970.

Black, Algernon D, *The People and the Police*, McGraw Hill, New York, 1968.

Bose, A C, *What is wrong with our police force*, Amrita Bazar Patrika, 28 January, 1969.

Bowes, S, *The Police and Civil Liberties*, Lawrence and Wishart, London, 1966.

Bramsted, Earnest J, *Dictatorship and Political Police,* Routledge and Kegan Paul, London, 1945.

Chapman, Brian, *Police State,* Praegar, New York, 1970.

Chatterjee, Sumit K, *The Police in Ancient India.* The Indian Police Journal, Centenary Issue: 1861-1961, 1961.

Clift, Raymond, E., *A Guide to Modern Police Thinking*, W.H. Anderson, Cincinnati, 1956.

Cox, Edmund C, *Police and Crime in India*, Manu Publications, Delhi, 1979.

Crame, James, *The World's Police,* Cassel, London, 1964.

Curry, J.C., *The Indian Police,* Faber and Faber, London, 1934.

Deb, R, *Malpractices in Law Enforcement,* The Indian Police Journal, XIX, 3, 1973.

Dwivedi, J N, *Police Power and Duties*, Allahabad Law Agency, Allahabad, 1950.

Erayil, A L & James Vadackumchery, *Police and the Society,* Kairali, Trivandrum, 1985.

Fitzgerald, M, *et al*, *Crime & Society,* Routledge & Kegan Paul, London, 1981.

Ghosh, S K, *Politics of Violence*, Ashish, New Delhi, 1992.

Gibbons, Don C, *Changing the Lawbreaker,* Prentice Hall, Englewood Cliffts, 1965.

Gouldsbury, C E, *Life in the Indian Police*, Manu Publications, Delhi, 1977.

Griffiths, P, *To Guard My People: The History of the Indian Police*, Ernest Barn Ltd., London, 1971.

Hale Charles, D, *Fundamentals of Police Administration,* Halbrook Press, Boston, 1971.

Hale, J, *Police and Law in a Democratic Society,* Indian Law Journal, Vol.28, 1953.

Holmgrem, Bruce R, *Primary Police Functions,* William Capp, New York, 1962.

Iyer, Krishna V R, *Police in Welfare State,* Asia Book Centre, Delhi, 1958.

Jeffrey (Sir) Charles, *The Colonial Police,* M Parrish, London, 1952.

Kanetkar, V G, *Our Police: Need for Drastic Reform,* Indian Journal of Public Administration, XXIV, Delhi, 1978.

Kenney, J P, *Police Management Planning*, Charles C. Thomas, Springfield, 1959.

Kulkarni, V B, *Police and the Politicians*, Indian Police Journal, Jan-March, 1971.

Lahari, S K, *Police Powers*, Law Book Society, Calcutta.

Lynch, W S, *The Police Function and Organized Crime*, CBI Bulletin, November 1975.

Mark, R, *Policing a Perplexed Society,* Allen & Unwin, London, 1977.

Mehra, A K, *Police in Changing India,* Usha, Delhi, 1985.

Misra, B B, *Police: Its Present Role and Tasks*, Orissa Review, August, 1970.

Misra, S C, *Police Administration in India,* National Police Academy, Mt Abu, 1972.

Mukerji, U, *Role of Police in a Democracy,* Indian Police Journal, July-Sept, 1968.

Millik, B.N., *World's Great Policemen,* Kalyani Publications, New Delhi, 1978.

Noorni, A G, *The Police Excesses,* Indian Express, Delhi, March 9, 1976.

Packer, Herbert L, *Policing the Police,* The New Republic, 4 Dec, 1965.

Pant, N C, *Role of Police in Promoting Secularism, Secular Democracy,* April, 1972.

Rajgopal, P R, *Communal Violence in India,* Uppal Publishing House, New Delhi, 1987.

Reiss, A J (Jr), *Police Brutality: Answers to Key Questions,* Transaction, 5 (Jul-Aug) 10-19, 1968.

Reith, Charless, *British Police and the Democratic Ideal,* Oxford University Press, London, 1943.

Remington, E J, *The Role of Police in a Democratic Society,* Journal of Criminal Law, Criminology and Police Science, Vol.56, 1965.

Ruchelman, L (ed), *Who Rules the Police?* New York University Press, New York, 1973.

Saksena, N S, *Police Unpopularity: Causes and Remedies,* Indian Police Journal, Oct-Dec, 1974.

Saksena, N S, *Terrorism: History and Faces in the World and India,* Abhinav Publications, Delhi, 1985.

Sharma, P D, *Indian Police: A Development Approach,* Research, Delhi, 1977.

Sherman, L W (ed), *Police Corruption: A Sociological Perspective*, Doubleday, Garden City (N.Y.), 1974.

Sinha, S K, *The Police in India*, USI Journal, April-June, 1970.

Thomson, Craig, *The Police State,* Dutton, New York, 1950.

Trilok Nath, *The Indian Police: A Case for a New Image,* Sterling, New Delhi, 1978.

Vadackumchery, James, *Police Enforcement Crimes and Injustice*, Gyan, New Delhi, 2000.

--, *Third Millennium Police: Take-off trends in India*, APH Publishing Corporation, Delhi, 2000.

Venugopal Rao, S, *The Police Service: Some Compulsions and Contradictions*, Indian Journal of Public Administration XXIV, Delhi, 1978.

Vohra, K B, *The Need for Reorientation of Police,* CBI Bulletin, February, 1973.

Wallerstein, J S and Clement, J W, *Our Law-abiding Law Breakers*, Probation 35 (April) 1947.

Ward, R H, *Police Corruption: An Overview*, Police Journal, Jan-March, 1975.

Westly, W, *Violence and the Police*, M.I.T. Press, Cambridge, Mass, 1970.

Whisenand, Paul, M, *Police Supervision: Theory and Practice,* Prentice Hall, Englewood Cliffs, N.J., 1973.

Wilson, J Q, *Dilemmas of Police Administration*, Public Administration Review, Sept-Oct., 1968.

Wilson, J Q, *The Police and their Problems: A Theory,* Public Policy, Vol.12, 1963.

Wilson, O W, *Police Administration,* McGraw Hill Book Company, New York, 1963.

Younger, Evells J, *Challenges to Police in a Changing World*, Indian Police Journal, Jan-March, 1970.

Index